THE ISLANDS

Also by Emily Hahn

Biography

The Soong Sisters
Raffles of Singapore
A Degree of Prudery: Fanny Burney
James Brooke of Sarawak
Chiang Kai-shek
Lorenzo: D. H. Lawrence and the Women Who Loved Him
Mabel: A Biography of Mabel Dodge Luhan

History

Love Conquers Nothing: A Glandular History of Civilization
China Only Yesterday: 1850–1950
Romantic Rebels: A History of Bohemianism in America
Breath of God: A History of Angels, Demons and Spirits
Fractured Emerald: Ireland
Once Upon a Pedestal: An Informal History of Women's Lib

Memoirs, Personal Journalism

Congo Solo
China to Me: A Partial Autobiography
Hong Kong Holiday
England to Me
Kissing Cousins
Africa to Me: Person to Person
Times and Places: A Memoir

Reportage

Diamond
The Tiger House Party
Animal Gardens
On the Side of the Apes
Look Who's Talking! New Discoveries in Animal
    Communication

Love of Gold

Novels and Fiction

Beginner's Luck
With Naked Foot
Affair
Steps of the Sun
Mr. Pan
Miss Jill
Purple Passage
Indo

Guidebook

Meet the British

Humor

Seductio ad Absurdum
Spousery

Children's Books

China A to Z
A Picture History of China
Francie
Mary Queen of Scots
Francie Again
First Book of India
Francie Comes Home
Leonardo da Vinci
Isaac Aboab
Around the World with Nellie Bly
June Finds a Way

Cooking

The Cooking of China

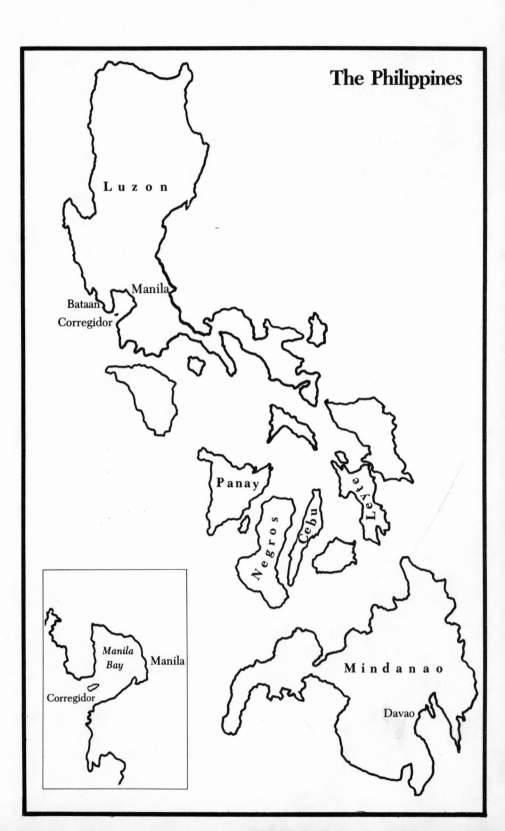

The Philippines

Luzon

Manila

Bataan

Corregidor

Panay

Negros

Cebu

Leyte

Mindanao

Davao

Corregidor

Manila Bay

Manila

The Islands

*America's Imperial
Adventure in the
Philippines*

by Emily Hahn

Coward, McCann & Geoghegan
New York

To my sister, Helen Hahn Smith,
with loving thanks for her patience
and helpfulness.

The author gratefully acknowledges permission to reprint the poem
"Mr. Matsuoka! Riddle deep for solving . . ." © 1940 Punch.
All rights reserved. (Rothco)

Library of Congress Cataloging in Publication Data

Hahn, Emily, date
  The Islands, America's imperial adventure in the
Philippines.

  Bibliography: p.
  Includes index.
  1. Philippines—History—1898–1946. I. Title.
DS685.H27   1981   959.9'03   81-3184
ISBN 0-698-11097-8   AACR2

Printed in the United States of America

Acknowledgments

I would like to thank the following for their help:

Alfonso Felix, Jr., of Manila, who has been most generous with his knowledge and stimulating theories; Lewis A. Gleeck, Jr., curator of the American Historical Committee of the Philippines, whose books contributed much to this one; Thomas Carter of the committee and his wife Mercedes for their sympathetic advice and hospitality; and the staff of the American Historical Collection Library. I am also grateful to the librarians of the Michigan Historical Collections and the Center for South and Southeastern Asian Studies of the University of Michigan, Ann Arbor.

I owe much to Morton J. Netzorg and his wife Petra, who run the remarkable Cellar Book Shop of Detroit, and know the Islands very well. Jock Netzorg's ideals about bibliographies, while hard to live up to, well deserve the effort.

Chapter One

"Three hundred and fifty years in a Spanish convent followed by fifty years in Hollywood—no wonder the Filipinos are schizoid." An American journalist is supposed to have said this, and I am unable to find the exact words, or even his name, but the thought is so applicable that I am using it anyway. My friend Alfonso Felix, Jr., of Manila has said the same thing in different words: that the combination of the two main educational influences in the Philippines, the Spanish Catholic friars and their successors, American Middle West schoolteachers, is surely cause enough for schizophrenia.

Somehow Americans don't think of the Philippines as part of the Far East, though according to the map they are as Oriental as, say, Malaysia. This is probably because our connection with the Islands has been close, though not necessarily affectionate. For half a century, more or less, the Philippines represented our first—or perhaps our second; let us not forget Hawaii—attempt at imperialism. If the attempt seemed to falter, it was because we, too, were

11

schizophrenic: many of us did not wish to think of ourselves as imperialistic, but many more had a strong impulse to be just that. They wanted to acquire control of the Islands not merely as a spin-off of the Spanish-American War but as a prize to hang on to. They thought we should occupy the archipelago for a while at least, staying a little longer, a little longer still, even perhaps forever. Hanging on was a question of good business, they said, or strategically wise.

But whether or not we were imperialists, our instinct to think of the Islands as Western was probably sound. The Philippines *are* of the West, having been influenced for centuries, first by Europe and then America. They are a Western country set down in the Orient, regardless of the fact that ethnologically the inhabitants are an Asian mixture. American schoolchildren know, or ought to, that the Philippines were not independent even before we came along with our steamboats and soldiers: they were a Spanish possession, and had been since— But let us begin at what, as far as we know, is the beginning.

The Spanish occupation of the Islands took place early in the sixteenth century, and was of a piece with other movements of conquering European nations on that side of the globe, soon after Christopher Columbus first landed on the strange soil of the Americas. Europeans were scrambling to claim as much Eastern territory as they could grab and hold. The Spaniards, occupied with the land they now held in America, did not at first loom large in this race to discover and conquer yet more territory, but they happened to back a disgruntled Portuguese adventurer and navigator, Ferdinand Magellan (or Fernão de Magalhães, to give him his proper Portuguese name), and he did it for them. He had first offered his services to the Portuguese king, Emanuel I, who turned him down, so he went to Charles V of Spain and divulged his reasons for wanting to sail to the East: he was convinced he could get there by way of a Western route. Like everyone else in his line of work, he wanted particularly to find a quick, comparatively easy passage to the Moluccas, or the Spice Islands, where an enterprising mariner could make a fortune with the right cargo: spices were enormously profitable in Europe.

In the words of historian C. R. Boxer, America had proved a disappointment in that respect. ". . . The new-found lands to the West at first seemed to yield little but stark-naked Amerindians, parrots, exotic woods, and some alluvial gold. America, in fact, for a couple of decades seemed primarily an obstacle to be circumvented in the quest for Cathay and spices." But Magellan was sure he could get through America at some place still unknown, and come out into the Pacific, known to the Spaniards as the Southern Sea, to reach the lands so glowingly described by Marco Polo and other early travelers. Of course Magellan was absolutely right in these important particulars; what he did not realize was the scope of the proposed enterprise, because the Pacific was a lot wider than anybody suspected.

Magellan presented the idea to Charles V in 1517, and the king was receptive to it. In 1518 he definitely approved it—even in those days it took a long time to get through official red tape—and Magellan had his way at last. On September 20, 1519, despite last-minute attempts to stop him by the Portuguese, who were having second thoughts, the navigator set sail from the Spanish port of Sanlúcar de Barrameda with a fleet of five ships and 265 men. They sailed directly toward South America, a route familiar to Europeans since Spain had installed settlements in Mexico and the subcontinent. After duly sighting land near Pernambuco, Brazil, they made their way down the coast, with Magellan looking out for some break in the land, some hidden way to the Southern Sea. In the quest he explored the Río de la Plata (in January 1520), but found no passage there. His plans to spend the coming winter, from March to August, in Patagonia for a rest were interrupted by mutiny among his officers, but that was a familiar hazard to explorers and he put it down promptly and severely. Not until October 21, 1520, did he prove his point at last by finding the passage now known as the Strait of Magellan. His ships threaded their way through, and slightly more than a month later the three vessels—two having been lost on the way—broke out into the Pacific.

Now for the Moluccas! They struck off into the vast Southern Sea in a northwest direction. For week after week, for two months, they came upon no land, until they feared they were doomed to wander forever in the watery waste, and had nearly run out of provisions when on March 5, 1521, they reached the Marianas, a group of islands they christened "The Ladrones," or "The Thieves," because of the pilfering propensities of the natives. The largest of the Marianas is the place we know better as Guam. Encouraged and replenished, they moved on to the vast archipelago now known as the Philippines, though Magellan dubbed them the San Lazaro Islands because he landed there on St. Lazarus's Day. Here, at the crown of his achievement, his luck ran out. Rashly he joined in a battle between two native tribes on the island of Mactan near Cebu, where he had decided to settle for a while, and was killed. This happened on April 27, 1521.

Because the surviving crews did not have enough men to handle three ships on the homeward voyage, they selected the *Conception* as the most worn-out vessel and burned it. In the two remaining ships, the *Trinidad* and the *Victoria*, they continued on their way, searching for spices. En route they put in at Borneo (which had close ties with the Philippines) and then came at last to the Moluccas. Here they got the unwelcome news that the Portuguese were already there, having sailed in from the other side, and were in occupation of Ternate. Nevertheless the Spanish mariners managed to fill their ships with spices, and then at last start their homeward voyage. They lost the *Trinidad* in a wreck from which only four men were saved, but the *Victoria* actually made it all the way, sailing across the Indian Ocean, rounding the Cape of Good Hope—never a small feat—and arriving safely at the Cape Verde Islands. As these belonged to the Portuguese they met with a chilly welcome, and thirteen of their men were detained by the authorities, but they got away with only eighteen left in the crew, and at last the *Victoria* weighed anchor at

Sanlúcar on September 6, 1522, almost exactly three years after setting out from that port, the first ship ever to sail around the world. Her cargo of spices was profitable enough to pay for the whole expedition, and her voyage gave mankind its first appreciation of how much water there is on the globe in comparison with land.

The Spaniards naturally followed up the Magellan expedition with others. Two of these, originating from Spain, failed to reach the East, but a third fleet under Alvaro de Saavedra, and a fourth commanded by Ruy López de Villalobos, succeeded in reaching the Islands, no doubt because, unlike the first two expeditions, they fitted out in New Spain (Mexico and High Peru) and thus got a head start. Saavedra's fleet touched at one or two of the southern Philippine Islands, and Villalobos's ships came into harbor at Mindanao on February 2, 1543. His fleet also visited Leyte and Samar. It was this commander who named the archipelago "The Philippines," after Prince Philip of Spain.

Magellan had found the island natives friendly—except, obviously, those who killed him. Antonio Pigafetta, who accompanied him on that momentous voyage and wrote a record of it, said that the Filipinos were fond of music and dancing, and that their favorite sport was cockfighting. As we have seen, even before the Spaniards landed, the Philippines were not completely cut off from the outside world. Ships from China, Siam, and Borneo constantly brought in goods to trade for Filipino gold, and in this commerce the natives had learned long since how to use weights and measures, in which technique they were very adept. (It took the Spaniards a long time to find the sources of Philippine gold, and they were disappointed when they did find them: the little mines were not as productive as the explorers had hoped.) The natives, reported Pigafetta, built good houses of wood and thatch and constructed many boats, as is to be expected of island people. The men wore loincloths and tattooed their bodies, and the women dressed in bark skirts and were fond of gold ornaments. The chieftains of the communities swathed their heads in turbans of cotton cloth or silk, and like the women decorated themselves with gold. They used golden dishes, and some even trimmed their houses with the precious stuff. There seemed to be no one overlord of all the Islands, but a kind of king ruled Luzon, and his son commanded the military and naval forces of nearby Borneo.

As to religion, said the chronicler, some of the natives were heathen and the others Muslim. In their colonizing, the Spaniards always followed the traditional pattern: they sought spices, gold, and converts to Roman Catholicism. They believed fervently that it was their duty, laid on them by God, to convert whatever unbeliever they came upon in their conquests, and had already put these precepts into practice in the Americas. The Muslims they encountered in the East were likely to prove as tough as other people of that faith and determined to remain Muslim, but the Spaniards never stopped trying.

Late in 1564 a fifth Spanish expedition set out from New Spain under the command of the remarkable Miguel López de Legaspi, a Basque who had served as town clerk of Mexico City. With him went Andrés de Urdaneta, an Augustinian friar in whose written account of the journey much of the story has survived. The Spaniards, with four ships and 360 men, stopped on the way at Guam to take formal possession of the Ladrones for Spain. On February 13, 1565, the fleet came to anchor off Cebu, which had been Magellan's choice of residence during his brief tenure. Here the natives at first threatened the strangers with bows and arrows, lances, and even a small cannon, but Legaspi decided to stay on nevertheless. In April that year his men came upon a memento of the famous navigator—a little figure of the Christ child which Magellan had probably presented to the queen of Cebu, and Legaspi took as a good omen. His dealings with the Filipinos were consistently low-key and gentle, and they soon dropped their hostility. In fact Tupas, king of Cebu, embraced the Christian religion and was baptized. Many of his people followed his example, and Legaspi shipped Urdaneta back to New Spain to carry the good news, to report on the expedition's success generally, and to ask for more men and munitions, which the little colony needed for defense less against the natives than the Portuguese who occupied territory nearby. The authorities agreed, feeling that the East was well worth the expense, as the spices now being shipped off to Spain with reasonable regularity continued to be profitable.

When his ships returned with the requested men and supplies, Legaspi decided to move his colony from Cebu to Panay, which was easier to defend. The chief drawback to the new locale was that many pirates infested the coastline of Panay, so Legaspi sent his grandson, Captain Juan de Salcedo, along with Martin de Goeti, to put them down. The officers were also instructed to explore the northern islands with special reference to Manila on Luzon. With them went a force of Spanish soldiers and Filipinos from the Visayan Islands near Mindanao. They were surprised by Manila, though they had heard a good deal about it, because it proved to be a strongly fortified city, which harbored a powerful Muslim chieftain named Rajah Soliman. Just across the Pasig River, along which the town was built, stood another strong city named Tondo, controlled by the Muslim chief Rajah Lacandola. Rajah Soliman was friendly at first and made the Spaniards welcome, but soon a large number of local natives attacked the Europeans and their forces, and the Spaniards fought back. They had superior arms and were better trained: the Muslims were soon driven off, but not before they had burned Manila to the ground.

In May 1571, Legaspi himself led a force of three hundred men to Manila and established the city again. He reconstructed the fort, built a government house, and made plans for an Augustinian monastery, a church, and 150 houses. Much impressed by Manila's superior tactical position, he declared it to be the capital city of the whole archipelago, and there and then settled in with his colony. Rajah Soliman did not accept the situation without resistance: he tried to expel the invaders and was killed in the attempt, but his neighbor Rajah Lacandola entered the Roman Catholic faith and gave no more trouble.

Little by little, Goeti and Salcedo conquered and brought under control all the rest of Luzon as well as most of the neighboring islands. The Spaniards were entitled to be proud of the fact that in a remarkably short space of time they had gained such vast territories for their motherland, but Legaspi and his men could not have accomplished such a feat if the Islands had been more thickly populated and better organized against invaders. As it was, in his time there were at most half a million inhabitants in the whole archipelago, hard as it is to credit when we look at today's swarming islands. What helped the Spanish, too, was that the priests who came with them as missionaries brought with them much ceremonial splendor, which attracted and awed the populace. The Filipinos had no similar priesthood to compete with the Church: even Islam, powerful as it was in neighboring countries, had not taken a very firm hold in the Islands, save in the country around Manila and the southern island of Mindanao. Wherever they were entrenched, they had to be reckoned with. The Spaniards, who dubbed all Filipino Muslims "Moros" or Moors, in memory of their coreligionists in the Iberian Peninsula, recognized without surprise that these people were as hostile to Christianity as their peninsular opposite numbers.

Though it is not the intention of this author to give a detailed account of the Philippines under the Spanish, some background must be sketched in so that one can see the kind of country the Americans burst into when their turn came in 1898. For one thing, it is important to remember that the Spaniards were not the only immigrants in the islands. Strictly speaking, of course, all inhabitants, even the so-called aboriginal or Negritos, can be classed as immigrants, but the same can be said about most countries as we know them. If the anthropologists are correct, the people found by the Spaniards when they arrived were chiefly of Malay blood with dashes of Chinese and Indian, whereas the Negritos are related to similar peoples in the Andaman Islands and Malaya. Nobody can be sure which place was their first home, but one thing is certain: they were low men on the totem pole when the Americans arrived. Dean

Conant Worcester, an early American visitor during the Spanish regime, was highly indignant at the treatment the Negritos received from the Malay-mixed Filipinos, who enslaved them as a matter of course.

The *Encyclopaedia Britannica* gives a description of the Filipino languages which is widely accepted: "All of the Philippine populations, including the Negritos, speak languages belonging to the widespread Malayo-Polynesian stock which includes most of the peoples of Oceania. . . . About 75 linguistic groups are found in the Philippines, and today language is an important identifying feature of Filipino ethnic groups. Three or four of these groups are major languages that are gradually absorbing their smaller neighbours. Tagalog, . . . the most important of these linguistic groups, is second in size, but its strategic position in central Luzon led to its adoption in 1946 as the basis for the national language, . . . Bisayan (or Visayan), the largest major language group, occupies the central islands but is split into three major subdivisions. In northern Luzon, Ilocano has become the dominant language."

Clearly, the picture is not simple.

Legaspi died in 1572, about a year after he rebuilt Manila. He bequeathed to his successors the task of defeating the Moros, but those warriors never stayed defeated for long. The fight was to continue, with complications—for a time, for example, the Moros teamed up with the Dutch in attempting to oust the Spaniards—until 1851, and might be described as one of the longest religious wars in history, a chronic struggle. The English, too, made attempts on the islands: Sir Francis Drake visited Mindanao in 1577, and in 1582 another English pirate, Thomas Cavendish, captured one of the Manila galleons. Five years later, on another freebooting expedition, Cavendish showed up again and tried unsuccessfully to take a spice-laden ship. He was not able to carry through on another attempt during the same visit, to get control of the shipyards at Iloilo.

Meantime, in 1574, Manila underwent a scare from another source when a Chinese sea-captain named Limahong attacked the city from the sea, and managed to sack a part of the place before he and his men were driven off. But this Chinese pirate was exceptional. Most of his compatriots who came to the Islands maintained a friendly attitude toward the Spaniards and Filipinos, and were interested in peaceful trade: as merchants they were free to come and go as they chose. The Spaniards recognized their value as hardworking, thrifty artisans and shopkeepers: they filled a need. Speaking generally, the Filipinos were not so industrious: if they resented the Chinese taking their place as hewers of wood and drawers of water, they showed no signs of it, but willingly stood back and gave up. Japanese traders, too, were made welcome, but the Chinese always far outnumbered them.

By the end of the sixteenth century the Dutch had become a palpable threat to the Spanish, supplanting the position of the Portuguese as the world's most daring navigators. They were busily trading in the Moluccas, which in 1605 they took outright from the Portuguese (though the Spaniards still maintained a foothold in some of the islands), and also made nuisances of themselves in Philippine waters, attacking all comers: Portuguese, Spanish, Japanese, and Chinese ships. As the conditions were very like those of formal war, nobody bothered to cry foul when in 1610 the governor of the Philippines fought and killed a Dutch admiral near Manila and took possession of some ships in his fleet. In spite of this setback, the Dutch went on from one success to another. In 1640 they occupied Malacca. The Spaniards evacuated their part of the Moluccas in 1662 because of the threat from Koxinga, a Chinese supporter of the Ming Dynasty who led his forces abroad and found refuge in Taiwan (Formosa).

In 1762 changes overtook even the quiet, backward Philippines, though not for long as these things went. The British, at war with Spain, occupied Manila. However, in accord with the Treaty of Paris, signed in 1763, Spain duly repossessed the city. Save for this interregnum, matters in the Islands moved with characteristic slowness, but one development was to prove overwhelmingly important—the growing power of the friars. Legaspi, as has been said, brought in the Augustinians. Urdaneta, who introduced the order, was accompanied by four others. Later came the Franciscans, Jesuits, Dominicans, and Augustinian Recollects, in that order, and by degrees all of them took possession of much of the land and wealth of the country. They held on, too, though the home government now and then suggested that they change their ways. Strictly speaking, priests of the Church should not acquire worldly possessions, but the friars were not the first of their persuasion to forget this admonition, and the homeland was far off. Nobody was in a position to check them. The greed and power of the friars were main grievances of the natives when at last, in the nineteenth century, the Filipinos revolted against their overlords.

In the meantime trade flourished for those in power. It was a triangular trade: Chinese vessels carried goods from China to Manila, and then the Manila galleons moved the same goods from Manila to Mexico, usually making the important voyage in each direction once a year—for, naturally, they did not return empty to the East, but brought payment in silver. The first galleon left Manila and sailed east across the Pacific in 1565, the last returned to Manila in 1815. In 1565, Philip II was king of Spain and his enemy Elizabeth Tudor was queen of England. In that same year, Pedro Menéndez de Avilés laid the foundations of St. Augustine, Florida. When the shipping line came to an end it was already five years after Miguel Hidalgo y Costilla began the revolt in Spain which was to create the Republic of Mexico, the United States had been a nation for fifty years, and Andrew Jackson had just won the Battle of New Orleans. In the years between, the sea had claimed dozens of the trading ships, thousands of men, and many millions in treasure. The English took four of the galleons: four more beat off English and Dutch assailants. The people of Spanish America called the galleons and their crews either the Manila galleons or the China ships, and welcomed their cargoes of silks and spices and other precious Oriental merchandise. The

Orientals knew them because they brought loads of silver in the form of Mexican and Peruvian pesos which in time became the accepted standard of value all along their coasts. "Dollars Mex" were still cited as units of currency in China until the Second World War and perhaps even later. The galleons were the first cause of exploration in California, and in Spain the ships proved in a practical way that in spite of Portugal's competition, she herself did indeed have an empire in the Pacific.

Just what articles were bartered in this trade? At the beginning the Islands were a disappointment to the Spaniards because they offered so little in the way of spices. A kind of cinnamon did indeed grow there, but not in great quantity nor of good quality, certainly not enough, said Legaspi in his reports, to justify the expense of colonization. There was a little gold about, as has been mentioned, but the Spaniards couldn't trace where it came from, and as for silk, though important natives wore it, its origin, too, was a mystery. Then it was noted that Chinese junks occasionally arrived at Cebu with silks and porcelains for sale, so the question about the silks at least was answered. In 1565, therefore, the first galleon starting out for Mexico from Manila was loaded with Philippine cinnamon, not because great profit was expected—nor was realized—but in order for the commander to discover a good, permanent return route for later ships. In 1572 one of Legaspi's vessels came to the rescue of a sinking Chinese junk off Mindoro, and saved the crew. These Chinese went home and told their compatriots about the Spaniards, and returned with friends and much merchandise. A year later two Spanish galleons carried rich cargo from China to Acapulco, and we have the records of it—712 pieces of silk, 22,300 pieces of fine gilt china, and many other porcelain articles. Soon Chinese junks in great numbers were sailing into Manila Bay to contribute to the next galleon's cargo. In a few more years the trade was humming: merchants even came over from Mexico to settle in Manila because the demand in Spanish America for Oriental goods rose and rose: there seemed no end to it. Situated at the crossroads as she was,

Manila prospered. Already a fine Spanish city, after a disastrous fire in 1603 it was rebuilt in even more splendid style, of stone with red tile roofs.

There was one bad effect of the galleon trade and its attendant prosperity: the Spaniards of Manila, having nothing to do between the ships' visits, became fat and lazy as well as rich. When a galleon came in, all would be bustle, the merchants gathering together the Oriental goods that had been brought in by junks. The goods had to be repacked in bales and chests for consignment, and there was tremendous activity on the part of the clerks making out invoices and registering the consignments with the treasury. But when all this was done and the ship was on her way, the men had nothing to do but wait for her return, when once again there was a pleasant bustle as the money was shared out. This lazy life was pleasant for the Spaniards with its luxury and self-indulgence, but the profiteers did little or nothing to improve conditions for the Filipinos, who badly needed instruction and help. No attempt was made to teach them modern methods of agriculture, industry, or anything else. The fact was that what with so many Chinese at hand, willing to fetch and carry and keep books, the Filipinos were not necessary for Spanish comfort. The clever, hardworking Chinese soon had a monopoly on local trade and handicrafts. According to a story noted by a contemporary Jesuit in the Islands, Diego de Bobadilla, they might sometimes have overdone the handicrafts. A Spaniard who lived in Manila had the ill fortune to lose his nose (possibly it was eaten away by syphilis), and he asked a Chinese wood-carver then visiting the city if he could make a new one. The Chinese produced such a good nose that the Spaniard, delighted, paid him very well. The artisan returned to China more than satisfied with the transaction—so much so that he returned to Manila the following year with a whole cargo of wooden noses in his junk. Alas, there were no more customers. As de Bobadilla said, to sell them he would have had to cut off the noses of all the Spaniards in the country.

All this time the religious orders gained more and more power and property, from which only the Church gained benefit. In fact, it was the Church rather than anything else that developed and grew: William Lyle Schurz said that the colony took on more and more the character of a vast religious establishment. Manila had become a warehouse of the Faith, and no official was powerful enough to resist it.

Any man rash enough to stand up to the friars and oppose them soon found himself in trouble. For a long time there was no help to be had from Spain, either: it was a long way off. However, during the reign of Charles III (1759–88) there was some relief: an attempt was made to broaden commercial interests in the Islands and develop their domestic resources. The local economy was given a long-delayed attention, and a few officials realized at last that the activities of Filipino peasants on the land in the last analysis had more importance than the comings and goings of trading ships, however immediately profitable. The cultivation of tobacco, copra, hemp, and sugar, all of which grew well in the Islands, might well mean more to the Philippines and those who owned them than external trade that made a few Spanish merchants wealthy for a while. And so, a year after Charles III died, there was a change, in that the port of Manila was opened to the world. At least that was the announcement made by the government, though on closer inspection this so-called opening did not amount to a great deal. To protect the galleons and their owners, foreign ships putting in to the port were permitted to trade only in goods of Asian origin: Manila remained closed to Dutch and English shipping, since Holland and England were still considered Spain's enemies, and the French were not welcome because the Spaniards didn't like them either. Naturally the leading European nations preferred to send their ships to more hospitable ports such as Batavia and Madras, and Manila's facilities, though superior, were ignored.

By the time the galleons ceased sailing, in 1815, the voyages had become worse than useless, hanging on by sheer inertia. The consul of Mexico was complaining to the king that they were just in the way, and pointed out that the Royal Company of the Philippines, which owned and operated the ships, was nearly defunct. All three of its galleons, he said, had been lying idle in Acapulco Harbor for a period ranging from one to three years, unable to get rid of their cargoes because the Americans and English were now trading directly with the west coasts of Spanish America, pushing out the Philippine merchants. Summing up the period, the most important fact about the galleons was that for 250 years they had carried shipload after shipload of silver to China, where the king of Spain was now known as the King of Silver. It was not good for the economic balance of Europe, this constant trickle of specie out of the West and into the East: belatedly, the Spanish were realizing it. In any case they were having other troubles with Mexico, not to mention Europe. In Europe they had the Napoleonic Wars, and in Mexico there was insurrection: Acapulco was actually burned down in 1813. In October of that year King Ferdinand capitulated and legally suppressed the Royal Company of the Philippines, and so, two years later, its last galleon left Acapulco for Manila.

One outstanding legacy of the galleon period remained in the Islands: the Manila Chinese, who have always been called (because of an Amoy word meaning "trader") the Sangleys. Because for so long they had monopolized retail trade and the skilled crafts, as the years went by they continued to do so. Some of them represented three or four generations of Chinese resident in the Islands, and many were intermarried with Filipino families. The historian William Lyle Schurz supplies statistics from 1935 to the effect that at that time Chinese operated 13,787 retail establishments in the Philippines, and Chinese merchants owned over 56 percent of the capital invested in that country. In 1932 they handled at least 50 percent of the total business of the archipelago. And these figures, remember, represent only the out-and-out Chinese. Of course the many intermarriages had their results, too: Chinese energy, Chinese intelligence, were imparted through inheritance to many officially Filipino families, the inquilinos or, as they were usually called, mestizos. Such, for example, was the background of the Philippines' most beloved hero, José Rizal y Mercado.

Chapter Two

Rizal was born in 1861 in Calamba, in Laguna Province, south of Manila. The political situation in which he grew up has been described by Father Nicholas Cushner, S.J., in his work *Spain in the Philippines*. In Spain throughout the nineteenth century a serious split existed between the liberals and the conservatives after Ferdinand VII wiped out (in 1813) certain reforms that had been put into effect by the Cortés, the Spanish legislature.

"In Spain liberalism had both political and religious overtones," wrote Father Cushner. It advocated absolute independence of the state from all positive religions, and encouraged anticlerical movements which led to the slaughter of friars and the burning of churches, a result which, though not advocated by the liberals, naturally led to their being equated with outright anticlericals: thus their programs of legislative reforms were suspected by both the moderate and conservative elements in Spain. After Ferdinand's death there was much upset and dislocation in the country, with rapid changes of government and rulers, and naturally this disorder

27

at home had its effect on Spain's overseas possessions. In the Americas, Mexico and Peru took advantage of the situation to declare independence, and though the Philippines, like Puerto Rico and Cuba, remained loyal, the home government feared they would follow Spanish America's example. Every change of government in Spain meant a corresponding dislocation in the Philippines, with a new governor arriving with his officials to displace the former appointee. It was a state of affairs that caused great dissatisfaction among the Philippine-born Spaniards. And the chaos in Spain had another bad effect on the Islands: economic development was even more neglected than it had been before. What growth that did take place on these lines was due to foreign capital.

The Spanish struggle between anticlerical liberals and conservatives was matched in the Islands in the late nineteenth century, the difference there being that the reformers attacked the friars rather than the Church itself, these clerics being described as "sly, avaricious, arrogant and impure" men who controlled the Church and state and preserved their power by deliberately refusing advancement to the native clergy. Cushner said it was probably true. The friars were masters of the country, especially in the provinces. Sir John Bowring, English diplomat and governor of Hong Kong, observed (as other travelers had done before him) that the religious orders in the Philippines were very rich, that their monasteries were almost palatial and their revenues enormous. The monasteries stood amid jumbles of pathetically poor huts, offering a dramatic contrast, said Bowring. But not everybody criticized the clergy in this fashion: at least one Spaniard pointed out that thousands of "Indians" (i.e., Filipinos) dwelt in peace and security though governed by a weak old man, a friar who inspired his flock with love and respect.

Perhaps. But there is no doubt that the religious orders had collected an awe-inspiring amount of land in the form of haciendas from which they derived large incomes, and these estates steadily increased in size. Some of the land was leased to Chinese mestizos, who in turn hired other people to do the work. Most of these lessors were absentee landlords. An upper class developed among the mestizos, and some of its members were affluent enough to send their sons to Europe to study. Sometimes the landholders raised their rent, and the antagonism that resulted from this action developed into anticlericalism.

"What is perhaps just as significant," wrote Father Cushner, "a pattern of tenant farming emerged which still plagues the agricultural system of the Philippines." (Today it is known as caciquism: the ruler of the village is the cacique.) Rizal's family was of this upper class of mestizos. Though not among the richest, they could afford to send their sons to Spain for their education, but José was only eleven, too young to go abroad, when a most important event took place. On January 20, 1872, a revolt broke out among the soldiers living in barracks in Cavite near Manila. A new Spanish governor, Izquierdo, had recently arrived to take over his post, and the authorities panicked. The revolt was not a large affair; only about two hundred soldiers and marines were involved. Moreover, it seems to have been over money rather than politics—the rebels had not been paid their wages. They were quickly arrested and punished, but the government took stern measures to deal with matters over and above that particular affair, and also arrested a number of suspect native priests as well as some local businessmen. Three of the Filipino priests, José Burgos, Mariano Gomez, and Jacinto Zamora, were tried by a kangaroo court, sentenced to death, and hastily executed. Burgos had been prominent in a struggle of Filipino secular priests against the transfer of parishes to the religious orders, and had long been under observation by the authorities. Zamora, like Burgos, was suspected of a connection with liberals in Spain. The youngest of the trio, Mariano Gomez, was a curate of Bacoor, Cavite, and nobody was sure afterward just why he had been singled out: the only common bond between him and the others was their antifriar sentiments. Yet Gomez was never at any time accused of anti-Spanish activities, and the Spanish government was never, then or later, explicit on the subject.

In addition to these executions, a large number of other clerics were imprisoned and exiled. It was rumored that the hated friars were the moving spirits of the whole affair, and people already inclined to rebellious feelings now had something of substance to serve as fuel to their fires.

Inevitably the affair resulted in the organization of the people against the friars. In Spain and the Islands between 1880 and 1896 a so-called Propaganda Movement developed, aiming for reform in colonial administration, but it still meant to confine its reforms (said Cushner) within the framework of the empire. Supporters of the movement in Spain were chiefly Filipino students abroad. They had a newspaper that advocated assimilation of the Philippines with Spain and representation in the Cortés for native Filipinos, but the newspaper staff soon divided into two camps, with Spanish mestizos (who were considered aristocrats) and Philippine-born Spanish on one side, and Filipinos with Chinese mestizos on the other. Rizal of course was to join the latter camp when he got to Madrid. As he said, he was almost bound to be a rebel after an experience his family underwent when he was still very young. It seems that the *guardia civil* arrested his mother on suspicion of being mixed up in a murder, and marched her twenty miles on foot to Santa Cruz, in Laguna. Though she was later cleared and released, Rizal never forgot his resentment against the incident. Also, his brother Paciano had reformist sentiments which he transmitted to José. Last, but certainly not least, was the affair of the three martyred priests.

José was brilliant. He studied first at the Jesuit Ateneo Municipal until he got his degree, then moved on to the University of Santo Tomas, which was run by Dominicans. There he decided to be a doctor, but he was still working toward the necessary degree when he broke off and went to Madrid, perhaps to take a more active part in politics. In the capital he found thirty or forty other Filipino students, but didn't think much of them as material for revolutionaries. He resumed his medical studies at the University of Madrid, and also did a lot of thinking—and talking, no doubt—about the

Philippine situation. The friars, he decided, were the real problem. In his first novel, *Noli me Tangere* (Touch Me Not), published in Berlin in 1887 when the author was twenty-six, he painted a most unflattering portrait of the friars, who are represented as venal, greedy, and sly, working on the superstitions of the simple Filipinos to keep them under control. The book came out in March: by June it was being eagerly read in the Philippines and scandalizing the churchmen. The archbishop of Manila himself sent a copy to the rector of Santo Tomas to show what his alumnus was up to. A committee was organized to study the matter, and on August 30 it announced that the book was heretical, impious, and offensive to the Spanish government. One could hardly be surprised by this. It was certainly all these things, and was intended to be, as far as the friars were concerned. Rizal was not only an angry young man: he was furious.

He was ahead of his times, wrote Father Cushner: *Noli me Tangere* contained nothing an educated Catholic would find fault with today. But this was 1887, and though the author was acclaimed by many of his colleagues for the book, he had become, irrevocably, an object of suspicion in the eyes of the Church and the government. However, as a full-fledged ophthalmologist he went home to the Islands and seems to have enjoyed a visit with the family without trouble. It was then, probably, that he cured his mother of eye trouble, which is one of the stories often told about him. Then he returned to Europe and visited England, and wrote and published articles about the Philippines. From there he went to Hong Kong and practiced medicine in that colony, and also organized the Liga Filipina, a nonpolitical society that aimed at unification of the Islands, protection of the members, defense against violence and injustice, encouragement of education and agriculture and commerce, and a study of reforms. All this would seem commendable but so vague as to be harmless to the powers in command. But no: evidently they could not forgive his attack on the friars, and when Rizal came back to Manila to open a branch of La Liga, he was arrested. They exiled him to the little town of Dapitan on Mindanao, where he lived for four years.

Father Cushner points out that though the formal Propaganda Movement did not survive Rizal's falling-out with its leaders, it had several important and lasting effects. Constant sniping at the friars did damage their overwhelming power and hindered their further acquisition of land. It also built up a new sense of unity among educated Filipinos, so that they no longer thought of themselves primarily as Tagalogs or Visayans or Ilocanos, but as Filipinos—and Filipinos threatened by the friars, who were themselves a visible manifestation of foreign political domination. Actually, however, Spain in the nineteenth century did not totally neglect the Islands: a few reforms were put into practice. Promotions and appointments were now based on efficiency and length of residence, elementary schools passed under government control, and the Church no longer kept such a firm grip on the education of children. There were a few other reforms as well, but by this time they were not enough.

During Rizal's exile a new organization called the Katipunan was formed by a fellow malcontent named Andrés Bonifacio, which went much further than the Liga: its aims were similar but the means differed. According to the Katipunan all Filipinos should consider themselves one nationality, and would petition for representation of the Islands in the Cortés, requesting equal rights for Spaniards and Filipinos. If these objects were not peacefully attained, an armed rising under the protection of the Japanese empire was recommended. Katipunan representatives called on Rizal in Dapitan, asking him to support them, but he refused, saying that the time for armed uprising had not yet arrived. In spite of this dusty answer they went ahead with their plans, and decided that the revolution was to commence on August 29, 1896. Then, worried because Rizal was in on the secret and might (they thought) betray them, they jumped the gun and started operations several days ahead of time, on August 26. In the meantime Rizal, incurably patriotic, embarked for Spain, because Spain and Cuba had just declared war on each other, and he meant to volunteer as a doctor in the Spanish army. He was arrested at Barcelona and returned to Manila. Tried in a great hurry for complicity in the Katipunan rebellion, he was found guilty and executed on December 30. So ended at an early age a most remarkable life, a man of many talents—doctor, poet, patriot. Few national heroes have been so worthy of admiration.

Rizal had foreseen that the revolutionary army could not win, and he was, of course, correct. At first it had some success in Cavite Province, near Manila: during that time only one man proved himself capable of leading such an inexperienced army—Emilio Aguinaldo of Cavite Viejo, who like most of his followers was a Tagalog. (He had been, for a time, mayor of Cavite Viejo, as well as a schoolteacher.) After May 10, 1897, when Bonifacio was captured and executed— probably, in fact, by order of the watchfully jealous Aguinaldo—the ex-mayor assumed sole leadership, but for all his talents he could not continue to hold Cavite against the more disciplined Spanish forces, and he took his men back to Biak-na-Bato in Bulacan. When word reached his army of the execution of Rizal, the insurrection took on fresh life, but on December 14, 1897, the Pact of Biak-na-Bato was finally signed by the contestants, the insurgents and the Spaniards, with some loyal Filipino troops, under General Fernando Primo de Rivera. Among other terms (including the expulsion of the friars), it provided that one and a half million pesos were to be paid to the revolutionaries, an indemnity was to be given to people who had suffered from the war, and the revolutionary leaders agreed to leave the country. Emilio Aguinaldo went with eighteen of his aides to Hong Kong on December 27, thus carrying out one of the very few treaty terms that were, in the end, observed. But the agreed sum was never paid in full, and the insurrection continued.

Chapter Three

Spain was overlord of Cuba as well as the Philippines, but before the Spanish-American War the two colonies had little else in common. After all, they were on opposite sides of the world. Every now and then some Cubans rose in revolt; every now and again the Spaniards felt that they had to crush some of the revolutionaries. It was inevitable that here and there a handful of Americans, drawing parallels between their history and that of the island so temptingly near their own territory, should work up indignation against Spain on Cuba's account. Thomas Jefferson, noting the island's geographic position, commented that if it ever came into British possession the Republic would be endangered. John Quincy Adams said that the laws of political gravitation were bound, sooner or later, to draw Cuba to the United States. In 1825 Henry Clay declared that America would never permit Cuba to be occupied by any other power than Spain. All in all, none of these gentlemen was a very good prophet.

But there the island was, still very close to the United States.

About the middle of the nineteenth century the American government made overtures to Spain about buying it. Spain, however, was not interested. In spite of this rebuff American gunboats continued to hang around the Cuban coast, and in 1852 Great Britain proposed a tripartite agreement to settle the matter and keep the peace, according to which we, with Great Britain and France, would agree to renounce any designs on annexing the island. The United States refused to consider such an agreement, saying that we had a special interest in Cuba. In 1854 three American ministers, to Spain, England, and France, met at Ostend, Belgium, and issued a manifesto the burden of which was that Spain should sell Cuba to us, that Cuba was necessary to the safety of the institution of slavery in our Southern states, and that if Spain continued to refuse to sell, thus threatening "our internal peace," we would be justified in taking it by force if we could. Pierre Soulé, our minister to Madrid, even pointed out that it was a good time to think of war with Spain, since England and France were fighting in the Crimea and wouldn't be able to interfere. However, this Ostend manifesto did not meet with general approval in the States, and the Republican government, realizing that public opinion was not ripe for it, dropped the matter.

Then, during the Civil War, Spain recognized the Southern Confederacy and the North was outraged. That was one reason why, when insurrection broke out in Cuba in 1870, Americans of the Northern states were ready to take sides against Spain: they still bore a grudge. They also still identified with the insurrectionists. That rebellion was crushed, but another one started up in 1895, and again plenty of Americans took sides against Spain. Two New York newspapers, William Randolph Hearst's *Journal* and Joseph Pulitzer's *World*, ran reports on conditions on the island that whipped up more anger on behalf of the *reconcentrados*, those unfortunate Cubans who were huddled into concentration camps without food, sanitation, or medicine. The reporters pointed out that while Spanish troops made war on Cuban guerrillas, thousands of the camp people were dying.

Of course it was not purely unselfish indignation that motivated some Americans to take sides in this struggle. The public was developing an appetite for aggrandizement. We had acquired territory (Texas, Oregon) and won a war with Mexico: why not take on Spain as well? At least one official in Washington was watching developments with keen interest and pleasurable excitement— Theodore Roosevelt, who was appointed assistant secretary of the navy in April 1897. He had already made such a name for himself as a fire-eater that the London *Times* commented unfavorably on the navy appointment, saying that his "extreme jingoism" seemed especially ominous in this context. Roosevelt, in indirect reply, had promised that he would be good and said to at least one reporter, "I am sedate now." But only a week after his appointment he was addressing President William McKinley on the subject of various improvements badly needed, he said, in the U.S. fleet. He prepared the way carefully for other matters connected with the fleet— territorial expansion both in the East and the West.

Roosevelt's superior, Secretary John D. Long, was somewhat ineffective, and willing to leave many matters in his aide's hands. Roosevelt was free, therefore, to indulge his taste for intrigue. He had joined, or perhaps one should say amassed, a group of like-minded men, who according to his biographer Edmund Morris, "consisted of Senators and Representatives, Navy and Army officers, writers, socialites, lawyers, and scientists." These people thought that the United States should free Cuba, annex Hawaii, and raise the American flag over the whole Western Hemisphere. None of these ideas was new. Many of Roosevelt's cronies had been urging certain planks of the program during the last days of the Harrison administration and all of the Cleveland presidency, but it took the dynamic assistant secretary of the navy to bring them all together and push for what they wanted. In the group were Senator Henry Cabot Lodge, Commander Charles H. Davis, who was chief of naval intelligence, Judge William Howard Taft, Charles A. Dana, who was editor of the *New York Sun*, and others. Also among them were Commodore

George Dewey and Captain Leonard Wood, who take leading places in the story of what happened later in the Islands. They were all aware that President McKinley needed pushing to do what they would like: for example, he was reluctant to acquire the Hawaiian Islands though they were ripe for plucking and Japan was rumored to have her eye on them. Even less did he want to go to war over Cuba. In his estimation, the United States had had enough war to last her for years to come.

But Roosevelt, in a stirring speech at the Naval War College in Newport, Rhode Island, on June 2, 1897, spoke urgently of the need for a rapid buildup of the navy. He told his enthusiastic audience, "It is too late to prepare for war when the time for peace has passed," declaring that in the case of any sudden attack from an enemy it would be six months before the States could parry it. McKinley read the speech and commented to a friend, "I suspect that Roosevelt is right, and the only difference between him and me is that mine is the greater responsibility."

Not long afterward the lobby managed to persuade the president to approve a treaty of annexation of Hawaii. There were protests from Japan, but none from Hawaii—none, at least, that were heard on the Hill. It was June 16, 1897.

George Dewey was elderly as officers go—sixty—and had seen action under Admiral David Farragut in the Civil War, but had done no active fighting since. Leonard Wood was an interesting man with a fine record from the Indian Wars: he had conquered Geronimo, and was also the assistant attending surgeon to the president. He and Dewey were in ardent agreement with Roosevelt's ideas: TR had plans for both of them. He knew, for example, that the rear admiral in charge of the Asiatic Squadron, Fred V. McNair, was due to retire in a few months, and he was determined to put Dewey in that place if he possibly could. His chance came on Labor Day, when Long was away from the office on a week's vacation. Working with his usual astonishing speed and efficiency, Roosevelt sent to the president his suggested plan for war over Cuba—"a two-stage naval offensive," the army following up the navy with a landing party, in which case it would probably be all cleaned up in six weeks. "Meanwhile," continued Roosevelt, "our Asiatic Squadron could blockade, and if possible take Manila."

On the following Monday a cloud appeared on the horizon, nothing less than a letter to Long which his assistant secretary managed to intercept. It was from Senator William E. Chandler, recommending that Commodore John A. Howell be appointed commander in chief of the Asiatic Station. Consternation! Roosevelt first tried to persuade the senator to withdraw his suggestion, but he refused. Next, the assistant secretary asked Dewey if *he* knew any senators, and Dewey, fortunately for the plan, did—Senator Redfield Proctor. Proctor consented to go to the White House immediately and interview Mr. McKinley in order to suggest Dewey's name before Chandler's letter should reach Mr. Long. The president accepted the advice without too much ado: he was not very interested in the navy's affairs at any rate. He duly wrote to Long suggesting Dewey as a replacement for McNair, and Long, when he came back to his office, naturally followed his direction: he could not very well refuse even though, as it happened, he would have preferred Howell.

So far, so good. Dewey was sent, by easy stages, to Hong Kong on December 7.

Still, in spite of public indignation over Cuba, it is highly probable that if there had been a referendum possible in the United States before February 1898, the cause of those in favor of a Spanish-American war would have been defeated. The nation—excepting Roosevelt and his group—was not naturally bellicose. Certainly President Cleveland in his time and McKinley after him would have voted against it. But 1898 brought changes. For one thing, because of a riot that took place in Havana on January 12, 1898, the American consul general there, nervous about the safety of American nationals in that city, asked for help, and the State Department sent the U.S. battleship *Maine* to stand by offshore. Ostensibly it was a friendly visit. McKinley had asked the Spanish minister in Washington,

Enrique Depuy de Lôme, if it would be all right, and was most politely reassured. Unfortunately, at about the same time de Lôme was writing to Madrid in less polite words about the president, saying among other things that McKinley was weak, a bidder for the admiration of the crowd. Somehow, the *New York Journal*, the Hearst paper, got hold of that letter (which never reached Madrid) and published it on February 9, resulting in ill will all around—as if there were not enough ill will already.

The *Maine* had arrived in Havana and anchored on January 25. Her welcome was so chilly that Captain Charles D. Sigsbee ordered that there should be no shore leave for the men, but nothing untoward happened until the night of February 15, when there was a gigantic explosion that sank the ship in the harbor, killing over two hundred men. Nobody was ever able to prove beyond a doubt that Spaniards were responsible for the calamity, though a group of so-called experts later claimed that they could detect traces of a mine placed under the vessel. But Americans did not need absolute proof to be furiously resentful. War fever hotted up. All over the country, citizens were chanting:

Remember the *Maine!*
To hell with Spain!

War seemed inevitable, and President McKinley bowed to public opinion and changed his mind: as a politician he could do no less.

After that, things moved fast—fast, that is, considering the times. On April 10, Queen María Cristina of Spain ordered the suspension of hostilities in Cuba, but on the next day the president asked Congress to give him the authority to intervene on that island. It did so readily, in addition passing a resolution which demanded that Spain withdraw from and pledge the independence of Cuba. If Spain replied to this action there is no record of it. On April 23 Congress passed an act authorizing the enlistment of volunteer troops. On April 24 Spain declared war on the United States; on the twenty-fifth, Congress retorted that Spain was too late, as a state of war already existed and had done so since the twenty-third, when the Atlantic fleet sailed for Cuban waters.

Already, on February 25, Roosevelt had taken advantage of Secretary Long's temporary absence from the office to cable to Dewey: ORDER THE SQUADRON, EXCEPT THE *MONOCACY*, TO HONG KONG. KEEP FULL OF COAL. IN THE EVENT OF DECLARATION WAR SPAIN, YOUR DUTY WILL BE TO SEE THAT THE SPANISH SQUADRON DOES NOT LEAVE THE ASIATIC COAST, AND START OFFENSIVE OPERATIONS IN PHILIPPINE ISLANDS. KEEP OLYMPIA UNTIL FURTHER ORDERS. Dewey was ready, therefore, when Long sent a cable of his own on April 24, ordering him to put to sea toward Manila. Within two days the squadron had vanished from its anchorage, on the way toward the Islands.

"The war thus begun was pathetically one-sided," comments the *Encyclopædia Britannica*. Though as a whole the American army was no better prepared than that of Spain, the navy, thanks to Roosevelt's frenetic preparations, was in good shape. The Atlantic Squadron possessed four new battleships, and in the Asiatic Squadron were modern protected cruisers against which Spain could marshal only seven antiquated vessels. Dewey led his fleet into Manila Bay early in the morning of May 1, picked off the Spanish ships one by one, and burned or sank all of them. It must have been an imposing sight, full of smoke and flame, yet in spite of all the words written by the United States newspapers of that time, and the gloating books, it was almost too easy to be sporting. Seven of our men were slightly wounded, 381 Spaniards were killed or wounded, and that was that. Dewey, idolized by a hysterically jubilant nation, was immediately promoted to the rank of acting rear-admiral.

Riding at anchor, he was able to see a city the like of which nobody in America, probably—nobody, that is, without experience in Europe—could have envisaged. The red-tiled roofs and stone houses built after Soliman's city was burned were still in evidence, as was the little city of fortifications, called Intramuros (or the Walled City), though the large population of Manila had now spilled over and outside. Around the splendid bay were other walls and other fortifications, with many useless guns pointed toward the floating ships. Two years earlier a British army officer and his wife came to visit Manila and other places in the Islands in order to produce a book about them: his wife took the photographs and Major G. J. Younghusband did the literary part.

"The bay of Manila," he wrote, "is so large that a strong wind from the west or southwest can raise a sea heavy enough to seriously retard landing operations. . . . Close to the point of landing stood, and stands to this day, a small, square, masonry fort called the Pulverina or Powder Magazine." Younghusband also described the dungeon of San Sebastian, a fort in Intramuros, which was below water level. The Spaniards, he recounted, had put 169 insurgents in there overnight. There was only one air hole in the place, and 54 of the prisoners were found asphyxiated in the morning. The survivors were led out and shot on the Luneta, the most fashionable promenade in Manila, on the shores of the Bay. This happened in August 1896; more prisoners were shot on September 12, in the presence of Spanish ladies strolling out to take the air, while the band played lively airs and a photographer was busy with his camera commemorating the occasion. They were not regular soldiers, said the major: among them were two jail officials, one chemist, two or three rich landed proprietors, a tailor, a schoolmaster, a doctor, and a merchant. Their arms and legs were bound and they were placed facing the sea and shot down from behind.

It is not clear whether the Younghusbands stayed right through until the Americans took over or merely went away and came back. In any case he knew Manila well, and saw the Americans there later. "The town of Manila consists of an old walled city, known as 'Intramuros,' and of various suburbs which have sprung up around it," he wrote. "It came into the possession of the Spaniards partly by conquest and partly by treaty in the month of May, 1570, upwards of three centuries ago. The walled city appears to have been built as a protection against the sea pirates about the year 1590 . . . and according to tradition Chinese labour was employed in the construction of the defences. The main bastions are built of huge blocks of faced stone, and even after three centuries of wear and tear would still form a protection against any but the heaviest guns. Of the suburbs, Binondo is the chief trading centre, and has indeed become a small town of itself, separated only from the walled town by the Pasig River. On the other hand, and connected with the walled town by the Luneta or public promenade, lie the combined suburbs of Ermita and Malate, where the English Club is situated, and where several handsome private residences are to be found. Both in the walled city and in Binondo the houses and streets are much the same as are to be found in any small town in Spain or France, architectural merit, such as it is, being reserved for the churches and cathedrals. The streets are narrow and paved with rough cobble stones, which must bring fond recollections of New York to the American heart, and the footpaths, except in the Escolta, the Bond Street of Manila, are rarely broad enough for two people to walk comfortably abreast. Mud, deep abiding mud, is prevalent everywhere for three-fourths of the year, and is replaced by dust during the remaining period. It is difficult to say whether the paved streets or the unpaved are the worst; both are execrable . . . The shops, especially in the Escolta, are surprisingly good for such an out-of-the-way place, and compare favourably with those of Hong Kong, Calcutta, or Singapore. . . ."

Dewey sent to Washington for troops to help him take the city, and in the meantime—a fairly long meantime, as troop transporting took weeks in those pre-aviation days—he placidly waited afloat. At least it was probably his intention to remain placid, but the Germans made this difficult. There were in the Bay at the time Dewey arrived two British ships, two German cruisers, one French and one Japanese ship. Almost immediately other German ships moved in, most impressive of which was the cruiser *Kaiserin Augusta,* the flagship of Vice Admiral von Diederichs, who from the first maintained an arrogant stance. William Cameron Forbes, later governor-general of the Philippines, thought his attitude might have been due to the fact that Dewey was still merely an *acting* rear admiral, whereas he himself was the real thing, but more likely it was merely his way of interpreting orders from Berlin, where officials were keeping a watchful eye on events in the Islands. Germany wanted at least a part of the territory there. The kaiser had plans for the Far East. Dewey had other reasons, too, for uneasiness: he knew that a Spanish squadron of destroyers and merchantmen (which were rumored, falsely, to be battle cruisers) had left Spain, aiming for Manila by way of the Suez Canal. Dewey's squadron had little ammunition and no access to any base of supplies. Nor, in spite of all Roosevelt could accomplish, had Washington as yet come to any conclusion as to just what the United States intended to do about the Philippines. The Treaty of Paris was not to be signed for another seven months. The German arrivals continued, until they had assembled in the Bay five men-of-war and naval transports with fourteen hundred men, nearly equal to the total number of Americans under Dewey's command. When Dewey asked the German admiral what his intentions were, all he got was the reply, "I am here by order of the kaiser, sir."

This was definitely disturbing. Dewey was fully aware that every nation had a right to protect its nationals; after all, we ourselves had kept the *Maine* in Havana Harbor for this reason. But in such circumstances as obtained in Manila, neutral nationals were supposed to observe certain laws of protocol, reporting the arrival of their naval vessels to the officers in charge, discussing the best places to anchor, and abstaining from interference between belligerents. The Germans ignored all these rules quite as if no U.S. squadron had vanquished the Spanish ships. Their officers visited the city whenever they felt like it (or could get shore leave, presumably), and were ostensibly friendly with the Spaniards. The German admiral officially visited the Spanish captain general, who returned the call. German officers visited the Spanish garrison, drilled their own men on land at Mariveles Harbor, and accepted the use of a large house for the convenience of Admiral von Diederichs, until Dewey wrote to him formally protesting this violation of the rules. Von Diederichs denied that the Americans had any special rights, and said he would submit the point to a conference of all the senior officers of the men-of-war in the harbor. To this conference only one officer, Captain Sir Edward Chichester of the British ship *Immortalité*, turned up, but he was completely in accord with Dewey, saying that he had directions from his superiors to comply with even more rigorous restrictions if Dewey imposed them. Chichester did not convince the Germans, and they continued to do as they liked until a German cruiser, ordered by the American dispatch boat to stop, failed to do so, and an American vessel sent a shot across her bows. It had its effect: the German cruiser halted. (Later, Dewey told Major Younghusband about that shot across the German ship's bows. Captain Chichester, he said, had pointed out to the German captain concerned that he had placed himself in the wrong by ignoring the American flag on Dewey's ship, and that a handsome apology was the best way out of the deadlock. Having thus smoothed German feelings, Chichester then went to Admiral Dewey and explained that the slight to the American flag was unintentional. It was probably due only to ignorance of naval etiquette, he said, adding, "You see, sir, the Germans have got no *sea manners*." That was good diplomacy.)

Next day von Diederichs sent to Dewey a staff officer with a list of grievances, to which Dewey returned an unequivocal reply, and the exchange seems to have settled matters: thereafter the Germans were less truculent. The Filipinos, or at any rate the Tagalogs, now found it expedient to continue the insurrection which had been interrupted by the entrance of the United States into the Islands. At the time of Dewey's action in Manila Bay, Aguinaldo and his companions were in Singapore, dutifully staying away from the Philippines and generally obeying the terms of the Pact of Biak-na-Bato, though they complained, with truth, that Spain was not carrying out her part of the bargain. Aguinaldo, in fact, was actually thinking of going to Europe, but paused when the American consul general of Singapore, Spencer Pratt, got in touch with Dewey, still in Hong Kong, and suggested that it might be a good idea for the commodore to meet the Filipino. After all, reasoned Pratt, they were on the same side, and a Filipino insurrectionist might well be useful. Dewey replied that Aguinaldo should come to Hong Kong as soon as possible. But then, of course, the commodore got his sailing orders and departed. Never mind, Aguinaldo reasoned, they would meet again in Manila, and in the meantime Pratt's attitude seemed promising. Aguinaldo went with three of his companions to the consul's house, where a meeting took place in the presence of an Englishman named Howard W. Bray, affiliated with the Singapore *Free Press,* who had lived a long time in the Orient and was very pro-insurgent.

Whatever was actually said at this interview—and there are several versions—the general outline is clear. It was on April 24, six days before Dewey's move on Manila. Everybody there, with the important exception of Pratt, recalled later that a provisional agreement was drawn up according to which Philippine independence was to be speedily proclaimed, a federal republic was to be established by insurgent vote, a "temporary intervention" of American and European administration commissions would be recognized, the members to be appointed by Commodore Dewey (who was now very nearly a rear admiral, but they didn't know it), and an American protectorate was to be established over the Philippines, to be recognized on the same terms as those fixed for Cuba. That was the general outline, but there were additional clauses. One of them stated that the agreement was to be ratified telegraphically by Dewey and President McKinley.

Was this agreement fact or fiction? Pratt was always to deny it, and the other Westerners, according to Albert G. Robinson in *The Philippines: The War and the People,* have produced no incontrovertible proof that it ever existed. He wrote, "The [Filipino] Junta in Hongkong assured me in emphatic terms that it was a fact. It appears to remain largely a question of personal veracity and I make no effort to determine which side has the rights of the matter." But Dean Conant Worcester, who served on both U.S. commissions after the signing of the Treaty of Paris and who knew the Islands for years before and after the war, did not hesitate to take sides, as will be seen in due course. Worcester was almost never known to hesitate.

Later, at any rate, Pratt received a cable from Washington

cautioning him against committing the U.S. government to alliance with any Filipino insurgent. The cable continued, in part, ". . . to obtain the unconditional personal assistance of General Aguinaldo in the expedition to Manila was proper if in so doing he was not induced to form hopes that it might not be practicable to gratify." The message ended on the same sharp, cautious note: if Pratt, consulting with Aguinaldo, had acted on the assumption that his government would cooperate with him in the furtherance of any plans of his own, or would consider itself pledged to recognize any political claims which he might put forward, "Your action was unauthorized and cannot be approved."

Worcester, in his book *The Philippines Past and Present*, goes into immense detail about this question. He had an enemy, one Judge James H. Blount, who took Aguinaldo's side in the controversy and went to such extremes, according to Worcester, that he himself took the trouble to get hold of the insurgent records and have them translated (they were, of course, originally in Tagalog, Aguinaldo's mother tongue). Blount, said Worcester, dwelt at length on promises, both expressed and implied, "which were consequently repudiated by Consul Pratt, Admiral Dewey and Generals Anderson and Merritt." Whether or not Dewey, Pratt, the U.S. consul general at Hong Kong, Rounseville Wildman, and the U.S. Consul C. F. Williams of Manila did (or did not) give assurances that a Filipino government would be recognized, the Filipinos, judging from their actions, certainly thought so, said Blount, and Admiral Dewey even gave them arms and ammunition.

Robinson, a staff correspondent for the *New York Evening Post*, like many of the newspapermen in the Philippines at that time, was pro-Aguinaldo. "There would seem to be but two possible interpretations of the situation," he wrote, "either the Filipinos were allies of the Americans and were so regarded by the Americans and by themselves, or they were looked upon only as convenient tools."

Not so, not so at all, said Worcester. At that famous meeting at Pratt's house, Bray had to act as interpreter because Aguinaldo knew very little English. Bray was keen on getting the United States into the affair, and it is impossible now to know what he told Aguinaldo. But consider, said Worcester, the ridiculous charges later made against Pratt and Dewey: that Pratt promised Aguinaldo recognition of the Philippine republic and that Dewey agreed. How could a consul take so much on himself? In his report, Aguinaldo said (in Tagalog, remember) that Pratt had assured him that because the Spaniards had not fulfilled the terms of the Biak-na-Bato agreement, his Filipino followers had a right to continue with their temporarily suspended revolution. Pratt then advised him—allegedly—to start fighting the Spaniards again. He said that the United States would help, and when Aguinaldo rejoined that he would like to see all this in writing, Pratt replied that he was going to telegraph Dewey asking for such an agreement. Dewey, he explained, was chief of the Philippine expedition, with great powers.

Pratt may well have said this, but he may not: we'll never know. We do know that he cabled the secretary of state on April 27 to say that he had sent Aguinaldo to Hong Kong to arrange cooperation with Dewey, and that next day he wrote at length explaining how he had come to meet the leader, and stating just what had been done. At the interview, he said, after learning from "General Aguinaldo" what object was sought by the present insurrectionary movement which, though he was absent from the Islands, he was still directing, Pratt took it upon himself, while explaining that he had no authority to speak for the government, to point out the danger of going along independently at this stage. ". . . and, having convinced him of the expediency of cooperating with our fleet then at Hongkong," he continued, "and obtained the assurance of his willingness to proceed thither and confer with Commodore Dewey to that end, should the latter so desire, I telegraphed the Commodore the same day. . . ."

Pratt arranged passage for Aguinaldo and his aide and secretary, under assumed names. They left on Tuesday the twenty-sixth. Just before leaving they had another interview with the consul, who wrote in his letter, "The general impressed me as a man of intelligence, ability and courage, and worthy of the confidence that has been placed in him. I think that in arranging for his direct cooperation with the commander of our forces, I have prevented possible conflict of action and facilitated the work of occupying and administering the Philippines. . . ."

As Worcester is careful to point out, Pratt explained to Aguinaldo that he had no authority to speak for the government. Also, there was no mention in the cabled messages between Pratt and Dewey of independence for the Islands, or indeed of any conditions on which Aguinaldo was to cooperate. In a later letter Pratt harked back to the second interview: "I enjoined upon him the necessity, under Commodore Dewey's direction, of exerting absolute control over his forces in the Philippines, as no excesses on their part would be tolerated by the American Government, the President having declared that the present hostilities with Spain were to be carried on in strict accord with modern principles of civilized warfare."

Aguinaldo, he said, agreed with all this, saying he was perfectly sure he could control his followers. He also stated "that he hoped the United States would assume protection of the Philippines for at least long enough to allow the inhabitants to establish a government of their own, in the organization of which he would desire American advice and assistance." To which Pratt appended the sentence, "These questions I told him I had no authority to discuss."

This does not sound as if the consul general promised independence. Again, after a meeting of the junta on May 4, 1898, Aguinaldo wrote a report of his installation as the president of the Philippines in which he repeated the story of his first interview with Pratt. Worcester added, "Note that there is here absolutely not one word of any promise of independence made to Aguinaldo by Pratt or anyone else." Nor is there. But Bray was not happy. He insisted that the promise was made and should be kept. The editor of the insurgent newspaper on Singapore took him to task on this question, said it was the first he had heard of Bray's story, and urged him to drop that foolishness. . . . But why go on? Such quarrels of history, as they move further and further from the actual occurrence, are arid. One thing that is obvious is that Aguinaldo himself certainly began to believe he had been promised independence for his country. He wrote about what happened when he and two attendants arrived in Cavite on the nineteenth, aboard the *McCullough* (which Dewey had ordered to bring him), to interview the admiral. "We anchored . . ." he wrote, "and immediately the launch of the Admiral—with his aide and private secretary—came to convey me to the *Olympia* [Dewey's flagship] where I was received, with my aide Dr. Leyva with the honors of a general, by a section of marine guards."

Later, in an inquiry conducted by the U.S. Senate, the chairman asked Dewey, "You, of course, never saluted the [insurrectionists'] flag?"

"Certainly not," said the admiral, "and I do not think I ever called Aguinaldo anything but Don Emilio; I don't think I ever called him 'General.'"

The chairman asked, "And when he came on board ship was he received with any special honors at the side?"

"Never," said Dewey.

There was more—a lot more—in Aguinaldo's memoirs, but the one that interests us now is his statement that the admiral had said, "America is rich in territory and money, and needs no colonies . . ." He added that Aguinaldo was to "have no doubt whatever about the recognition of Philippine independence by the United States." He said the same thing in slightly different words, and the Senate chairman again tried to track it all down:

"There was no recognition of the republic?"

"Never," said Admiral Dewey. "I did not think I had the authority to do it and it never occurred to me to do it. There was a sort of reign of terror; there was no government. These people had got the power for the first time in their lives and they were riding roughshod over the community. The acts of cruelty which were brought to my notice were hardly credible."

He had reminded Aguinaldo that he was supposed to treat his prisoners well, and Aguinaldo had replied that he would. When Dewey heard that U.S. troops were soon arriving he asked

Aguinaldo to withdraw from Cavite and make room for the Americans.

"He demurred at this," said Dewey, "but finally withdrew and established headquarters across the bay at a place called Bacoor, from which place on the 15th of June he sent me a proclamation declaring the independence of the Philippines. . . . That was the first intimation; the first I had ever heard of independence of the Philippines."

The chairman asked if Aguinaldo had ever hinted of his intentions. No, said the admiral, not a word. "He had done what I told him. He was most obedient; whatever I told him to do he did. I attached so little importance to this proclamation that I did not even cable its contents to Washington, but forwarded it through the mails. I never dreamed that they wanted independence."

But, of course, they did. After protesting to no avail that his men should have back the trenches the Americans took to use in their siege of Manila, Aguinaldo lost patience with the argument. He smoldered under the indignity of his position. Filipinos, even his brave Tagalogs, were permitted to come into and go out of Manila as they chose, but were not allowed to carry arms in the city, though now they felt entitled to claim it as theirs. In September he took his immediate supporters and withdrew from the environs of Manila to Malolos, twenty miles away, and there he set up a government of his own, with his chief adviser Apolinario Mabini by his side. On June 12 they issued a declaration of independence from Spain and at the same time proclaimed a provisional republic, with Aguinaldo as president and Malolos their capital—at least for the moment. He was in a reasonably strong position, the pro tem protocol having stated that U.S. forces should occupy the city, Bay, and harbor of Manila pending the signing of the Treaty of Paris. No other place was mentioned. Cavite, too, was occupied by American troops, but the western and northern territories of Luzon were firmly held by the insurgents. On June 29 the rebels in Malolos ratified Filipino independence—in form.

Chapter Four

Dewey's position during his long, long wait for reinforcements was unenviable. Manila was still a Spanish city, and his authority, as he said bitterly, extended just as far as he could throw a shell, and no farther. News from terra firma was not cheerful: the insurgents were busily entrenching themselves, and though they obeyed his orders to stay out of Manila, he knew they resented him. He knew the reasons for the delay: the United States was simply not prepared for transport of troops on such a large scale for so long a voyage. Ships had to be found to carry the men who, for that matter, also had to be found. To campaign in the Philippines, they decided in Washington, would necessitate an army of twenty thousand men, and there weren't that many under arms in the whole country, let alone near the West Coast. All our regulars were busy in the Atlantic. Hurriedly the administration began enlisting volunteers and scraping up ship transport. It was to take the first installment sixty days to arrive, late in June. Major General Wesley Merritt, a West Pointer and a Civil War veteran, was given command of the Pacific forces, but he couldn't go with the first lot: this was commanded by Brigadier General Thomas M. Anderson. They were volunteer troops from Oregon and California, as well as a portion of the 14th United States Infantry. Aboard the cruiser *Charleston*, they set sail from San Francisco on May 25th, but were not the first to arrive, because of orders to meet up with the second contingent in Honolulu and proceed to Guam, which meant they didn't get to Cavite until June 30. On June 20 the *Charleston* was dutifully sailing into Guam harbor and, like a proper war vessel, she shot off a few rounds to show the Spaniards that she meant business. But only a few officers inhabited this lonely port, and they had heard nothing from Manila for six months: they didn't even know a war was on. When they heard the shots they assumed that the ship was paying a courtesy call and that the noise was a salute. The chief officer and his aides immediately put out from shore in the official launch to pay his respects and to apologize for not having replied to the *Charleston*'s salute with one of his own. The fact was, he explained, they had no ammunition left. It was by the Americans that he was brought up to date.

The Spaniards stayed where they were, waiting, like Dewey, for whatever was to happen next—in Manila mostly, but also in other towns and camps. Considering the busy depredations of the insurgents there must have been more anxious times for them than for Rear Admiral Dewey. But Anderson arrived at last, and a second detachment, under General Francis V. Greene, came along after another two weeks, followed on July 25 by General Wesley Merritt— at last!—and his men.

The end of July brought General Arthur MacArthur, Jr. This particular arrival merits special attention. The general had a young son named Douglas, born in 1880, who at that time was a cadet at the West Texas Military Academy, and as we know, Douglas was fated to be heavily involved in the Philippines. All the MacArthur men were service people, all, that is, but the founder of the family in the United States, who was a judge in Milwaukee. Considering what was to follow, it is interesting that General Arthur MacArthur, Jr., was totally ignorant, when he got his orders to sail, of what and where the Philippines might be. He knew about Cuba, of course: every American military man knew about Cuba, and naturally he assumed he would be going there—until he read his orders. The Philippines? He sent out for a map from which he learned a few salient facts. (And, as in the famous story about Winston Churchill, he might well have asked what those damned dots were.) This story is not intended to cast aspersions on MacArthur's general knowledge of geography, because it was quite as good as that of most of his countrymen. As Chicago editor Finley Peter Dunne's creation, Mr. Dooley, observed on the subject of the Islands, "'Tis not more than two months since ye larned whether they were islands or canned goods." MacArthur was soon to learn what they were. His expedition consisted of four thousand men, mostly volunteers, and like all the others they sailed from San Francisco. It was a preearthquake San Francisco, not yet ruined by fire: one wonders what impression the men had of the city as they marched through its streets.

When Merritt arrived he was told by Dewey that there were twelve thousand men in Manila, and that the city was in bad shape because of the insurgent blockade: they were running short of food and water. About six thousand Americans—army people, not naval—occupied the shore from Manila to Cavite. Dewey was of the opinion that the taking of the city should wait for the transport *Monterey* and its third detachment; in the meantime, they had better get Aguinaldo and his followers out of the way if possible. Aguinaldo was beginning to feel resentful, said Dewey. General Greene was detailed to carry out this task; he was told to prove to Aguinaldo that the Americans were better armed than the Tagalogs. The attack began on the night of July 31. On the following day MacArthur's troops came to help push the insurgents back. They pushed forward steadily for six days and nights, until August 7. Greene wanted to mount an all-out offensive, but Merritt insisted on waiting for the *Monterey*. It arrived on the seventh, when Merritt with Dewey decided the time had come.

On that day the Spanish captain general, Fermin Jaudenez,

received notice through the go-between, the Belgian consul, that the Spaniards had only forty-eight hours to prepare for battle, the warning being given, Dewey explained, for the sake of the many noncombatants who had taken refuge in the city and must now be removed from danger. Not to be outdone in courtesy, the captain general thanked his enemy but replied, reasonably enough, that he could hardly move out the noncombatants, seeing that the city was surrounded by insurgents and that a large number of wounded, sick, women, and children were already crowded within the city walls. In that case, replied the Americans, surely it was the captain general's duty to save the city from the horrors of bombardment? The captain general agreed, but both officers knew he would be in dire trouble, as would Governor-General Augustin, if he made things look too easy for the victors. The captain general had assumed command under a rather perplexing order from Madrid that he must preserve the Philippines to the sovereignty of Spain. So he played for time until the Belgian consul conveyed to him a threat that if he didn't surrender, the Tagalog insurgents would be permitted to come in and sack the city, possibly putting the inhabitants to the sword at the same time. On the other hand, promised Dewey, if the Spaniards surrendered and did not fire their Luneta guns, he wouldn't bombard Manila at all. Jaudenez replied with a face-saving statement that he would hold his fire if the American ships didn't come too close: after a token shelling of the forts, he said, the Spanish forces must be given time to withdraw. A white flag was to be displayed on the city wall when the right time arrived. Above all, the Spaniards wanted to be reassured that the insurgents would be kept out. He need not have worried; it was not the intention of General Anderson to permit those insurgents to take any part at all in the investment of Manila, but Jaudenez didn't know that, and he did worry until he got his assurance.

In the most gentlemanly way possible, therefore, the forces agreed on the date—August 13. It was chosen because on that day the tides were propitious for fording the estuaries that cut off the Spanish fort and trenches from the surrounding land and water. With great care General Merritt arranged the approaching allocation of troops once they were in the city, making it evident (as the historian James Le Roy was to write) that what he had in mind was not merely ordinary policing, but keeping out the insurgents. According to his instructions, General Anderson also sent to Aguinaldo, on the evening of the twelfth, the following message:

"Do not let your troops enter Manila without the permission of the American commander. On this side of the Pasig River you will be under our fire."

Everything took place more or less as planned, though here and there insurgents did confuse the picture by accompanying the American forces uninvited. Manila fell honorably enough to satisfy the Spaniards, almost, if not quite, without meeting resistance from the defenders. (The governor-general escaped in the *Kaiserin Augusta*.) Just afterward the United States and Spain signed their protocol, to fill in the time before the treaty should be settled. In the summing-up, the American casualty list was gratifying low, though as things were planned there should have been no casualties whatever. In spite of all precautions there were a few exchanges of shots, as a result of which four American troops were killed and three officers and thirty-two men were wounded, while among the Spanish forces thirteen men were killed and seven officers and fifty-seven men wounded.

Before Manila was occupied, the U.S. Army forces that had already arrived in the Islands amounted to 470 officers and 10,464 enlisted men. They found in the city 13,000 prisoners of war and 22,000 arms. Some of the soldiers, in the act of surrendering as they had been ordered to do, threw down their rifles with such force as to break them, poor angry fellows. Others burned their standards.

Now that his chief task was accomplished, General Merritt did not stay long in his new post of military governor of the Islands: on August 29 he was relieved by Major General Elwell S. Otis, who in his turn—but this is looking into the future. Even today, with communications so much better, capturing a country and settling it down is not a simple matter, especially when the capture is accompanied by conditions that do not please one's so-called allies; after all, the Tagalogs *were* supposed to be allied with the Americans. Certainly the Filipino insurgents were not happy with the situation, especially after they were forbidden to take any part in the proceedings. Aguinaldo and his companions were very indignant, and pointed out that if it had not been for their help the capture of Manila could not have taken place. Indeed, most of the American high brass would not have disputed his claim. In Dewey's *Autobiography* the admiral paid the insurgents a sincere compliment, saying that they had fought well and were important in isolating from Spanish attack the United States Marine forces at Cavite. He added that they were equally important in preparing a foothold for the American forces who had not yet arrived. Merritt agreed. He estimated a number not far short of twelve thousand of the tough little soldiers—rather a lot, especially if they happened not to be of a friendly disposition toward American troops, but that was one of the things people didn't yet say.

At any rate Manila was taken, the armistice was signed on the same day, and the Spanish-American War, to all intents and purposes, was over. The combatants had still to wait for the Treaty of Paris, which was not signed and settled until the next year, but, as has been said, a protocol was settled there and then. The real war, with the Tagalogs, was only beginning, though green Americans could hardly be expected to know that.

A resident of Manila today, Mr. Thomas Carter, who came originally from Oregon and takes a keen interest in the history of the Islands, has published a number of papers in the *American Historical Collection Bulletin* of Manila. In the July–September 1979 number of the *Bulletin* he sums up (under the title "Webfeet Volunteers") the 441 days passed by these volunteers from door to door, or, as he explains, from San Francisco to San Francisco, during their adventure in the Islands. The body was called the 2d Oregon U.S. Voluntary Infantry and was commanded by Colonel Owen Summers, who ordered its history written after the men's return to the United States. Carter points out that the 2d Oregon was the only organization among American army detachments in the Philippines that actually had a chance to do a soldier's duty on the battlefield of the Islands. The rest manned posts and all the rest of a soldier's duties, but they didn't fight.

"The regiment was the first to land in the Philippines," said Carter, "the first to enter the walled city of Manila, and the first to return to the United States. From August 13, 1898, until March 12, 1899, it was one of the three regiments performing the trying, difficult, and dangerous duties of provost guard in Manila. It took part in forty-two battles, engagements, and skirmishes, marching five hundred and thirty-eight miles in three months." He adds some interesting statistics. In all, the regiment numbered 1352, including 56 officers. Their average age was just under twenty-five; eighty-nine were married. They were students, clerks, lawyers, bookkeepers, carpenters, farmers, laborers, mechanics, teachers, merchants, ministers, and college graduates (whatever that might mean on closer inquiry). Five hundred and thirty-one were church members. Thirteen were killed in action, three died later of wounds, three were captured and killed, forty-three died of diseases while in the service, one was drowned, and one died by some other accident—a total of sixty-four deaths altogether. All the men had been enlisted at Portland, Oregon, but only 35 percent had been born in that city, the rest having come from Iowa, Missouri, Ohio, Pennsylvania, California, Illinois, Canada, Scotland, Ireland, and Denmark—in other words, a typical American gathering.

Evidently they were an unruly crew, but then army volunteers tend to be hard to manage. Seventy-five percent of them, during their tour of duty, faced summary courts on charges of drunkenness and/or absenteeism for more than twenty-four hours. One man in Company A was had up for such sins seven times. Another, from Company G, was tried seven times and another from the same company was in court eight times. But the champion, says Carter, was the man from Company M who had to face the court ten times. Evidently he got bored with the whole thing after that, because he deserted.

It was May 28, 1898, when this group sailed from San Francisco: they arrived in Manila on June 30, '98. On the famous date of August 13 they were the first American troops to march into the Walled City, received the surrender of the Spanish army, consisting of thirteen thousand officers and men. So far it was peaceful, but then the real fighting started, with the insurgents. The first battle of that war was fought on February 4, 1899, and the last for the Oregonians was at San Ysidro on May 20, 1899: 106 days in all, during which they fought forty-two battles.

Twenty-one members of the regiment elected to stay in the Philippines when the rest of the boys went home. So much for that regiment, but a good overall description of conditions for the average American soldier in the Philippines is given by another writer, Victor Hurley, in his book *Jungle Patrol*. Hurley was fiercely pro-Aguinaldo and angry with the American decision to stay and occupy the Islands, but when he got around to writing his book in 1938 a good deal of it was history. The American authorities, he alleged (and there is no reason to doubt his word), at the beginning were ignorant of the most basic facts of tropic sanitation, and the troops were not properly clad for their destination. They were in heavy service uniform with blue shirt, and actually carried overcoats across their arms. As if this were not bad enough, they wore heavy winter underwear. Since it was before shoulder pads had been adopted by the army, all their equipment was slung from the hips—a galling weight, said Hurley, which included canteen, haversack, and the regulation double row of a hundred cartridges.

Perhaps the people most to be pitied at this time of readjustment were the Spaniards, who according to the terms of the protocol were supposed to hang on in various other parts of the Islands until June

1899. The governor of Mindanao, General de los Rios, was now reassigned from Madrid as Spanish military governor and acting captain general until June 1899, with HQ at Iloilo. In Manila there was to be a Spanish commission to take care of such matters as repatriation of officers, men, and matériel. But the insurgents quickly discouraged General Rios's garrisons and officials, attacking them until they left the Visayas and Mindanao in order to concentrate at Iloilo with the governor. Ultimately they all took the prudent course and moved to Zamboanga, which was much easier to defend when the time should come. And in Iloilo, since there were no U.S. troops occupying it, the Filipino insurgents moved in and filled the vacuum. By the end of 1898 all of Luzon except Baler, which was still held by a small Spanish garrison, and all the Visayas next door, had been evacuated by the Spaniards, and their government was supplanted by Tagalogs. By the end of May 1899, all of Mindanao was in a similar situation.

"After the capitulation of the Spaniards," wrote Younghusband, "the whole civil government of Manila and its suburbs was taken over by the Americans, the general officer commanding becoming Military Governor. To undertake such a task is indeed a formidable one, especially for an army situated far from its base and unable therefore to draw at once on home resources for trained officials. But perhaps no military force is better situated for meeting such a demand than is an army composed of the material which fills the ranks of the American Expeditionary Force. There are here the best part of 18,000 volunteers, men drawn from every rank of society, lawyers, merchants, postal clerks, tradesmen, office hands of all descriptions, university men, and, indeed, it would be difficult to say what trade or calling is not represented. From amongst these men it was possible to draw fairly proficient officials to man the Customs, Postal, and Police Departments, whilst the Provost-Marshal-General became Chief Magistrate of the borough and executed functions accordingly . . . the working of the city police came as a new and startling innovation to Spaniards and Filipinos alike; the infraction of the laws of sanitation and public decency became a finable offense. Old residents, male and female, who from time immemorial had been accustomed to perform the offices of nature in any convenient spot in the public streets, now found that the continuance of such habits was a luxury which, pecuniarily speaking, they could no longer afford, for even the most opulent would hardly care to pay a couple of dollars on each occasion. The custom of emptying slops out of window was also severely discountenanced, and one Spanish officer who happened to hit an American sentry in this way, spent the night in the guard-room, and, in addition, had to pay a handsome fine in the morning. . . . To give an instance of the absolute filth of Spanish ways of living, it is only necessary to allude to their household arrangements. Here the only 'place of resort' is a small room at the top of the house, with a hole in the floor. To this common and awful retreat ladies and gentlemen of the highest birth and most distinguished bearing resort, and it is a solemn truth that this pit of iniquity is never cleared out . . . and that a solid column of this decayed filth, standing sometimes as high as the second storey, forms part and parcel of the houses of even the richest and most distinguished Spaniards." An American officer, he continued, would bear him out on this matter, for he—the American—with a fatigue party took three weeks clearing out these "appalling monuments of uncleanliness" in a block of buildings occupied by his men. Nor, went on the major in his English way, did the Spaniards ever bathe. Or hardly ever.

Younghusband gave good word pictures, as well as rather smudgy old photographs, of other than the sanitary conditions he and his wife encountered. He spoke of course of cockfighting, the great Filipino sport, and how the Americans tried sternly to repress it as well as lotteries and gambling houses. Filipinos were used to all these ways to lose money and did their best to circumvent the new law. The loss to revenue was considerable, as all these pastimes paid for licenses, and even the English of Hong Kong and Singapore, even those from as far away as Calcutta, liked to have their little flutter in Manila.

The Filipinos of the towns, especially Manila, copied their

masters, the Spaniards, as much as possible. The women wore a kind of mixed Spanish-native dress, with plenty of skirts; the men wore long tunic shirts over white trousers, somewhat less formal attire than the Spanish, but not very different. Spaniards, in other words, set the styles. Spanish men selected mistresses from among the Filipinas, or sometimes the Chinese, and treated the children of such marriages as if they were European. There were rich Filipinos and poor ones, but all of them, except the pagans in the hills, were Roman Catholics, and Rizal's picture of the great power held over them by the friars seems to have been accurate. When a rich Filipino built a house, it was as Spanish in style as he could afford it to be. In nobody's memory was there any time when the Spaniards had not been masters, so Manila was really a Spanish city with Oriental overtones. Even the transport could have been moved to the continent of Europe without attracting much attention—save, of course, the slow-moving carabao carts used by the peasants in the country.

Streetcars, with their central meeting-point at the bridge over the Pasig River, ran "weakly wailing" out to all the suburbs and also to the walled city, the driver blowing continuously an instrument suggestive of lost souls. These cars were built much like other streetcars in other cities abroad, and for four cents you could go as far as you pleased. The ponies pulling them were very small, barely thirteen hands high, and though plucky and willing, one pony this size could hardly be enough for a car holding twenty to twenty-five people. Spaniards had no compassion for animals, said the Englishman: the Americans would have to do something about that. The public vehicles apart from streetcars were divided into three kinds, with moderate charges for all. The first-class carriages were double-ponied open victorias like those the Dutch in Java called "milords"; the second class were called "quiles" and were very like the jaunting car of Dublin, and were drawn by one pony; the third class consisted of small, one-ponied, hooded traps with seating for two behind the driver, facing the pony.

There were several fairly good restaurants in Manila at which the

63

charges were very moderate—about one dollar a meal, including red Spanish wine. "Of saloons and bars there is a sufficient quantity," continued the major. "From one bedroom window it is possible for a fairly dextrous man to flick the stump of a cigar into four, whilst a fifth is only about twenty yards out of range, and a sixth, seventh, eighth, and ninth could be reached by the most infirm person in a few seconds from our bedroom door. Each saloon is filled with small tables, and at each table are seated permanently four American soldiers, and in front of each warrior is a pile of monkey-nuts and a glass of beer. As the bar keeper rakes in 40 cents, or about tenpence, on each of these glasses of beer, it is obvious that the bar keeper's eldest daughter is a lady worth marrying. The majority of these saloons are now in the hands of Americans, but a few Spaniards are still holding on, aided by American assistants—heaven preserve us from calling them waiters. The beer drunk is almost entirely American, and is delicately brought to the attention of consumers by humourous advertisements. Thus one brewer asks: 'How is your pulse? Is your tongue dry? Do you expectorate cotton? IF SO, LOOK OUT, MY SON!! or you are a gone goose. ———'s beer will cure you and make your tent a happy home. ———'s beer is what you want; insist on having it, and kick if you don't get it.' A rival gentleman retorts: 'How about icebergs? Next to icebergs there's nothing so cooling as a glass of ———'s beer. When it is cool it is so chilly that you must keep it away from YOUR MOTHER-IN-LAW, or the old girlie will make it hot for you.' And a third merchant prince informs the public that his beer 'kills the sun's heat. Try it, boys,' and to do them justice, they do."

There were Filipino stringed bands in many of the saloons, Major Younghusband observed, and the Filipino musicians played exceedingly well and entirely by ear.

The Americans, he continued, had already started four newspapers in Manila: there were three dailies and one biweekly. Considering their youth and restricted circulation they had a very good service of foreign telegrams and contained many useful and instructive articles on local and American topics. He enjoyed the advertisements especially. "'Holy Gee,' exclaims one organ, '200 new subscribers in one hour! Walk in, boys, beer ain't in it with newspapers. Dump down your dollars and secure an intellectual feast for one month, anyhow.' But the beer man is not to be defeated, for on the back of the same paper he holds out most inviting suggestions of celestial bliss to those who drink his beer, thus: — 'Beware of microbes. The little demons that down a strong man. There's NO MICROBES in S——'s beer, and don't you forget it. If by accident a microbe should fall into S——'s beer, he would reform and become an ANGEL. Who would not be an Angel?'"

Major Younghusband recounted with relish his first meeting with a genuine dyed-in-the-wool American soldier, who happened to be working as a waiter in one of those saloons that were so numerous. A brilliant row of five electric lights led to a gorgeous interior, a huge square hall in which there were what must have been one hundred small tables, and at least four hundred soldiers drinking cold beer (which, he admitted, was usually excellent). Three individuals sat above the crowd, enthroned and chewing cigars in a superb and kinglike manner. They might have been royalty, but in fact they were merely having their boots shined. Younghusband couldn't find anywhere to sit down until an elegant individual in a decidedly unwashed jersey, with a remarkably dirty towel around his neck, got him a place and a beer, sat opposite him, and said, "I calc'late there's no dam good at people settin' opposite each other and wonderin' who's who; my name's Crosby, an' I got an ignominy discharge from the army three days after landin'; and who may you be?"

The major told him. The waiter said, "That so?" and departed to distribute drinks and disseminate this information. Later he insisted on buying Younghusband a drink. That was the major's first contact with the troops: later he had many more, and seems to have enjoyed the acquaintance. Approvingly he said that his wife, when walking out alone, instead of being subjected to insults and bad language, met with nothing but courtesy and helpfulness.

Where were the Americans to go from there? It must have been a long wait for everyone concerned, but at least in the United States, at the White House, time was whiled away, however anxiously, by the urgent question of just what America was to do with the Philippines now she had them. Roosevelt and his party thought they knew very well—of course, they said to each other, the Islands would be added to United States territory and to her glory. But President McKinley was not of their mind. It hardly needs saying that the U.S. government did not know a great deal about colonial matters. The Americans themselves had burst out of the colonial chrysalis not much more than a century earlier, and had been engaged only lately in a fierce war to keep the whole edifice together. For President McKinley the question of the Philippines had been settled too quickly for proper thought. It seemed only a day or two between the decision to go to war against Spain on behalf of poor little Cuba, and presto! there he sat with a whole archipelago in his lap. He didn't want it there, but he saw no way to disembarrass himself of the burden, what with the Roosevelt pack baying all around him.

"I had every reason to believe, and I still believe, that the transfer of sovereignty [by the Treaty of Paris] was in accordance with the wishes and the expectations of the great mass of the Filipino people," he said in 1899, in his annual message to the commission he had sent out to the Islands. "If we desert them we leave them at once to anarchy and finally to barbarism. We fling them, a golden apple of discord, among the rival powers, no one of which could permit another to seize them unquestioned. Their rich plains and valleys would be the scene of endless strife and bloodshed. The advent of Dewey's fleet in Manila Bay, instead of being, as we hope, the dawn of a new day of freedom and of progress, will have been the beginning of an era of misery and violence worse than any which has darkened their unhappy past. . . ." People did talk that way in those days, and Americans no doubt actually felt that way. McKinley continued that Philippine independence under a protectorate was impossible because it would involve at the outset a cruel breach of faith. It would place the peaceful and loyal majority at the mercy of the minority of armed insurgents. It would make us responsible for the acts of the insurgent leaders and give us no power to control them. It would charge us with the task of protecting them against each other and defending them against any foreign power with which they chose to quarrel. In short, it would take from the Congress of the United States the power of declaring war and invest that enormous prerogative in the Tagal leader of the hour.

Cuba, which had started all this, was a different matter. Her future was already arranged, and had been from the beginning of the war: after a short period of readjustment, she was to have independence. But even so, McKinley had never wanted the war, as we know, and now that the distasteful affair was over, he still wanted no part of the spoils. As one writer commented, when the peace negotiations started in Paris, the president was still not ready to say whether the Islands should be returned, released, or kept. Obviously, by the time he delivered that message to the commission he had done a lot of thinking on the matter, consulting now and then with members of his party, most of whom advised him to hang on to the territory.

In the *Dictionary of American Biography* the historian Professor Frederic Logan Paxson, harking back to the affair, wrote that we should not lay on the archipelago the blame for having started the United States on the road to imperialism. It was Cuba that should be held responsible, in his opinion, or at least our actions in Cuba. There, Leonard Wood, presiding over the formulation of the island's new constitution, found the freshly liberated citizens behaving in a manner that seemed to him (considering all that had gone before) distinctly refractory. They were feeling their oats, he thought, and being downright unfilial, just as if they felt no gratitude for what we had done for them. For this reason, included in the constitution was the Platt Amendment to the Army Act of 1901, which conceded to the United States the right "to protect Cuban independence and good order." It may seem a rather odd way to protect independence, but it is not the first time that a governing body has so reasoned.

Professor Paxson has observed, "The legal beginnings of a new imperialism were laid down in this provision," and we see his point.

"In [Spain's] place we see planted the youngest of nations preparing to face fresh obligations and ready to start on the new road which destiny appears to have pointed out to her," says Major Younghusband, a trifle pontifically. "That America should hesitate before making so new and momentous a departure is not to be wondered at. The whole policy of the nation, since it became a nation, has been to avoid all foreign complications and all foreign obligations, to live self-contained and self-supported, aiming at no man's property abroad and pledged to resist interference from without. The annexation of the Philippines marks the parting of the ways. . . ." Then he quoted a number of prominent Americans who were all sternly against annexation—Andrew Carnegie, Carl Schurz (editor of the *Yale Review*), and others. Carnegie's argument was that the United States still had a continent of its own to develop and populate. In England there were 370 persons per square mile, in Belgium, 571, and in Germany, 250, whereas we Americans had only 23. "A tithe of the cost of maintaining Americans away over in the Philippines would cover the expense of an immense number of important public works in America which now await funds," he wrote. Her internal water communications could be improved, her harbors deepened and protected, a waterway from the Great Lakes to the sea could be constructed, a canal constructed across Florida— an endless number of improvements awaited doing at home. Annexation would not even benefit trade. Even loyal Canada trades more with America than with Great Britain; she buys her Union Jacks in New York. "Trade does not follow the flag in our day—it scents the lowest price current," said Carnegie.

As for Carl Schurz, he argued about the political rights accorded to all American citizens. Annexations, he said, bring on the problem of determining the status in the Republic of large masses of tropical people who are utterly different from the Americans in origin, language, traditions, and habits, with no hope of assimilation. Either they must be admitted to Congress or be despotically governed, thus overriding the republican principle that governments derive their just powers from the consent of the governed. Finally, he considered that American divergence from her past policy would be the old tale of a free people seduced by false ambitions, and running headlong after riches, luxuries, and military glory, till they head down the fatal slopes to vice, corruption, decay, and disgrace. The *Yale Review,* he said firmly, objected to annexation on the grounds that America was unprepared for a colonial policy, having, unlike England, no trained Indian and colonial civil servants.

Younghusband found it interesting that American army officers supported these opinions. They felt that such military strength as the nation possessed should be concentrated at home, not frittered away in foreign stations. To garrison the Philippines, they pointed out, the American standing army would have to be raised at once to twice its present strength, for it would be hopeless to rely on volunteer regiments to supply the deficiency, and once the novelty had worn off, the American people would resent the increased taxation involved. They felt these things in spite of the fact that annexation would most certainly lead to their own advancement in an army where advancement was slow and pay poor.

The Treaty of Paris was agreed on at last, and signed in that city on December 10, 1898. According to its terms Spain gave up the Spanish West Indies to the United States (with Cuban independence granted) as well as Guam and "the archipelago known as the Philippine Islands." For her part the United States agreed to pay to Spain, within three months of the signing of the treaty, the sum of twenty million dollars. There were other, comparatively minor, terms: for example, for ten years from the date on which the treaty was signed Spanish ships and merchandise were to be allowed into Philippine ports as freely as were American ships and merchandise. Congress was to determine the civil rights and political status of the Filipinos. Free exercise of religion was assured to the inhabitants of all the territories over which Spain was relinquishing her authority, and so on.

During the following February, on Valentine's Day, the U.S. Senate passed a resolution that their ratification of the peace treaty did not mean that the inhabitants of the Islands became citizens of the United States, "nor is it intended to permanently annex said islands as an integral part of the territory of the United States; but it is the intention of the United States to establish on said islands a government suitable to the wants and conditions of the inhabitants of said islands, to prepare them for local self-government and in due time to make such disposition of said islands as will best promote the interests of the citizens of the United States and the inhabitants of said islands."

By that time, though the Senate had no way of knowing it, the Philippines' second war was under way, and had been for ten days.

American officials close to the Philippine problem held long discussions as to how to control the natives without the use of force—a question that would seem in crying need of an answer at the time the discussions took place, in 1899. Among other effects the talks marked the beginning of what became known as the Open Door Policy, framed to hold in check the various European powers with interests in Chinese waters. Though the United States had acquired the Hawaiian Islands somehow or other along the way, it did not seem such a barefaced act of expansionism as it might, since the only inhabitants to resent the action were non-Hawaiians such as the ubiquitous Japanese. The Hawaiian Island group became a consolidated nation under King Kamehameha I, who died in 1819. In 1820 a large group of American missionaries went in and did their work so efficaciously that the inhabitants willingly accepted their nationalist as well as Christian ideals: they adopted a constitution modeled on the American one in 1840 and a more liberal document in 1887. King Kamehameha had been succeeded by other rulers in their turn, but they were never absolute monarchs, since the Hawaiians also had a

70

cabinet and a two-house legislature—nobles in one, representatives in the other. Queen Liliuokalani, who was crowned in 1891, was not satisfied with the amount of power she held, and tried in 1893 to remedy matters, but the people did not approve of her changes, and she was deposed. Earlier, the Hawaiians seem to have preferred annexation to the United States, and President Benjamin Harrison assented to the idea, but President Grover Cleveland, suspicious (and rightly) that the pro-annexationists had been coached by American businessmen, turned down the idea. However, the Hawaiians declared themselves a republic on July 4, 1894, and on July 7, 1898, formal annexation by the United States at last took place. This, argued the expansionists, was merely tidying up the situation at last, but some Americans now looked askance at the record. Hawaii, Puerto Rico, Guam, and the Philippines all coming under the Stars and Stripes in one galaxy? Controversy and clamor were aroused.

During the presidential campaign of 1900 William Jennings Bryan raised the cry of "Imperialism!" This, with its companion term "Expansionism!" was a dirty word to many citizens. The idea of a dependency on the farther side of the Pacific was wholly new to the majority of Americans, and repugnant to many of them. The dissidents didn't want to give statehood to the Islands either, as this would have bestowed on them too much power as a balancing force between American political parties. It would be conferring on the newest entrant the highest possible position that can be imagined, which would never do. Then what *was* to be done with the Philippines? We had no idea how to take care of dependencies: we knew only that the word "colonial" jarred on our ears. No doubt McKinley was in full sympathy with these sentiments. Nevertheless, politics being what they are, he took the Philippines under our wing. After all, technicalities such as statehood did not have to be settled immediately.

Plenty of Americans were not preoccupied with principle in any case. These were the people who saw commercial possibilities in our annexation of the Islands, and though it would be unfair to picture the entire administration as a moneygrubbing or power-hungry body, some officials might well fall into that category. Frank A. Vanderlip, assistant secretary of the treasury in 1898, went on record in expressing the thoughts of this school:

"Together with the islands of the Japanese Empire, since the acquirement of Formosa, the Philippines are the pickets of the Pacific, standing guard at the entrance to trade with the millions of China and Korea, French Indo-China, the Malay Peninsula, and the islands of Indonesia to the south. Australia may even be regarded as in the line of trade. The possession of the Philippines by a progressive, commercial power, if the Nicaraguan Canal project should be completed, would change the course of ocean navigation as it concerns a large percentage of the water-borne traffic of the world. The project is alluring."

Colonel Charles Denby, a member of McKinley's first Philippines Commission, gave even less thought to the wishes of the Islands' natives: "The cold practical question remains: will the possession of these islands benefit us as a nation? If they will not, set them free tomorrow and let their peoples, if they please, cut each other's throats."

Those of us who live in a more brutal age may wonder what is wrong with that. Most of the insurgents probably wanted such freedom, at least if they didn't want American government.

Though McKinley hesitated at first out of moral compunction, he soon had good reason to cease hesitating. The strategic and commercial importance of the Islands, while hardly a secret, especially after Theodore Roosevelt started talking, had simply not seemed at first to matter to Americans who felt secure in their isolation and their underpopulated lands. Now they started to study maps and think about such matters. As long as we had the archipelago, some of them reasoned, we might as well use it where it would do most good. The general public still paid little attention to geopolitics, but developments in the Far East made the annexation of the Islands more significant than had at first appeared. Manila Bay, according to Roosevelt and Senator Henry Cabot Lodge, would be an ideal outpost for our ships at just the right place. And wasn't it time that Oriental trade should cease being monopolized by other nations? Wasn't it high time American businessmen should have their chance, too?

In 1898 the transpacific carrying trade of the United States was represented by six small steamers of the Pacific Mail Steamship Company, with a handful of Americans doing business in various Asiatic ports, because the considerable commerce of the East was fairly well monopolized by Europeans. China, too, was being cut up and swallowed by European nations. By 1900 Great Britain had Hong Kong, Kowloon and Weihaiwei on ninety-nine-year leases. France, already holding Indochina, now had the Bay of Kwangchow Province on a similar lease, and both Great Britain and France held China's promise not to cede nearby territories of these leaseholds to any other power. Germany held a ninety-nine-year lease on Chiao Hsien and various other advantages, such as the right to build two railways in Shantung Province. Russia had a twenty-five-year lease on Dalny, Port Arthur, and the southern half of Liaotung Peninsula. Japan had a grip on Formosa and the Pescadores, Korea was independent, and Portugal owned Macao "in perpetuity." Small wonder that the Boxer Rebellion should have begun to bubble up . . . and just then we, the United States of America, got possession of the Philippines.

Our Secretary of State John Hay, at least, saw the implications of what was going on in the neighborhood of the Islands, and in the autumn of 1899 he did something about it, writing to all the nations involved (and Italy as well) to request formal assurance from each government that any new claims made by them to spheres of influence in China would not interfere with any vested interest within such spheres, and that the Chinese tariff then in force would apply to all merchandise, of no matter what nationality, landed or shipped to all ports within such spheres. The duties levied thereon should be collected by the Chinese government. No discrimination whatever should be made in the matter of harbor dues or railroad charges within such spheres as to vessels or merchandise belonging to the citizens or subjects of any other nationality.

This, in other and shorter words, was the Open Door Policy, and all the concerned nations agreed to it. It was settled in March 1900 (to look ahead a little), just in time for the Boxer Rising of June of that year. What happened then is an important part of history: the involved nations were able to collect relief forces that marched on Peking from Tientsin. They included American troops—two regiments from the Philippines—who could now be spared, because things were settling down in the Islands. Americans were thus made conscious as never before of China as a market for export, and they were no longer indifferent to the advantages of digging in so close by, in what now appeared to be a convenient, comfortable city—Manila.

Back to 1898. When Manila was taken, the United States was faced with a double problem: her own soldiers and the insurgents. Sometimes it appeared as if the insurrection was the lesser of these evils. To the Americans it seemed clear that the war was over, and they wanted to celebrate.

"Soldiers who had won a war were entitled to relaxation," wrote Victor Hurley in *Jungle Patrol*, "and it was a land where señoritas smiled from shaded balconies." In no time three hundred saloons had opened, and there were brawls and rackets everywhere. The soldiers forgot all about Spain: they also forgot the Filipinos, who were not forgetting anything. The war had been supposed to bring them independence, but all they had gained so far was a change of masters. Things became so noisy and undisciplined that the generals imposed a curfew according to which all troops were to be off the streets by 7:00 P.M. To enforce this rule, the 20th Infantry was detailed to military police duty. They didn't like it, but orders are orders. The other soldiers made up a song that irritated members of the 20th so much that it was enough just to whistle the tune to start a fight. It began:

74

The Bridge of Spain
Will groan with pain
When the 20th goes to battle

Soldiers will be soldiers, one might say philosophically, but a lot of the natives were not inclined to be philosophical about the Americans' behavior. They were shocked. As James Le Roy commented, drink was not one of their national failings, and their erstwhile masters, the Spaniards, had not gone in for hard liquor either. Said Le Roy: "The American—already well advertised to the Filipinos by the Spaniards as an intemperate, irreligious product of mixed ancestry, who had ruthlessly slaughtered the red man of his own continent and was engaged in lynching the black men whom he had held in slavery till late in the century—was not slow in putting in evidence his Anglo-Saxon contempt for people of any other color than white." In a long footnote he quotes a letter from Manila (an American letter) dated the end of August, which said that the soldiers were spoiling for a fight and hated the Filipinos for having lied to and cheated them. They were inclined to treat the native as a burly policeman treats a ragged street urchin. A Manila newspaper complained in November that the suburbs of the city, heretofore pleasant residential districts, were being overrun by laundries and tailor shops set up for the convenience of the troops. Besides, there were no thriving businesses anymore except those that dispensed food and liquor—"restaurants, bars and taverns, cafés and saloons of recreation."

Moreover, it seemed as if the war was not over after all. Americans had gone into it, at least as most of them thought, out of altruism, but now it seemed that altruism was not enough, and it began (in Hurley's words) a slow fade into the background. Henry Cabot Lodge actually said aloud that the States made no pretense of being interested in the Islands solely on account of the natives. "We believe in trade expansion," he added. This did not sit well with such Filipinos as could understand him. Never mind American ideals, they thought: they wanted independence. They didn't want to be annexed by anybody, even an idealistic Western democracy. Those who were politically aware, no matter how dimly, of how these things happen decided to take steps.

The beginning of the insurrection against the United States can be pinpointed on February 4, 1899. It was at night when a private in the Nebraska Volunteers, on guard with his companions at an American outpost in Manila, heard the cautious step of an intruder and called out, "Halt!"

There was no reply. He called again, "Halt!" and out of the darkness came the reply in a strange accent, "Halto!"

"Well, I thought the best thing to do was to shoot him," said the private later when he was interviewed, and so he did. Two more men then sprang out of the dark from a gateway about fifteen feet away. One was dropped by the guardsman next to the first private, and he killed the other. The two guards then retreated to the next line of six, and the first man said, "Line up, fellows, the niggers are all through these yards."

Then the waiting Filipinos began firing, and the insurrection was on.

MacArthur was being repeatedly frustrated by what seemed to him (and the other generals) the indolent complacency of his superior, Major General Otis. Now he saw his chance. Through hard work and watchfulness he waged war against the occasional invaders as effectively as he could, but Aguinaldo, too, was very busy, mobilizing against the Americans he now regarded as enemies. MacArthur thought Otis should consult with Aguinaldo while they were still on consulting terms and, if possible, come to a useful understanding, but Otis would not be budged. Nothing, he declared, could be discussed until the insurgents had laid down their arms, as they had been told to do.

"The stage was set," wrote William Manchester in *American Caesar*, "for a new, gorier war between the 'goddamns,' as GI's of that era called themselves, and the 'gugus,' their word for natives, a precursor of 'gooks.'"

In Paris they were still haggling over the terms of the treaty. One of the suggestions made to McKinley was that he should take only Luzon and leave the other islands of the Philippines to their own devices. Luzon was the center of trade, it was pointed out, and by far the most important part of the archipelago, but this idea was obviously impractical and after a lot of discussion it was abandoned. Meantime in the Philippines the insurrectionists grew busier and busier. Over and over Otis was asked by Washington how they were getting on over there, and each time he said, quite falsely, that they were fine, thank you. The time for the volunteers to go home was drawing close, and Otis was supposed to tell Washington how many more men he was going to need as they departed: each quotation of numbers that he gave erred grossly on the side of optimism and underestimation. The American public was not informed of the truth, that under Aguinaldo and his intelligent friend and adviser Mabini the insurgents had things very much their own way, and would continue to do so unless troops and more troops were thrown into the struggle. The Filipinos, agile fighters, were operating on their own ground, whereas the Americans were strangers, inexperienced at that, who had to learn under fire.

Early in 1899 two regiments of regular infantry arrived under the command of Brigadier General Henry W. Lawton, who relieved General Anderson. Lawton, who was placed in charge of the first division, had distinguished himself in Cuba and was of a very different caliber from Otis. Unfortunately the latter was his superior officer who could and often did cancel the judgments of the former. It was Lawton who was responsible for the taking of Malolos, the seat of Aguinaldo's government, though the blow was not heavy, since the insurgents easily escaped into the neighboring swamps and hills. MacArthur in the meantime advanced toward Kalumpit. Through it all one gets the impression that fighting the Filipinos was only a secondary task for the generals: their real struggle was with Otis, who could hardly ever be budged from his do-nothing posture. Then Lawton was killed in battle at San Mateo on December 18. As Hurley said bitterly, at least this death proved that the war was by no

77

means over when Americans at home were claiming that it was.

Officially the war ended in November 1899, but unofficially it sputtered on until the middle of 1902, and even then it wasn't finished, though the words were different: the Islands now entered an era of banditry, or "ladronism" as it was called. Why such misinformation from the high brass when they said the Islands had been pacified? Because, said Hurley, the American people were not sympathetic to President McKinley's colonial aims. With seventy thousand men still in the field the American people could hardly believe that the Islands were really pacified; something had to be done, and that is why twenty-five thousand troopers were disbanded and sent home. (This writer holds no brief for Hurley's theory, but that is what he said.) "The United States was to experience a period of chill and ferocious guerilla warfare that was to reach across decades of time, and they were to learn that the regular troopers of the United States were not adaptable to the dripping jungle that was the terrain." And the Filipino, he added, was a sturdy jungle man, easily aroused to fanaticism—a doughty fighting man, like his cousin the Moro. Like other American writers Hurley was much affected by the incident of Tilad Pass, on December 2, 1899. Major Marsh, head of a battalion of the 33d Volunteer Infantry, was technically victorious here, but the account of sixty Filipinos who fought the Americans at the pass is the one that lives. Aguinaldo had sent the sixty: only seven returned to tell him they had failed. Their general was a youth of twenty-two named Gregorio del Pilar; he was among those shot down.

It wasn't just an insurrection, continued Hurley, it was a legitimate war of protest. He quoted with approval an interview that Mabini gave the *Chicago Tribune* war correspondent Richard Henry Little: "The Filipinos realize that they can expect no victory over the American forces. They are fighting to show the American people that they are sufficiently intelligent to know their rights. The Filipinos maintain their fight against the American troops not for any special hatred, but in order to show the American people that they are far from indifferent to their political situation." Were they really? At any rate Mabini was far from indifferent.

The heroic death of Pilar and the continuing struggle taught the Americans something—that they had better change their approach, and they did: the so-called jungle patrol came into being. Policemen of the jungle was what Hurley called them, men bred in the bush, or at least well trained to survive in it. They knew how to survive traps and ambushes, because many of them had fought in the Indian Wars in the States, and they trained the others. They understood the ways of the so-called savages and knew how to fight them. Hurley describes them as large men with drooping mustaches, who spoke slowly; it is a stereotype, but probably a reasonably descriptive one. They were outfitted with linen uniforms with red epaulets and their arms were not of the latest sort. In time they got their title—they were the Philippine Constabulary. They were organized about the middle of 1901. Sometimes they cooperated with the regular forces, but often the regular forces didn't want to bother with them, out of a snobbish objection to some of their ways. For one thing, the constabulary made an effort to enlist Filipinos, and when this succeeded they armed the new recruits. A foolish, risky thing, said the regulars: it can lead to no good to hand out rifles like that. Those "niggers" were sure to desert with their arms at the first opportunity . . . but they didn't. In the end, according to Hurley's claim, the constabulary were the men who won the war for us.

"The so-called Filipino Republic is destroyed," MacArthur had reported to Otis in November 1899, but he was wrong, and he probably knew it. He was urging Otis to offer amnesty to all insurgents and even pay them thirty pesos apiece for each rifle they turned in. Otis, it need hardly be said, refused to consider the suggestion, while Aguinaldo and his party went to ground in Bataan. The war must have looked endless to MacArthur at that point. However, relief was at hand. Otis was relieved of his post and MacArthur was given it, on May 6, 1900. It would be logical to suppose that now with a free hand, the general could quickly finish the job. It would be logical, but that didn't happen. From the time he succeeded to Otis's place to the genuine end of the war, when Aguinaldo was caught, took more than two years—twenty-eight months, to be exact. The United States had to send 150 Americans in pursuit of those maddeningly agile natives, who fled when they were cornered and simply returned, as soon as the Americans moved on, to occupy their old haunts once more. The cost of the war was enormous: the American public was getting very restive.

The only encouraging factor throughout those months was that the insurgents never got a genuine foothold in Manila itself. This does not mean that the city was a peaceful or salubrious place. Uncomfortably crowded, it was unsanitary as well. Fortunately for general well-being, the American authorities lived up to the reputation they had earned, and grappled firmly with the forces of disease and pestilence: very soon United States Army doctors were busy vaccinating everyone within reach against smallpox—an effective precaution, though the Filipinos wondered at it. As for the crowding, it did lead to trouble, especially among the soldiers: racism was always breaking out. The soldiers quarreled with the Filipinos because they were brown; they quarreled with their own comrades-in-arms when—and because—they were black. Still, things might have been worse.

Chapter Five

Historians have sometimes asked themselves and each other how Aguinaldo did it. What kept him successfully harrying the enemy for so long, when many other leaders failed? Many of their number thought that the answer was not Aguinaldo at all, but Mabini, who had a truly remarkable intellect, and whose only reason for not occupying the place of Emilio Aguinaldo was that he was badly crippled. LeRoy wrote that at the end of active hostilities in August 1900, General James F. Bell, who was in charge of the temporary government of Manila, had a series of personal interviews with Mabini and tried to persuade him to consent to peace. Bell pointed out that as long as the guerrillas continued to kill American soldiers there could be no independence for the Philippines, whereas if the "assassinations" would only die down for fifteen or twenty years, why, the Islands could be as independent as they liked. To which Mabini replied, "When the 'efforts and sacrifices' of the Americans cease to be merely for their aggrandizement, the Filipinos will show their gratitude."

This remark was not only exasperating, but seemed so wrong-headed to General Bell that he could scarcely think of a fitting rejoinder. He gave up and the interview came to an end, but the fact was, Mabini and Aguinaldo were keeping a shrewd weather eye on the approaching presidential election in the United States, which they were convinced would be won by the Democratic party, headed by Bryan. In such a case, they reasoned, why should they try to stay in favor with these lame ducks in Manila? That they misjudged the public mood in the United States is not surprising: that they should be able to form opinions at all on a situation geographically so far removed from them is perhaps more startling. But Filipinos are very keen and observant when it comes to politics, even with politics not their own.

But before that, in the spring of 1900, even the most optimistic guerrilla must have felt in his bones that the war could not be carried on much longer. There was obvious trouble among the higher echelons of the Filipino forces, Aguinaldo and Mabini having fallen out. At last Mabini, whose health was never good, retired, and this was a serious loss to the insurgent movement, almost its death blow. Another loss was that of General Antonio Luna, one of the best and most talented officers under Aguinaldo. He was, evidently, too talented for the leader's taste, because he was cut down and killed by Aguinaldo's guards, ostensibly in error. Rot was setting in generally. Besides, as we have seen, the Americans, slowly but inevitably, were learning and making headway. In short, the independence movement had sunk to a few scattered bands of Filipinos who stayed in the hills, emerging only for lightning raids against their compatriots as well as the official enemy—for they needed supplies, and a lot of people had now got used to the American regime and accepted it. Aguinaldo's whereabouts, though not pinpointed, were known to within a hundred miles: he was hiding out in difficult terrain to the north of the city. It was known by practically everyone that he had with him his wife and three other women who were in flight from the foe, and the Americans were also aware when these females dropped out and took refuge in barrios, or villages, here and there. The leader made no bones about sending his wife and her near relatives to live in comparative safety when things got really rough for his band—and the Americans knew that, too.

Now that Otis was no longer there to stop him, MacArthur on June 5 was able to put into action his long-deferred plan and proclaim an amnesty, which included the thirty-peso idea for each surrendered rifle. It helped a little: a few stragglers from outlying bands came in for their money, but it didn't lure Aguinaldo from his hidey-hole, though the general had half thought it would. Finally Colonel Frederick Funston volunteered a plan by which he might go out and catch the fugitive, and MacArthur agreed that it was worth trying. With a few picked men from the American ranks and a larger group of natives known as Macabebes, they set out. The Macabebes had always shown an unusually friendly spirit toward the Americans, because of which it was rumored that they weren't genuine Malays, but descendants of a tribe of American Indians. It has proved impossible to trace this fascinating legend and tie it down, much less to prove it, but in any case the Macabebes, for whatever reason (and being Indian hardly seems a convincing one, now that we think about it), were on the side of the Americans. The truth may lie in the fact that during the Spanish regime they were loyal to Spain, and this loyalty was simply transferred to us.

Funston set out with his band in what he was assured was the right direction. It was. A day's march from where Aguinaldo had set up camp, the Macabebes took over and put into effect the planned stratagem: they tied up their American allies and the whole party then resumed their march, at last reaching Aguinaldo's camp. There, when challenged, they explained that they had come upon the American party by accident and conquered them in fair fight: they claimed a reward for this effort and for turning over their prisoners, thus lending an admirable touch of verisimilitude to their narrative. At first Aguinaldo was suspicious, but in the end he was convinced, and gave the Macabebes permission to spend the night on his territory in order to guard their captives. During the dark hours, the so-called prisoners were set free and got quickly to work. Aguinaldo was captured at last. For a time Funston was the hero of the war, especially when he brought the Tagalog leader back to Manila. That is to say, he was a hero to his mates, but in the United States things were not so clear-cut. The many American correspondents who were on the side of the Filipinos lent strength in their writings to the anti-imperialists at home. As so often happens, they themselves were carrying on a war with the military who were supposed to be on their side. They declared, often truthfully, that their dispatches were being censored, and that they could not get the full story out except by mail (far too slow) or by cabling from Hong Kong (complicated, not to say delayed).

"All sorts of base motives were ascribed to the American officials principally connected with the Philippine undertaking," wrote James LeRoy, "while Aguinaldo and certain other Filipinos were magnified into great statesmen, as well as heroes and patriots." Other newspapers and speakers treated such reports with scorn and contumely, and called the anti-imperialists traitors. And so, in a manner of speaking, they were, since the insurgents were well aware of the discussion going on in the United States, and probably put too much stock in it, thinking that their cause was nearly won. Before he was captured, some Americans actually wrote direct to Aguinaldo, praising him and urging him to hold out. Some of the figures given by LeRoy explain, in part, the increasing unpopularity in America of the war in the Philippines. As hostilities stepped up, so did the number of casualties, especially in northern Luzon.

"Of the total of 2729 casualties (509 killed and 2220 wounded, of whom 170 also died) in the American army from February 4, 1899 to June 30, 1900, there had been a monthly average of 174 killed and wounded between the date of the outbreak and the end of March, 1900 (during which time the force averaged 41,000 men), as compared with an average of 93 casualties during the succeeding three months (with an average force of 63,500 men). But something of the character of the warfare (commonly from ambush) was indicated by the increase in proportion of Americans killed to those wounded; during the period when a more or less organized force was encountered behind trenches or in the open, about 1 American was killed where 4 or 5 were wounded. . . ." In 1900, however, the odds changed, one American killed to two wounded. Moreover, the climate began to tell: the Americans had many more sick. Three times as many were dying of disease as were killed by wounds. They suffered from dysentery and malaria. During the first seven months of 1900 there were 995 deaths among the troops, 654 from disease. In that time 1560 men were sent home, 110 of them certified insane.

With Aguinaldo neutralized, his followers could not carry on indefinitely, and in time the whole nation was quiet—except, of course, for the Moros. The Moros were always an exception. Their struggle was somewhat different from that of the others. It goes without saying that they were against the United States, but they also waged war on the other natives. They were against non-Moro Filipinos, Spaniards, or any other peoples who did not share their fidelity to Islam. They considered their hostile actions holy war. The Americans called it piracy.

One American who played an important part in the earliest uneasy stages of what one might call peace was Dean Conant Worcester. Unlike the others, Worcester already knew the Islands, and in a peculiarly thorough fashion. As a young zoologist he was at the University of Michigan, studying under the head of the Department, Professor Joseph H. Steere, an enthusiastic traveler who loved to hold forth in class about foreign places he had visited—the Amazon, the Andes, Peru, Formosa, the Moluccas, and the Philippines. In the spring term of 1886 Steere announced that he intended to return to the Philippines and resume work he had started there some years earlier, and he said that any student who could pay his own way was welcome to come along. Worcester had very little money, but he managed to raise enough, and two other youths joined the party, one

85

of them being his good friend Frank S. Bourns. It was a memorable journey. The party got off whatever paths had been beaten—there were not many in those early days—and Worcester wrote of his adventures in a book that was published much later, in 1898, *The Philippine Islands and Their People*. In this he said that to see the country properly one must leave the cities behind and plunge into the wild.

This was not easy. Between the largest islands it was comparatively simple to get around, since mail and merchant steamers plied from port to port, and sometimes native sailboats were all right for the less traveled areas—as long as you could trust the weather. But weather was always a question. In his report Worcester was not so easygoing on the subject of land transport. "In the vicinity of the larger towns one occasionally finds what purports to be a carriage road," he wrote. ". . . In the rainy season it is sure to be impassable . . . Many of the paths which by courtesy are called roads are reduced to ditches, pools, and sloughs during the rains, and are utterly impracticable for a man on horseback, while there are plenty of 'roads' on which a horse is worse than useless at any time. Although the lack of bridges is, of course, not so serious a matter for a rider as for one who attempts to drive, it is not at all uncommon to encounter streams too deep and swift for fording and swimming. Even in crossing fordable streams one needs to exercise care, they are sometimes infested by man-eating crocodiles." This was the country into which we sent volunteers from the farms of Oregon and Nebraska.

One reads quite a lot about horse riding in those days, but as the natives were not in much of a hurry and there were not a lot of horses anyway, they preferred the carabao, or water buffalo, which is much slower. A carabao will go where a horse cannot, said Worcester, but he is a most uncomfortable ride and his disposition makes him rather unreliable: "He has an inborn prejudice against white men, and the smell of one is sometimes enough to stampede all the buffaloes in a village." Worst of all, a carabao flatly refused to work at all in the heat of the day, but made for whatever mudbath he happened to see and soaked in it, regardless of who or what happened to be loaded on his back. All in all, the writer concluded, one is better off depending on one's own feet.

Once an American found himself treed by a carabao when for some reason he was walking alone in the country at dusk. Perforce he sat in the tree, the carabao snorting below, and there was no other human being anywhere in sight or, evidently, within hailing distance. Every so often the beast seemed to doze, and then the American would try stealthily to come down, hoping to make a run for it, but every time he moved the carabao woke up and sprang, or rather lumbered, to attention. It was a most uncomfortable night he spent perched up there, but at last came the dawn, and with it a little girl, a very little girl, who couldn't have been more than four years old. She greeted the carabao, slipped a rope around his neck, and led him off without the slightest difficulty.

The Spaniards described the seasons in the Philippines as *"seis meses de polvo, seis meses de lodo, seis meses de todo,"* or "six months of dust, six months of mud, six months of everything." But, said Worcester, when it's muddy in one place it might very well be dusty elsewhere. He found the soil astonishingly fertile. Even when crops were taken from it year after year, he said, it wasn't used up. Productive areas were not found only in valleys: quite often they were better on mountainsides. (The Philippines are volcanic in origin, which means that one might find patches of favorable soil practically anywhere.) The most important agricultural products Worcester reported in the time of the Spaniards were sugar, abaca (Manila hemp, much in demand for rope and other nautical purposes), tobacco, rice, coffee, maize (Indian corn), cacao, yams, coconuts, and bananas. There were all sorts of bananas, in many varieties of size and sweetness. Various attempts to grow abaca elsewhere than in the Islands have failed: it remains one of the most profitable and satisfactory crops of the Islands. Cacao was introduced from Central America. There were excellent beans, guava (which grew over the whole area because it was spread by birds), and

87

cotton—good, long-stapled cotton—though at the time of Worcester's first visit the government had made the cultivators switch over to tobacco. He found the chief luxury offered by the Islands was their great variety of fruit, some specimens enormous and others only large enough for one delicious mouthful. In the extreme south, as in Mindanao, a popular fruit was durian, "which in spite of its abominable stench is the king of all tropical fruits," said Worcester. Mangustan (or mangosteen) also flourished in the southern islands, as did papaws (papayas), several varieties of oranges and lemons and limes and citrons and shaddocks (a kind of thick-skinned grapefruit), jackfruit, breadfruit, custard apples, lanzones, tamarinds, and lichees.

He observed that the value of forest products was potentially enormous, and he gave a very long list of the species he could recognize; there were many others he couldn't. Though he had no doubt that the mineral wealth of the Islands was great, he admitted that it had never been properly developed: the Spanish authorities were much given to legal quibbling, which delayed such matters. He wrote often, complainingly, of the lack of transportation and communication: there were no railroads and no ordinary roads, lacks which held the Filipinos back. But the final and greatest problem to colonization, the securing of good cheap labor, had not been surmounted, and Worcester saw little hope that it ever might be. He had seen much good rice and sugarcane spoiling in the fields for want of men to harvest it.

"The Native is a philosopher," he explained. He worked when obliged to, and rested when he got the chance. His wants were few, and nature supplied most of them. The Native found it possible to rest most of the time. Any laborers one needed could usually be got only from a considerable distance (why? He did not explain), and had to be paid in advance. A progressive nation could do something with the situation, said Worcester: the Spaniards were unable to.

It was during a second visit to the Philippines that the writer ran into incidents involving the Moros of Mindanao. He described them as being much dreaded. Mindanao was nominally divided into provinces, but in fact Spanish control was effective only in narrow strips along the sea and near a few rivers which afforded the only means of communication with the interior. There were no roads at all—the old story. The Spaniard who was in charge of all the Islands at that time, the notorious General Valeriano Weyler y Nicolau, who had introduced concentration camps into Cuba, determined for some reason to send an expedition into this impassable country and (as he thought) settle the Moro problem once and for all. He concentrated all available forces and marched them into the forests of Mindanao, but they were never able to overtake the Moros, who simply ran away as they approached. Besides, the Spanish soldiers suffered terribly from starvation and fever, and 80 percent of them were soon out of commission. Worcester saw the expedition when it returned, and described it as a wreck. All the priests that could be assembled from neighboring towns were not enough to hear the confessions of the dying, and sick men were sent off by the shipload. Weyler himself, said Worcester bitterly, was perfectly safe: he had directed operations from aboard a dispatch boat offshore. Several glorious victories were celebrated in the streets of far-off Manila, with processions and fireworks.

The traveler reported that all male Moros, if they were more than sixteen, went around armed unless they were explicitly forbidden by the Spaniards to do so. They made their own weapons, too, of beautifully finished steel: weapons called barong, kris, and campilan. (Most of us today are familiar with the kris and its undulated blade.)

Not all of Worcester's experiences were as painful as those afforded by the Spanish army versus the Moros. At Ayala he and Bourns found a village of decent, civilized natives completely under Spanish control. But he collected and told many stories about bad friars: one, for example, exacted so much money for burials that the natives were forced to do without, and instead left the bodies of their dead exposed to the elements. Another friar, during a famine, sold rice at an exorbitant price. The schools in the provinces, which were the responsibility of the friars, were woefully bad. According to the old laws of the Indies (as he sometimes called the Islands), the Christian doctrine was to be taught to the natives in the Spanish language, and every now and then since the early discoveries of Spanish navigators a new decree to that effect had been published, to no avail: Spanish was hardly ever taught. In 1887 something, at least, was done about it when the governor-general communicated with the archbishop of Manila "somewhat pointedly calling his attention to the duty of himself and his subordinates in the matter, but nothing resulted." The simple fact was, said Worcester, that it didn't suit the purposes of the friars for their parishioners to speak Spanish. (Here it should be said that this observation seems to have applied to all of the Islands. When the Americans took over, very few Filipinos spoke Spanish. The exceptions were of the upper classes, educated men and women. It was the elegant language, possession of which showed that the speaker was aristocratic and privileged.) Yet it would have helped to have one common language in a country where there was, in Worcester's words, an endless multiplicity of native dialects, so many that few of the Spanish officials attempted to learn even one, especially as they were almost sure to be transferred from one place to another before they had made much headway.

The friars were different. They usually spent all their lives at one post; they were forced to learn the local language. As a result, such a friar became the most convenient bridge of communication between official and native, and he liked it that way. Few native schoolmasters dared to go against his wishes; thus the "education" of most Filipinos "consists of a little catechism and a few prayers, which they learn in their own dialect. The more fortunate get some knowledge of writing and arithmetic, with, possibly, a smattering of Spanish." From these accusations the American absolved only the Jesuits, who, though they were kept out of the Far East for years, from 1768 to 1852, while there actually did educate Filipinos and also established missions among savage tribes. Many met death at the hands of Moros.

*　　*　　*

This was not the whole prewar experience of the Islands enjoyed by Worcester. The first year had sunk into his soul, as it had into that of his friend Bourns, and when they returned to America, though they agreed that they had had quite enough of the Philippines, it was not true. Worcester was ill and had to recuperate with his family in Vermont. When he was cured he returned to his job at the University of Michigan, but soon he was trying hard to raise money for a return trip to the Islands. Bourns, who shared his longing, joined in the campaign, and they actually raised the sum of ten thousand dollars in various grants—enough for their plans. It was May 1890 when they set out once more. This time they stayed two and a half years and added a good deal to their knowledge of the archipelago. They found that Visayan, the language they were best at, was useful in most places, and they also grew more fluent in Spanish.

Unfortunately while he was alone, Bourns having gone to Borneo, Dean Worcester contracted typhoid. It is a slow-acting disease and he didn't realize at first what was wrong with him. He kept going on at his work as long as possible, inspecting villages until he was nearly dead. Finally the complaint was properly diagnosed and he went back to the United States, gloomily certain that this time his experience with the Philippines was over for good. He could not have been more mistaken.

In 1898 when war with Spain seemed inevitable, Worcester was back in Michigan, cured of his typhoid, though weakened by it, and occupying a professorial chair. Knowing as he did the faults of Spanish government in the colonies, his sentiments were with the Cubans: so strongly did he favor going to war over the island that many of his friends called him a jingo. If health had permitted, he thought, he would certainly have enlisted like Frank Bourns, who sailed for the Islands on the second steamer carrying American troops. In the Philippines, Bourns served as interpreter as well as chief medical officer, and he was present at the surrender of Manila. He wrote constantly to Worcester. In the meantime that gentleman, still convinced that life in the Islands was impossible for him, swallowed his regrets as best he could and arranged to take his family instead to Europe, where he planned to study. But on the way to the East Coast he stopped in Washington to tell President McKinley his ideas. He was afraid there would be an outbreak of hostilities between the Filipinos and the Americans, and he had ideas on how this could be avoided. Later, he confesses in his book of memoirs, he realized that he was mistaken in several important particulars. There certainly were hostilities, but not the ones he had prophesied. His main experience with natives had been with Visayans and the so-called wild tribes, whereas the trouble when it arrived was from the Tagalogs.

In those simpler days the president was actually glad to meet the professor from the Midwest, and listened attentively to him. Worcester wrote, "President McKinley very kindly gave me all the time I wanted, displayed a most earnest desire to learn the truth, and showed the deepest and most friendly interest in the Filipinos. Let no man believe that then or later he had the slightest idea of bringing about the exploitation of their country. On the contrary, he evinced a most earnest desire to learn what was best for them, and then to do it if it lay within his power."

At the end of the interview came a surprise: President McKinley asked Worcester if he would go to the Philippines as his personal representative. Worcester thought it over for a week, no doubt wondering if going back to the Islands would not imperil his health. Finally he agreed. There were now new developments. McKinley had evolved his idea of sending out a commission to run the Islands for the time being. Would Worcester be willing to go as a member of that commission? Again he said yes. The European trip was indefinitely postponed, and the family returned to Ann Arbor so that he could get himself ready for a much longer voyage. The names of the other commissioners were now announced: Jacob Gould Schurman, president of Cornell University, our old friend Major General Elwell S. Otis, still the ranking army officer in the Philippines, Rear

Admiral George Dewey, and Colonel Charles Denby, who for fourteen years had served as the United States minister to China. This, by the way, was the president's first commission, and was not intended to last a very long time.

Denby was detained in Washington, so Schurman and Worcester went ahead. They reached Yokohama, Japan, on February 13, 1899, where they got the news that hostilities had broken out on the fourth. Hurrying on, they reached Manila on March 4 and were joined by Denby about a month later. They were uncertain as to just what was expected of the commission: McKinley himself probably didn't have definite ideas. Soon they ran into trouble with one of their number, Jacob Schurman. When he arrived he was all in favor of sternness with the natives—"A stern and bloody policy," as Worcester said—but a trip up the Pasig with Dewey changed his mind completely: he had had no idea that war was like that. Horrified, he was with difficulty dissuaded from cabling McKinley to stop the carnage and the war instantly. The other commissioners prevailed on him to maintain calm and at least talk it over in the morning after his return, not on the spot as he was eager to do. He did calm down by morning, but he did not change his mind or give up. He learned Spanish very quickly, enough at least to converse with the locals, and he took to having long, private conversations with various Filipinos. The others too, said Worcester, had such conversations—after all, that was an important one of their duties— but always as a group, and once when Schurman tried independently to cable to Washington the other commissioners felt they had to tell him that this simply would not do. After that he practically dropped out of the proceedings, but he didn't resign, and he did manage to get other reports through, unilaterally, from time to time. The others saw less and less of him. He moved by himself around the Visayas and southern islands, and on his return to Manila he announced his departure for the States, pleading the opening of the fall term at Cornell as an excuse—not the first nor the last gentle academic to falter in the face of war's brutalities.

93

Anyway the first commission's task was now finished, but soon McKinley appointed a second one, and he asked Worcester to stay on and join it. Worcester did. Without a day's break he resumed his duties with the new lot, with William Howard Taft at the head of the commission. At home Taft was a judge with an excellent reputation in his field, and though he had not yet tried his hand at administration or executive duties, when President McKinley asked him to take on the work he willingly accepted the post. He got to Manila early in June 1900, a man of enormous girth and considerable mental power, who was destined to be president of the United States for one painful term. He had been brought up in Ohio, but his background and training were of New England. (As a matter of fact, one could say the same of most native-born Americans in the eastern half of the country.) Taft had served well on the Ohio Superior Court; when he was only thirty-two some of his colleagues thought that he might be appointed associate justice of the U.S. Supreme Court. He himself pooh-poohed that idea, yet in the same year President Harrison named him solicitor general. That was in 1889, and he assumed office the following year. (In 1892 he became a U.S. Circuit Court judge.) During the next nine years he did extremely able work, though in the field of labor relations he gained a reputation for conservatism that his biographer Henry F. Pringle pronounces unfair. Taft believed firmly that labor had the right to organize, and in this belief he was a considerable distance ahead of most of his colleagues.

He had just received an offer from the Yale Corporation to consider election to that university's presidency when McKinley's invitation arrived. It did not conflict, because as he explained he could not have accepted Yale's offer in any case: he said that he was a Unitarian, and the Yale alumni would not have cared for that religion in their president. Besides, he didn't feel that he was qualified for the post. Little time was spent discussing the matter, as McKinley's offer merited serious thought. Very soon Taft resigned his seat on the bench and, early in 1900, set out for Manila, where he was soon settled in the governor's palace, or Malacañan. It was a happy choice both for the archipelago and for Taft. From the start he liked the

Philippines and the Filipinos. It was he who coined the phrase "little brown brothers," which so annoyed other Americans who did not share his fondness for the natives. Soldiers stationed in the Islands sang,

> I'm only a common soldier man in the blasted Philippines.
> They say I've got brown brothers but I don't know what it means.
> I like the word fraternity, but still I draw the line—
> He may be a brother to William Howard Taft, but he ain't no brother of mine.

The other members of the commission were Luke E. Wright of Tennessee, Henry C. Ide of Vermont, Bernard Moses of California, and, as we have seen, Dean Conant Worcester. Their task was to establish civil government in the Islands, and they had a definite program to this end: after some ninety days of observation the commission was to become a legislative body, though executive power continued to be vested for the time being in the military. They arrived on June 3 and were greeted, if that is the right word, by a very frigid General MacArthur, who (said Worcester) seemed to regard their arrival in the light of an intrusion. He actually kept Taft waiting for a full hour when that official arrived. The general had been told to provide suitable office space for them, which turned out to be five desks, one for each commissioner, and five private secretaries, all crowded into one little room in the Ayuntamiento, or town hall. MacArthur made no bones about his opinion of the commission: in his first long interview with the members he told them that they were an injection into an otherwise normal situation. Later he said that what the Filipinos needed was a military government pinned to their backs with bayonets for ten years. To be fair, in good time he was to withdraw that remark, but according to one of the party Taft was never to forgive him for his behavior on that first day.

95

For some reason there happened to be a preponderant number of men from Michigan on the commission. It is said that Taft, when he became official governor general of the Islands on July 4, 1901, opened a meeting of his cabinet by saying, "The Michigan University Alumni Association of the Philippines will come to order."

"The back of the rebellion is broken," he reported cheerfully in a letter to Washington soon after he arrived. As he saw it, the first thing to do—the very first—was to end military rule over the Islands: MacArthur's instinct had been right in looking on him as a threat. The rest of what Taft wanted to do sounded simple enough, though not necessarily easy. Education was the thing, he said, the fundamental thing, but there were two other projects for the commission to get busy on right away. They must pacify those natives who were still rebellious, and somehow they must make the friars disgorge the lands they had taken over the years. In one of his first reports to Washington he summed up what he had learned about this difficult question. In the earlier insurrection many friars had already paid with their lives for the wrongdoing of their predecessors: the others had fled to Spain, leaving to the insurrectionists the enormous area of four hundred thousand acres in pieces of land that they had held and rented out to Filipino tenants. The land had to be settled again, but the friars should not come back—of this Taft was firmly convinced. His suggested solution to the problem was for the U.S. government to buy the lands and sell them to the natives at what would be considered fair prices, and this, ultimately, was done. It took a long time, a lot of traveling (to Rome, to consult with the pope), and the sum of $7,200,000, but in the end the matter was finished with a reasonable amount of goodwill.

All this, however, was yet to come when the commission first arrived and tasks allotted. One is awed by the duties they set themselves—so much work for so few men. Wright was dubbed secretary of commerce and police, Ide became secretary of finance and justice, Moses was the secretary of public instruction, and Worcester found himself the secretary of the interior. On that same day three Filipino members were added to the commission—Dr. T. H. Pardo de Tavera, Benito Legarda, and José R. de Luzuriaga. Until October 16 in 1907 the commission continued to be the sole legislative body of the Philippines. Then the commission was transformed into the Upper House of the Philippine legislature, and the Philippines Assembly, composed of eighty-one elective members, constituted the Lower House. But that was still a long way off.

Taft's biographer denied the allegation that the head commissioner was a sentimentalist, as some of his opponents alleged. Persistent lawbreakers, Taft declared, when they were caught, should be either hung or banished to Guam, but he did not consider executions necessary.

In July 1901 he was made civil governor of the Philippines, and the military authority of the Islands became secondary.

Chapter Six

Worcester's story might almost be called that of the American Philippines in their early days, though it doesn't cover quite everything in detail. Certainly he tried to do that, but his work load was tremendous. The question of public health was of first importance, and he organized what he rightly claims to have been an effective campaign against the bubonic plague, smallpox, and Asiatic cholera, all of which were endemic in Manila. He also had to struggle against the foot-and-mouth disease and rinderpest, more than particularly distressful in an agricultural country like the Islands in that they wiped out a large number of badly needed horses and cattle. From the beginning, too, he was responsible for the enforcement of marine and land quarantine regulations, which made him generally unpopular until people could be convinced of the wisdom of these precautions. But the portion of his many-faceted job that was obviously nearest his heart was the carrying out of his duties as head of the Bureau of non-Christian Tribes, under the heading of which all the aboriginals (about an eighth of the entire population of the archipelago), pagans, and Moros were lumped. Worcester, who was really an ethnologist at heart, much enjoyed the trips he had to make to familiarize himself with the people in his care.

Later it was probably Bernard Moses, as secretary of public instruction, who bore the responsibility for education in the Islands, but at the very beginning it was on the direct orders of Taft that the United States armed forces, in what might be called the strangest shift of policy in American history, became schoolteachers overnight. Yet, though a trifle unconventional, it was a logical move. Here was this nation kept—hitherto—in the direst ignorance. Well, they had to be taught, and in the quickest way possible. Three weeks after the American occupation of Manila, therefore, seven public schools were opened, each in the care of an American soldier who taught the children English. Father William D. McKinnon, chaplain of the 1st California Regiment, was put in charge of all Manila's schools. (Father McKinnon later became a regular army chaplain resident in Manila. For months he also served as a communications medium between the Spanish archbishop and the American troops: the large number of Catholics among the Americans was a pleasant surprise to the Spaniards, who had earlier thought all the soldiers were naturally Protestants, beyond the pale.)

Catholic or Protestant, it might seem odd that our soldiers were given this task. And, if it came to that, why was the English language chosen for the first lessons? Frederic Marquardt wrote in *Before Bataan—and After*, "The soldiers were specially chosen for the job—at the specified request of William Howard Taft, who had become convinced that the best way to 'pacify' the Filipino was to offer him the tool by which he could govern himself, namely, education." As for English rather than Spanish, well, how many Americans spoke Spanish? Besides, as has been observed, few of the Filipinos were at home in that language either. There is no doubt that pacification was desirable, on both sides of the fence. As Marquardt, among others, has reminded his readers, during hostilities the forces had used a marching song deemed so offensive that the higher-ups ordered that it should not be sung. The chorus, sung to the Civil War tune "Tramp, tramp, tramp, the boys are marching—" goes,

Damn, damn, damn the Filipinos,
Pock marked, yellow skinned ladrones.
Underneath the starry flag,
Civilize them with a Krag,
And return us to our own beloved homes.

The "Krag" was the Krag-Jorgenson repeating rifle used by American troops.

Fortunately the soldiers' attitude, generally speaking, was not like that after all. In a publication in Manila edited by Attorney Alfonso Felix, Jr., for the Historical Conservation XXIV Society and published in 1973, we have the memoirs of Captain Arlington Ulysses Betts, Company E, 48th Regiment. According to Lewis E. Gleeck, Jr.'s, book, *Americans on the Philippine Frontiers*, which cannot be faulted for its careful collection of facts, this Betts was one of the few native Americans among the volunteers to have studied in Europe, having received a military education in Europe in the time of Bismarck. (Betts was born in Ohio in 1867, and came of a well-to-do family.) He had started a rubber plantation in Mexico which he sold to the Firestone Rubber Company when the Spanish-American War broke out, then he went home and organized the Buckeye Regiment of Ohio volunteers. The men were comparatively well armed with Springfield rifles. They sailed from San Francisco in four ships, straight to Legaspi, defeated the Filipino forces who stoutly defended the beach, and landed on January 29, 1900. Let Captain Betts's account take over from there.

Some of the men burned Albay and Daraga, and on February 2 there was another engagement at Legaspi. Six days later they took the port of Tabaco, which was temporarily deserted. There were a few more battles in the vicinity, but at Tabaco they were met and aided by a "splendid Spanish priest" who did everything he could to

101

induce the people to come home. He held Mass every morning and rang the church bells at the accustomed hours, but for a few days nobody appeared. Then at last a few old men and beggars straggled in for Mass. Nobody bothered them, and when they went back to the hills to rejoin their fellow villagers in hiding, they took with them provisions from the Americans, hard tack or canned salmon or sardines. Encouraged, the others began coming in, each time more and more of them staying at home.

On March 15 the Americans made up an expedition to Bacacay, "a thriving town," Betts called it, on the south shore outside Tabaco Bay near Sula Pass. The Americans had long tried unsuccessfully to catch Bacacay's inhabitants at home and persuade them that no harm was meant: that they (the Americans) merely wanted to establish a civil government there. This time Betts moved a detachment of soldiers into the countryside at night and they managed to surround the town undetected. In the morning, when the people got agitated, Captain Betts took his officers to walk slowly through the principal streets, greeting everyone with a *"Buenos días"* and a smile. Then the party called on the priest at his convent and reassured him. He was persuaded to tell everyone at early-morning Mass that the Americans meant no harm, but only wanted to organize a civil government. After Mass the cordon of troops around the town was lifted, and the soldiers entered Bacacay, mingled with the people, and made friends. There was never any more trouble in that town.

Under the date "March 20th 1900" the captain continued: "I then conceived the idea of opening a school to induce parents with children to return. Free schools were something new to them. I gave orders that all children returning to town must go to school. We took a large building and converted it into a school. Our soldiers painted blackboards and I found among our troops were plenty of school teachers with experience. I appointed teachers of experience. The school proved to be the key that unlocked the whole situation. The mother instinct to improve her child in this experiment of opening free schools [sic]. In a few days mothers with whole families came marching into town and occupied their former homes and finding nothing that they had left had been disturbed, we further gained their confidence.

"The days following their entrance to town, all their kiddies went to school. There was no such thing as books, papers, pencils, slates, etc., there were no seats or benches, but every fellow sat on the floor and recited as well as he could, the English pronunciation of the letters which the teacher placed on the blackboard. There was no chalk but we discovered that decayed coral off the beach made a very fair substitute and the yellowish-white mark it made was easily visible. I discovered then that if we got the child we were sure of the friendship of the mother and if she was with us, it would be but a short time before the father, who was no doubt a soldier in the Insurgent Army, would come in and surrender and join his family.

"In a very short time we had 10,000 people back into the town and I had to open three more schools. You see, there never had been public schools or in fact, schools of any kind, so there was no such thing as school supplies. The question of a copy book was soon solved by the little fellows themselves. They made copy books out of the leaves of the banana plant. The veins in this leaf were just like ruled paper and the underside of the banana leaf takes ink just like real paper. They made pens out of quills and ink out of berries. Every little fellow showed up each morning with a fresh four leaf copy book which he had made himself. They laid on the floor to copy the lessons from the blackboard. So, I have always held that the free schools was the key that unlocked the whole situation for us in the Philippines. It was the key then, and is still the key."

Tabaco grew so large that Captain Betts wasted no time in installing a "provisional municipal government," with president, vice-president, treasurer, police force and all. They used the old Spanish Tribunal for the municipal building. They had no funds, so Betts and his helpers suggested that they first clean the city and put it into a sanitary condition. Tabaco had been built on the old Spanish system, with open sewers on each side of the street: property owners were required to clean the sewers running past their houses. With army prisoners he repaired the old dam that had supplied the town with running water in canals and the streets, and they got the water back. A light had to be hung outside every house and every business place. "We now had a lighted and clean city, with good sanitation, clean streets, public schools, good police protection and good fire protection, workable sewers with free running water and it had not cost us a centavo of direct tax."

A market was constructed, with the help of the prisoners, and now at last money entered the picture: space in the marketplace was rented off. With this income they were able to pay native school-teachers, salaried municipal officers and the police force, as well as the expenses of the city's prisoners. "The American teachers, of course, received no salary," said Betts. The soldiers made benches and a stage, and presto! there was a town theater. "Vaudeville and athletic performances were provided by the Filipinos," said Betts. "They always played to full houses."

On April 21 the troops, having heard that the insurgents' main headquarters were at Bantayan not far from Tabaco, marched over and drove them out, having spiked all their guns. It took three more expeditions, however, before these insurgents were driven out for good. These activities were necessary, the captain explained, because the Philippine hemp ports had been closed for several months by the U.S. forces, and since the Islands supplied most of the hemp for the world's market, there was a great shortage of the fiber and prices had gone sky-high, from six pesos a picul (133.33 pounds) to fifty pesos a picul. Besides, the hemp storage space in all the hemp ports in the Islands was overcrowded.

All in all, Captain Betts had to learn a lot. There was the affair of the priest of the town of Malilipot who, he was reliably informed, was really an insurgent officer and actually wore the insurgent uniform under his church robes. He often pretended to give the U.S. officers information about the insurgents' doings, but he seemed to know exactly when they came to see him and was waiting at the front door when they arrived. Finally one of Betts's aides managed to lift the hem of the priest's skirt. Sure enough, under it he was wearing military boots and striped trousers tucked into them, just like those of insurgent officers. The Americans said nothing, having no intention of arresting him. They said good-bye, mounted their horses, and rode away, when they heard people yelling that the priest was escaping. He had taken alarm, grabbed the church's golden Mass implements, and tried to escape. He was riding a fast pony. The American detachment chased him, but the chase came to an end when the priest and his pony began to cross a temporary bridge made of woven split bamboo over a deep gorge. The pony stumbled and fell over the side of this makeshift bridge, the priest of course went with him, and both were killed. The golden service set was returned to the people of Malilipot, who told them then that the priest had been head of that locality's secret service. As if worried that his readers might think him antipriest, Captain Betts hurriedly added, "I made it a rule never to interfere with other people's religious beliefs and liberties. I was also very fortunate in having in my district a most tolerant, progressive lot of priests who aided me in every way possible. . . . I was not of their faith and they knew it, but they did not let that interfere with our friendship. I have always looked back to those early days with a great deal of pleasure, when with their help, we were able to solve all sorts of vexing social problems in establishing law and order. My being a Mason, no doubt, was a hard nut for them to crack, but it seemed to have made no difference with our friendship."

Captain Betts took his discharge at Manila on June 18, 1901, to accept an appointment as governor of the Province of Albay. But before this happened, toward the end of 1900, he accompanied his men to the town of Lagonoy in that province. ". . . the people of this province were exceedingly poor," he wrote, "and had scarcely any of the advantages of the average Municipal government. I decided to put into effect the same plans I had used in other districts in organizing a local Municipal government and opening Free Public Schools." He did so, and the same story followed. They got a large two-story building, their soldiers painted blackboards, "and I selected a well trained and experienced school teacher from my

105

company of soldiers. . . . Native teachers were selected and trained to be able to take over the school when we were withdrawn from the district . . . I finally found a very bright young man about 28 years old who had been well educated in one of the Spanish Universities in Manila and I offered him the job of Superintendent of the Schools and he gladly accepted the position. He was a wonderful find. He was from this district and knew the dialect and the people. He put his whole heart into the work and did wonders in getting the schools organized and operating under a system . . . Of course the American teachers did their work gratis and seemed only too glad to help out and make the experiment a success. In fact they also became enthusiastic over the work and sacrificed much of their time to the cause. Our newly appointed Superintendent was working himself nearly to death and so were the native teachers.

"I knew of course that they could not keep up their work much longer without some compensation for they had to live. I finally consulted the Superintendent and asked his suggestions. He informed me that for himself he asked for no compensation for he had a little income from his small plantation. He suggested that we ask the parents of the school children to contribute something to the native teachers and it mattered not how little just so it was something. I knew how very poor the mass were and I told him I doubted if it could be done, but he could try it. It worked like a charm. Soon the native teachers had more chickens, eggs and rice than they knew what to do with. I was so pleased that I felt I should do something, so I told him I would contribute P4.00 a month to each of the native teachers from my private purse."

There were of course no school supplies. Betts suddenly remembered that back home in Toledo, Ohio, the city board of education had "tons" of used schoolbooks in fair condition, but which were not reissued for sanitary reasons. He wrote to the Toledo board of education asking for those books, telling them all about the Philippines schools and enclosing a number of the banana-leaf books used by the Filipino children in his town. Two months later the sergeant in charge of army supply stores at the port of Sabang telephoned to say that he had sixteen packing cases all addressed to Betts, the heaviest he had ever handled. Betts, who had heard no word from Toledo, asked him to forward them, and in due course there they were—enormous and heavy packing cases.

"Suppose they wanted to surprise us," said Betts. They knocked off one of the lids and found the box filled with books, slates, pencils, tablets of paper, and plenty of chalks and copybooks. The superintendent was so happy that he cried like a child, and Betts admitted that he might have shed a few tears himself. One box was delivered to each of their sixteen schools of the district. The next day Betts and the superintendent visited each school to unpack the case and hand out the books, slates, pencils, and so on. There was general joy, and the spirit of giving seemed to spread, because the men of Betts's company, with whom the superintendent had become very popular—he helped them to write Spanish letters and so on—passed the hat around for him, calling it the Company E monthly contribution. It amounted to thirty pesos a month, and Betts joined the movement with his contribution.

"Sometime later I was sitting in my quarters when I noticed a long procession coming down the main street and it seemed everyone was carrying a flag," he wrote. "It proved to be the schools and each little fellow had taken a bamboo stick about 4 feet long and split it on the end and stuck in the split an American flag that he had made out of a sheet of paper on which he had drawn with berries an American flag."

They paused at Betts's gate. The superintendent, who headed the procession, asked him to come down to the gate, and there he unrolled a scroll written in Spanish and read to Betts their letter of thanks to the Toledo schools. "It was a masterpiece," he said, "and contained all the flowery words that can be expressed only in Spanish." This, explained the superintendent, was to be forwarded to Toledo. But there was more to come. The children wanted to make a present to Betts himself, something they could afford to give.

107

The line then started marching past him, and each boy as he reached Betts bowed and handed him an egg. When they had gone Betts had received more than four hundred eggs. Soon afterward duty called him away.

Thirty-five years later a new road was opened which made it easy to get to Lagonoy by car. Before then it had been necessary to take a steamer, and what with one thing and another Betts had never made the trip. But now, when all he had to do was drive it, he decided to have a look at the old place. It was Sunday, and the town was very quiet when he arrived at one in the afternoon, but the Municipal Building was open: they were registering voters there. He spoke to one official about forty-five years old, and asked for several of the former important men of the town by name. They were dead, said the official, looking puzzled, all dead a long time ago, but when Betts asked for Captain Andrace, who had been old even in the old days, he had more luck.

"There's his house," said the other man. "By the way—I beg your pardon, but aren't you Captain Betts?"

"Why, yes," said Betts. The official raised his voice and shouted to the other men around the place, "Fellows, it's Captain Betts!"

They crowded around him. At least half of them had been schoolboys in his time, and they were overjoyed to see him. They followed when he went to see Captain Andrace, and in the general jubilation he wondered how on earth they could have recognized him. He weighed about fifty pounds more than he had in the old days, he was not in uniform any longer, and his hair had gone gray. But Captain Andrace explained: among his souvenirs was a framed photograph of the school in the old days, complete with the superintendent, dozens of boys, and Betts himself.

He didn't get out of Lagonoy for three days. "It certainly was a reunion I shall never forget," he wrote.

What he did not mention about the years in between is told in the Gleeck book. "Civil Government was proclaimed in 1901, and after two years as military Governor, Betts found himself elected for four years to the office of Provincial Governor. . . . Betts was capably assisted in his work of reconstruction by Lt. Governor Roman Santos, who succeeded him in office in 1905, and by an able secretary, Joaquin Tomas, from a prominent propertied family of the province, whose daughter he married.

"Betts never left Albay. A man of means himself, an intelligent and capable businessman who married into a wealthy family, he acquired plantations, real estate, a coal mine and sawmills. Five children were born of his marriage, the eldest, Joe, taking over management of the family business and property. Although Betts suffered severe property losses while with the guerrillas in the Albay hills during the Japanese occupation, the family resumed its prominent place in provincial life after the war. In 1957, aged 91, Arlington Betts died."

For the commissioners the business of education couldn't stop with soldier teachers, who were merely a temporary expedient. In Washington and Manila it was decided that the Civil Service Commission should collect bona fide American-trained teachers willing to volunteer, to be sent out to the Islands as quickly as possible. (Gleeck calls them the first Peace Corps.) They volunteered all right, and in numbers. Most of them, obviously, were motivated by the missionary spirit, but were also young and eager for adventure in strange lands. Perhaps it was not made clear to them that most Filipinos were already Christians, but never mind. The first of these people, men and women, were in a batch of thirty-eight who disembarked at Manila in June 1901, from the U.S. transport *Sheridan*. They were followed two months later by the famous *Thomas* (famous, at least, among Philippines schoolteachers) which carried a thousand more. Because they were so many, all imported teachers in time came to be known as "Thomasites," and the name of the *Sheridan*, like that of another teacher-carrying transport, the *Buford*, was forgotten. As soon as they had arrived and were somewhat acclimated they were sent off to their posts, many of them in the wilds, to sink or swim. Two Filipina women, Geronima Pecson and Maria Racelis, have gathered reminiscences of the early days of Thomasites in *Tales of the American Teachers in the Philippines*.

109

Their accounts have much in common with Captain Betts's. In Manila, too, there were no textbooks, no paper, and no pencils: very seldom was there even a schoolhouse. Those already built by the Spaniards were being used as storerooms for military supplies, a use for which, according to one writer, they were better fitted anyway, being dark and gloomy.

"Old ruins were cleaned up and provisional sides and roofs were made of bamboo, coconut leaves, or grass. . . . Short bamboo uprights were sunk into the ground and on top of these were fastened a network of long bamboo poles. . . . When the pupil became tired sitting on the bamboo he could kneel on the ground and use the bamboo for a desk. Later, overcome by fatigue brought on by irregular habits, lack of nourishment, and the repetition of a strange language, a tired little head used the bamboo as a pillow." R. G. McLeod, superintendent of the School of Arts and Trades, 1914.

Supplies had arrived by 1903, but the teacher's hours of work were not shortened. On the contrary: he had to teach at least five hours a day and then use another hour instructing Filipino schoolmasters in his craft—for the idea from the beginning was to train native teachers as speedily as possible and then depart. The American teacher also used three evenings a week to preside over adult classes. He was expected to supervise village schools and village teachers, as well as join in the social life of the community. It was a strenuous schedule. The typical teacher lived miles from any of his compatriots, and mail from home was, at best, irregular and infrequent. His only reward was that he was meeting a challenge, and meet it he did. Some twenty-five years after the beginning of the system, a high official from the United States, addressing the International Institute of Teachers College, Columbia College, in Geneva, said that in a survey he had made of the different school systems, he found no other country that could compare with the progress in education made by the Philippines.

And the system did not remain very long in the hands of American teachers. In 1902 there were 1074 of them; in 1910 there were 773, with 8275 Filipino teachers. The ratios continued to alter swiftly, until in 1950, the last date in the printed table of these statistics, only 8 Americans were left as compared with 85,396 Filipinos. In 1951 the last actual Thomasite, Miss Mary E. Polley, died at her residence in Pasay City—for many of the teachers, having spent fascinating years of their lives in the Islands, chose voluntarily not to go back to the United States.

In the anthology is an article by Julian Encarnacion, dated 1953. He claimed that education was no new thing for the Filipino even before the arrival of the Spaniards, since one generation passed to the next its folklore, crafts, customs, and beliefs, taught first by the parents and then by the village elders, "more or less self-appointed teachers by virtue of their age and experience." As boys outgrew their home surroundings they joined their age groups in the house of some village elder who taught them to read, write, figure, master a craft, and learn their people's religion and customs. Girls, too, went through an educational process, learning how to be wives and mothers. Encarnacion mentions "the ancient written dialects of the Filipinos" and says that the Spanish were surprised to find that practically every other native could read and write.

This, if true, certainly would be surprising to the early Americans, who saw nothing in the Islands but illiteracy. But remember, says the writer, the literate Filipino had to undergo a complete change in his mental habits after the Spaniards arrived. He had to be a Christian, he had to use European letters, and he had to accept a new classification in the social sense. The Spaniards had established European-style colleges and universities, accepting as students only the children of Spaniards, mestizos, and the more well-to-do Filipinos. Schools for women were academic or vocational and belonged to one of two extremes: they were either run for the benefit of poor or wayward girls, or they were finishing schools for exalted señoritas.

Then in 1863 a royal decree declared that the Philippines were to have popular education from that time on, with one teacher for every 5000 natives. The schoolteacher was usually a mestizo with Spanish blood and a very strong sense of the dignity of his position. He conducted his class like a military martinet, rod in hand. Pointing his finger, he would tell the pupils what lesson to prepare for the next day, and he insisted that they be ready with their recitation of the textbook pages they had been ordered to memorize. Those who failed in their recital had their hands slapped, or were ordered to kneel on large, knobbly seeds. The schoolmaster came next to the priest in the village hierarchy. He belonged to the elite, and seems to have been one of the least popular officials of the old regime. At least this was indicated in the record left by people who took part in the first insurrection against Spanish rule, when they, too, declared a republic. In the second rebellion, against the Americans, it is interesting to note a kind of echo of this sentiment: the constitution drawn up at Malolos in the Tagalog language provided for a school "free from friars." It was in other ways, too, a revolutionary document. For one thing it claimed the right for women to hold university degrees. For another, as the government was thoroughly anticlerical, it decreed that Christianity should have no part in school teaching. Instead, it asserted that pupils should study the history of the Philippines. But then came the Spanish-American War, the insurrection, and other interruptions, and when the smoke had cleared away, all these changes, good and bad together, counted for nothing.

One of the teachers was Dr. Gilbert S. Perez, an American, not a Filipino. He wrote of the Thomasites and the others, "In 1901, America sent a new Army that was unarmed—an army of American teachers which had a task to perform equally as difficult as that of its military predecessors. These pioneer American teachers found that their pupils reacted to a recitation of Lincoln's Gettysburg Address and Patrick Henry's speech to the Virginia Assembly exactly as the pupils at home would react, and the seeds of democracy sown in those early days of American occupation fruited gloriously at Bataan, Capas and Fort Santiago." No other country had sent out an army like this, said Dr. Perez, never in the history of the world, and perhaps he was right at that time. They (the army) were scattered all over the Islands like soldiers, each fighting his own battle with meager equipment. Many remained after their first work was done, having become truly Filipino. Dr. Perez himself was one of those. Like the tenderfeet they were, they suffered at first from tropical illness of various kinds, and worked splendidly during the cholera epidemic of 1902. In many cases, said Dr. Perez, the teacher was the only American in town, and in more than one place there was no native or even a Spanish doctor to help him. But the teachers knew a few fundamental rules of hygiene, and they learned more, and they taught what they knew as if they were health officers, born to the work. Many illnesses as well as cholera became more manageable through their efforts.

In his enthusiasm Dr. Perez gave—perhaps—too much credit to the teachers regarding the defeat of smallpox, though the main thing was that it was well and truly defeated, regardless of who was responsible. He gave some striking statistics in his paper. In 1909, he said, the faces of 20 percent of seventh-grade pupils in the Philippines public schools were badly pitted with the telltale scars, but in the sixth grade the percentage was only 12 percent, in the fourth grade, 5 percent, and in the lower grades there were no scars at all. This dramatic fall in the disease that had been the scourge of the Islands for as long as visitors could remember was due in large part not so much to the teachers as to the remarkable Dr. Victor Heiser, whose memoirs, *An American Doctor's Odyssey*, were a best seller in America in the 1930s. Heiser arrived in Manila as chief quarantine officer in the Philippines in 1903. As any good health officer would be, he was horrified by the sanitation conditions he found there. The British, French, and Dutch, he said scornfully, with all their long experience of colonization in the Far East, had always held that it was a waste of time and money to bring sanitation to Orientals.

"Across the street from my office," he wrote in the *Odyssey*, "was smallpox, to the right was plague, and to the left cholera." He added that 40,000 people were uselessly slaughtered every year by smallpox. Dr. Heiser, who was to become an outstanding figure in the history of the American Philippines, organized a vaccination campaign which was in a large part responsible for the astonishing change in national health within a few years. Unfortunately he arrived too late for some of the American teachers' army. Often they came into the cities and backwoods without any medical protection or disease prevention whatever, since the withdrawal of American garrisons from many towns meant the disappearance of their surgeons with such help as they were qualified to give. Dr. Perez printed a sad little list of casualties that he compiled from the records of the first twenty years after the American teachers came. Of these, seven died of cholera, four of smallpox, two of dysentery, and six by ladrone action (that is, killed by thieves).

In all of the chorus of praise received by the teachers in the book about the Thomasites there is, not surprisingly, little mention of the embarrassing but inevitable fact that they were not rapturously received at first. Most Filipinos at the beginning were not all that keen to be taught.

"Attendance was irregular and the amount of tardiness appalling," said Dr. Perez severely. He admitted, too, that while some pupils came out of curiosity (though they remained to be enrolled), other children had to be brought in by the police. But by 1904 it had dawned on the parents, at least, that in education lay the means of self-improvement through jobs, possibly in the prestigious Civil Service, and enthusiasm mounted so rapidly that some aspiring students had to be turned away for lack of places until the authorities scraped up more money for schools.

Like upper-class Spaniards and Chinese aristocrats, the Filipinos looked down on manual labor. Even those people who worked with their hands—and they were many, since most natives, of course, were agriculturalist—had the firm idea that sending their children to school was a leg up in the social scale, and therefore these children should not have to work as their fathers did. The families went to a lot of trouble to save face for the young students by finding friends and relatives who could carry their books and other impedimenta to school for them. The American point of view that manual labor was right and proper for everybody was strange to them, and shook them badly. Dr. Perez tells how a schoolmaster in San Miguel, Bulacan, disillusioned the village in this respect at least, though it took rather a lot of time. He wanted to start a school garden with the children, so he ordered a load of bamboos with which to make a fence around the plot. According to local custom, the bamboos when delivered were left in the river below the school.

"Next Monday morning," the master told his big seventh-grade boys on Friday afternoon, "we will carry those bamboos up the hill and get started."

On Monday morning the boys arrived, each accompanied by a helper, a father or uncle or full-grown cousin meant to do the hard work so that the student need not sully his hands. With some difficulty the teacher dissuaded all these well-meaning people from joining in, and sent them home. Then he and the students, *with the supervisor and the principal*, carried the bamboos up the riverbank and onto the garden plot. It is to be hoped that the boys got the idea then and there. Other teachers had many similar experiences. One girl, it is said, was at the beginning accompanied by a servant whose duty was to carry her books from one classroom to the next.

Tales of the American Teachers contains a lively section from the writings of Mary H. Fee, one of the women who arrived aboard the *Buford* in 1901, a week before the *Thomas* got there. These passages come from her 1910 book, *A Woman's Impressions of the Philippines,* one of the best pieces of popular writing to come out of that period of Philippines history. When the *Buford* came to anchor, Miss Fee and her companions were housed in Intramuros, in a place formerly occupied by a training school for girls. That afternoon, untroubled by the modern complaint of jet lag, they went out together for an exploratory walk.

"The narrow streets with overhanging second stories; the open windows with gaily dressed girls leaning out to talk with amorous swains on the pavement below; the swarming vehicles with coach-

115

men shouting 'Ta-beh'; and the friales (friars)—tall, thin, bearded friales in brown garments and sandals, or rosy, plump, clean-shaven friales in flapping white robes—all made a novel scene to our untravelled eyes," she wrote. They climbed some mossy steps and found themselves looking across the moat to the beautiful avenue called the Bagumbayan. It was the hour when everyone walked or rode or drove in the city, toward the park called the Luneta.

When the time came for their duties to be allocated and they were told (after the arrival of the *Thomas*) where each one was to go, Mary Fee found herself assigned to Capiz in the Visayas (now Roxas City). Frankly she looked forward to it, though a number of the other women, whose courage failed, made a fuss when they discovered that they were to leave Manila. Miss Fee said she didn't really care where she went, except, as she said, she wanted to go alone, or at least without a female companion.

"I had my doubts about the advisability of binding myself to live with some one whom I had known for so short a time, and subsequent experience and the observation of many a quarrel grown out of the enforced companionship of two women who never had any tastes in common have convinced me that my judgment was sound," she wrote. Perhaps it was in sheer relief that the powers on high granted this request. It must have been a hectic couple of days in Manila: "Great was the wrath that swelled out the Exposition Building!" said Miss Fee. "The curly-haired maiden who had fallen in love with a waiter on the *Thomas* wept openly on his shoulder, to the envy of staring males. A very tall young woman who was the possessor of an M.A. degree from the University of California, and who was supposed to know more about conic sections than any woman ought to know, was sent up among the Macabebes. Whether she was embittered by the thought of her scintillations growing dull from disuse or from scintillating head axes, I know not, but she made little less than a tragedy of the matter. The amount of wire-pulling that had been going on for stations in Manila was something enormous, and the disappointment was proportionate."

Then there was the inevitable eagerness with which the young

American males of Manila tried to meet all the young ladies who had just arrived. The women preferred the uniforms with which the city abounded to plain dull youths who were trying to get a foothold in the business world. Miss Fee understood and was sorry for the dull youths, but she wouldn't introduce them to the schoolma'ams. It was against the rules.

She had to wait to go to Capiz. The first stage of the journey (on which she was accompanied by two or three other teachers) was by a vessel of the Compañia Maritima which took them to Iloilo. They set out on the seventh of September, fortified by a few words of pidgin Spanish which they had picked up in Manila. It was enough knowledge for Miss Fee to understand the words that were used more often than any others; *"Segura mañana"(sic)* or "tomorrow for sure." Time meant nothing in the Philippines, and she and her companions had to wait for some days in Iloilo, long drowsy days of doing nothing, until at last the party could move on. Capiz at last!

"There were the great, square, white-painted, red-tiled houses lining both banks of the river; the picturesque groups beating their clothes on the flat steps which led down to the water; and the sprawling wooden bridge in the distance where the stream made an abrupt sweep to the right. On the left of the bridge was a grassy plaza shaded with almond trees, a stately church, several squat stone buildings which I knew for jail and municipal quarters, and a flag staff with the Stars and Stripes whipping the breeze from its top. Over all hung a sky dazzlingly blue and an atmosphere crystal clear. . . . I knew that I should like Capiz."

The division superintendent and the male teachers started out in the morning, he to place the others in their respective stations. There was already an American teacher in Capiz who taught at the boys' school, but as he spoke the language and was needed as an interpreter, Miss Fee was left to take over his work for the time being. (The boys' school was the only one yet organized.) She found the school, which consisted of two one-story stone buildings. An American flag floated over one, and a noise like a boiler-factory proceeded from the other.

"The noise was the vociferous outcry of one hundred and eighty-nine Filipino youths engaged in study or at least in a high, throaty clamor, over and over again, of their assigned lessons," she reported. It was the old Spanish custom still in force. As she entered, the boys rose as one and shrieked, all together, "Good-morning, modham." They were so delighted at her surprise that they yelled it again and again, but at last she got them settled down and began on a quieter method of teaching. There were many unfamiliar aspects of the work for her. Goats were one problem, though they did not seem so, evidently, to the boys. Goats came in through door and window, and when she asked her pupils to eject them, they showed such fervor that she found it better just to ignore the visitors.

The boys' teacher eventually returned, and shortly thereafter a girls' school was opened. At first things went very slowly; the concept of regular education for females was new to Capiz's inhabitants, and little girls seemed reluctant to come to class, or at least they were not encouraged with any enthusiasm. But once they got started there was a flood of them, and Miss Fee had to turn the tables and call on the former teacher for a bit to help her handle the numbers. Some of the pupils brought their dogs, but the dogs were well behaved and quiet. At first all teaching took place in one enormous room, in which classes had to be switched back and forth. This was inconvenient, and ultimately the room was cut into three parts, the children were dissuaded from learning their lessons at the tops of their voices, and things generally became more orderly.

So far, so good. In her domestic arrangements, however, Miss Fee did not settle down so comfortably. She had a cook and general servant in one, a man named Romoldo. One day he came and asked if he couldn't hire a female servant to help him. She would be very handy for the mistress, said Romoldo, and besides, she was newly orphaned. Miss Fee agreed to take in the poor child, and the orphan appeared—rather a surprise she was, being older than Miss Fee had expected. She was also very unattractive, being heavy-browed and pockmarked. Her name was Tikkia: she had long oiled hair and scanty clothing. It never occurred to the innocent schoolteacher that any romance was going on between the two domestics, until one day a friend's servant, another man in the village, was so rude to her that she asked for an explanation, and found to her surprise that Romoldo had "stolen" Tikkia from this other man, her husband. Miss Fee spoke to the sinners about it. Tikkia explained volubly that it was all right because she and her husband had not been married in church. Earnestly Miss Fee tried to make her see the error of her ways, but it was no use. Finally another American living in Capiz said to her, "What on earth have their morals to do with you? If the servant suits you, that's that."

Romoldo did suit. Thinking it over, Miss Fee saw where she had been wrong, and gave up her attempts to manage her household's private life and reform the Philippines. In any case Tikkia finally settled it by leaving both her suitors *and* Miss Fee. Teaching on the Islands, it seems, was educational on both sides.

One wonders, looking at photographs of those earnest men and women from the United States, how long it took some of them to habituate themselves to the climate. The pictures show them dressed much as they would have been on summer days at home in Illinois or Nebraska, the men in jackets, collars, and ties, the girls in long skirts with small waists, high collars, and even, some of them, the pancake hats that were in the mode at the time, riding high on their pompadours. One hopes that during the warmest season they relaxed, even if only to let their stays out.

Chapter Seven

The assassination of McKinley in September 1901 left the way open for Vice-President Theodore Roosevelt to succeed. This was at the time that Taft and his commission were organizing the civil government in the Islands, and as Taft stood high in Roosevelt's estimation (then, though things changed later on), little happened, probably, that would have been different under McKinley. There was much to do. Elihu Root, secretary of war, had written out for Taft a letter of detailed instructions as to revenue, administration of justice, religious freedom, education—everything, in fact, that might be involved in the government of a country under new management.

"The powers of the Governor-General were extremely wide," wrote Cameron Forbes, "much more so than is usual in democratic countries where the power is derived by delegation from the people." Incidentally, the governor's title did not become "governor-general" officially until 1905. "The Organic Act of Congress in 1902 granted the Governor-General certain powers in addition to those remaining in the Military Governor after the transfer of legislative power to the Commission September 1, 1900. Except as otherwise provided by Congress, these were the powers of the Spanish Governor-General, of which the United States Supreme Court decided that an act was legal unless there was a law or order specially prohibiting it, and held that 'the existence of power, being usual, will be presumed, and the absence of it, being exceptional, must be shown.'"

In Washington the War Department housed the Philippine government, Elihu Root feeling that this arrangement was most efficient. It was there that the Division of Customs and Insular Affairs was organized, chiefly by the assistant secretary of war—assisted by Captain John J. Pershing, who later went to the Islands as major and assistant adjutant general.

It had been decided that the laws passed by Congress for the United States were not to be automatically applied to the Philippines. The division—or, as it soon became, the Bureau of Insular Affairs—was watchful that this rule be carried out. Special consideration was given to such legislation as seemed good for the Islands, for example the Pure Food Law: in these cases the laws were adapted for special application and incorporated in the Islands government. And there were many other laws necessary to the Philippines for which Congress in Washington had no versions. For example there was the question of currency. The United States had its own arrangements, but the system in the Islands was a mess. The Filipinos and Chinese used several kinds of coin, Spanish Philippine, Mex, U.S. paper scrip (which was circulated originally by the troops, who were paid in it), and anything else the Chinese traders might import. Something had to be done about the situation, and at long last, in 1903, Congress in Washington authorized (especially) a new system based on a peso that was worth fifty cents U.S. gold. (The fact that this peso did not exist was not permitted to discourage the currency reformers.) The actual circulating medium was to be the Philippine silver peso, which was declared legal tender for everything. At first it didn't work. The banks would not cooperate and the businessmen, usually Chinese, insisted on discounting the Philippine peso because it did not hold as much silver as the Mexican dollar. But such rebels were quickly brought into line. The army stopped paying out its paper money: the maverick Spanish Philippine and Mexican coins were collected and sent to San Francisco to be reminted, and the government issued new paper money of its own. There was a flurry when silver values went up in the world market and the new silver peso became worth more than—well, than a peso. People hoarded their pesos then, and exported them, until export was prohibited. But these matters settled themselves in time.

The commission also got busy on taxation, raising it on luxuries and lowering it on necessities. Incidentally, or perhaps not so incidentally, the expenses of running the Islands were not paid out of American pockets. From the beginning the Philippines were expected to pay their own way, and did. This fact was not well publicized in the U.S. press, but it was a fact.

There were dozens of other tasks connected with government— postage stamps had to be designed and printed, government bonds were advertised and sold, railroads were contracted for (Worcester was very keen on railroads in the Islands' future), and experts acquired in every field. Behind it all was the knowledge that the people of the Islands were to be educated and trained to look after these matters for themselves one day. "In the words of President Roosevelt," wrote Cameron Forbes, "it was a programme of changing a government of Americans assisted by Filipinos into a government of Filipinos assisted by Americans, or, as expressed by Governor Taft, a policy of making a government which was at the beginning strongly paternal as rapidly as possible less so."

One of the first constructive acts of the commission, said Forbes, was the creation of the Civil Service Bureau, and examinations were given to qualify Filipinos, first for the lowliest positions and then, as they learned their work, for higher and higher posts. This resulted in a steady, continued Filipinization of the service. Men were promoted according to merit and efficiency, "though this was not rapid enough to satisfy the ambitious young Filipino impatient for advancement." This policy was all right, on the whole, for the Filipinos, but it led to angry feelings among the Americans who had come out with the army and decided to stay in the Islands and make their lives, to say nothing of their fortunes, there. As we have seen, most of the business they carried on in the latter stages of the insurrection depended almost wholly on the troops—tailor shops, restaurants, and bars. As the effects of war receded so did the army, and these merchants, who considered themselves stranded through no fault of their own, were resentful and bitter.

"An American commercial firm in Manila even inserted in a Manila paper a large-sized advertisement consisting of Governor Taft's picture and below it the words: 'This is the cause of our leaving the Philippines.' The firm, however, continued profitably in business in the Islands," wrote Forbes serenely.

Politics had to be considered: politics is second nature with most Filipinos, and now that the Spaniards had gone, the science flowered as never before. Taft thought it wise to organize a pro-American political party before something less helpful made its appearance. Late in 1900 the Federal party made its appearance, its members consisting, among others, of onetime insurgent leaders who had started out with Aguinaldo but had eventually disagreed with him and moved into Manila. Among the onetime Malolos men were solid citizens such as Dr. Trinidad H. Pardo de Tavera and Don Benito Legarda—both of them were later members of the commission—as well as the Honorable Cayetano Arellano, chief justice of the Supreme Court; Felipe Buencamino who was to be the first director of the Civil Service; Luis Yangco, a wealthy merchant in the city; and Arturo Dancel, later governor of Rizal. There were others who had not been first with Aguinaldo. "Some of these men had lived in foreign countries and most of them had held offices under or otherwise identified themselves with the Spanish government. Generally they were accredited members of the learned professions, or large property owners, or both." Their Federal party stood for peace and annexation, the immediate acceptance of American sovereignty in perpetuity, with increasing autonomy leading up to admission as a state. Was all this approved of in Washington? Not unanimously, but the general feeling was that it was a beginning where a beginning was badly needed. And in spite of disapproval among many Philippine-based American businessmen, it had a beneficial effect on events in the Islands. After the Federal party was formed, insurgent activity gradually ground to a halt. Señor Arellano prevailed on Aguinaldo himself to take the oath of allegiance to the United States, and though here and there, in pockets of resistance, hostilities continued, the insurgents' activities slowed down. Cameron Forbes makes the interesting comment: "Philippine property owners and conservatives were inclined to accept permanent American sovereignty, not only because they feared continued danger to life and property under a weak government, but also because the idea of nationalism was new. There was no general demand for independence among the common people." Some Filipinos did keep up the cry for independence, encouraged by bandits who cloaked their depredations under this demand, and some of the outlaws were strong enough in certain regions to make it dangerous to speak up for the Federal party there. In this, said Cameron with some indignation, they were encouraged by the activities of the Anti-Imperialist League in Boston. As time went on the political opponents of the Federal party took up the clamor for independence—"the increasingly popular slogan of nationalism" Forbes called it—when the time came to seek votes, but this did not happen until 1907. No general elections took place during Taft's incumbency, but Roosevelt called him back in 1904 to be secretary of war. Taft thought it over, then accepted because in that post he could continue supervising the affairs of the Islands. His successor was Vice-Governor Luke E. Wright, who, after all, knew the country and was well schooled in his erstwhile superior's philosophy. When Filipinos chanted their slogan of the Philippines for the Filipinos, he would retort that though he thoroughly agreed: "Our job just now is to make the Philippines worth something to the Filipinos." He altered Taft's policy in one respect: he did not confine his Civil Service appointments to members of the Federal party, but went on the theory that the most meritorious man should be chosen no matter what his politics. Under

125

Wright there came an end at last to guerrilla warfare and brigandage.

Before we go into the traumatic affair of political changes in Washington, it might be as well to see what life in Manila was like for Americans before the transition. Under the section in Gleeck's *The Manila Americans* called "The Escolta: Clarke's," is a collection of descriptions of Manila in 1903 and thereabouts, with American civilians arriving to take over, in some part, from the more raucous soldiers. The Escolta was about five hundred yards long and had for centuries been the city's main shopping street—a sleepy, awning-covered street which in the old days had looked like a towpath between two rows of tents. The American troops changed all that, turning it into a jumble of honky-tonks. The noise of orchestras, cornets and clarinets and the combardino, amply compensated for the lack, in those early days, of Gramophones and automatic pianos not yet imported from America. The bars were very busy. . . .

But Governor Taft changed all that. One of the first things he did was ban saloons in the Escolta, and it became again a quiet shopping center. "Otherwise, photographs of the time show that the street now had a distinctly small-town American look," writes Gleeck. Close to the foot of the Bridge of Spain, slightly upstream from today's Jones Bridge, Clarke's soft drink, candy, and ice-cream parlor faced Beck's American Bazaar, Manila's first American-style department or general store. . . .

"At one of Clarke's tables today, a steamy morning in August, sat H. E. Heacock, one of the rising American businessmen, who would later abandon Manila (leaving behind a jewelry business which would in the Thirties become the biggest department store in Manila) for other, more inviting business opportunities elsewhere in the Orient. His companion was Harold Pitt, already successfully launched in business as a leading mineral water salesman. (It is difficult, so many years later, to appreciate what a problem, and thus also business opportunity, potable liquids presented to the early Americans.) . . ." Lewis Gleeck pictured Customs Commissioner Morgan Shuster arguing above the coffee cups with these gentlemen over one of his confiscations of undervalued merchandise, and, at another table,

Clarke himself conversing with Einar Peterson, a Danish prospector, about funds to develop a promising mining claim to be called "Benguet Gold Mining."

Leaving the Escolta, Gleeck leads us to a girls' school in Calle Nueva, later Mabini Street, where there was meeting the second District Conference of the Methodist Church. Presiding was Homer C. Stuntz, one of the best known American preachers in Manila and the pastor of the American Church. Though the church authorities naturally wanted to make converts among the Filipinos, they were on that day primarily worried about the spiritual welfare of the American soldiers on their doorstep. One of the ladies had, the year before, reported, "Gross evils have rushed to our shores, surrounding our boys with great temptations. We, as Christians, must help to supply some alternative for these evils which lie close at hand. We must be ready with a cordial handshake, a word of friendship, an open door for a social evening, good literature and some alternatives for the ice cold beer to quench his thirst. . . ."

Every evening, during the comparatively cool hour of the day, almost everyone went out to promenade on the Luneta, the public park which in those times was a narrow, grassy oval surrounding a bandstand near the sea: it took in a popular stretch of beach. Around the grass ran a roadway lit by gas lanterns. The Luneta reached from the Intramuros walls for about a quarter of a mile. During the day, children and their guardians played on the sand, but in the evening the Luneta belonged to Manila's society. Wrote Gleeck, "In the hours before dusk, the affluent and the near-affluent, in carriages of various kinds (after food and drink and stevedoring, livery stables were the first considerable American business activity) drove around and around the oval with its bandstand, where an excellent band concert was given nearly every evening. Mrs. Taft particularly enjoyed the Luneta and the exuberance of the open air play of the school children, American and Filipino, from the American school of its day located on nearby Calle Victoria, just inside the walls."

Had Taft wished to avail himself of his rightful prerogative, he could have driven to the right, against the popular stream. His

127

predecessor, the royal governor, would have done this, and in a coach-and-four at that. So could an archbishop. But Taft, of course, rode with the others, in a carriage-and-pair. Round and round they all went, bowing right and left to their acquaintances, most of whom they had probably met during the day, and more than once. Taft was very serious in his democratic principles.

Not everyone among the regular inhabitants of the city was as decorous as the governor or the missionaries would have liked. Even when we have discounted the servicemen, Manila would not have been the same without the almost notorious "Mayor" W. W. Brown, who had been proprietor of a famous saloon on the Escolta, until like the others he had to move out. This was the Alhambra, popular not only among service officers but newspapermen, lawyers, business-men, planters, and showgirls. Brown himself, enormously fat, was a teetotaler, but he was lavish with his hospitality to those who drank. What made him noteworthy, said Gleeck, was that "Mayor" Brown openly and a trifle contemptuously defied the Puritanism that the Americans had brought to the Islands. "As early as 1901, the apostles of virtue were trying to apply stateside social taboos to the social life of local Americans at the same time as they sought, sometimes pathetically and somewhat ludicrously, to impose their own moral standards on Philippine society." While Manila's American news-papers lectured the world on the sins of the *querida* (sweetheart, i.e., concubine) system, and American preachers thundered against gambling and cockfighting, they apparently saw little wrong in the Americans' own heavy drinking, though this often scandalized the Filipinos. "Mayor" Brown did not accept this viewpoint.

"Not that most of the Americans of his time were compulsively moralistic," said Gleeck. Bachelors, miners, and planters, those on the fringes of domesticity, lived as boisterously as they liked, but in Manila the American wife and the American preacher, fighting for morality, segregated the moral from the immoral and the acceptable from the unacceptable. Sometimes, therefore, they segregated large parts of the nonofficial American community from Filipino society, and that was not a desirable effect.

Summing up the year 1901, Gleeck saw that the Americans in Manila had as yet no sense of community. But they did have a sense of identity, and they already had businesses, newspapers, churches, schools, and clubs. It would not be long before they were in fact a community.

In 1903 the proportion of Filipinos employed in the Civil Service was 40 percent. In 1913, after the upheaval of the Democratic administration was reflected by Francis Burton Harrison as governor-general, it was 71 percent, which means that the Americans who were out had to look elsewhere for work unless they left the Islands altogether. But never mind that story as yet: we are looking at statistics only. There had been a great increase in the number of Filipinos who took their entrance examinations in English. In 1903, 97 percent of those examined took their tests in Spanish, but in 1913, 89 percent chose to be examined in English: the total number examined was 7755. Almost all appointees for ordinary clerical work were—by that time—Filipino, but the supply of other workers than clerks, i.e., bookkeepers, stenographers, civil engineers, physicians, veterinarians, surveyors, chemists, bacteriologists, agriculturalists, horticulturalists, constabulary officers, nurses, electricians, mechanical engineers, and other scientific employees, was still insufficient to meet the demand, and no wonder. Only one Filipino, for example, had passed the stenography examination since the beginning of the Civil Service ten years earlier, so it was still necessary to bring out many American stenographers every year. But each year a few Filipinos passed the junior stenography examination, and their numbers were rising: in 1913 there were eight.

The salaries paid executive officials, chiefs of bureaus and offices, chief clerks and chiefs of divisions often equaled those paid to their opposite numbers in U.S. government service. In the legislative branch, the Speaker was paid $8000 annually. Members of the commission without portfolio got $7500. Members of the Assembly got $15 a day for every day in session. In the executive branch the secretaries of departments got $15,500 each, including their $5000 as members of the commission. At the time of the change in administration in the United States, in 1913, the ranking executive officials of the insular government were a governor-general, a secretary of the interior, a secretary of finance and justice, a secretary of commerce and police, and a secretary of public instruction. All of these were appointed by the president, subject to Senate confirmation. The secretary of finance and justice was a Filipino; all other secretaries of departments were American.

The legislature consisted of two houses, the Philippines Commission, or Upper House, and the Philippines Assembly. There were nine members of the commission—the governor-general, four secretaries, and four more appointed by the president, subject to the usual Senate confirmation. Four of these members were Filipinos, the other five Americans. The Assembly or, as we might call it, the House of Representatives, was composed of eighty-one members, all elected and all Filipinos. They represented thirty-four of the thirty-nine provinces into which the archipelago was then divided. The two houses of the legislature had equal powers: neither had any special privilege in the matter of initiating legislation, and affirmative action by both was required in order to pass it. The Moro Province, the Mountain Province, and the provinces of Nueva Viscaya and Agusan were not represented in the Assembly nor subject to the jurisdiction of the Philippines legislature. The commission alone had legislative jurisdiction over them, their population being largely Moro or other non-Christian tribes.

In this time of postwar and political activity, one tends to lose sight of what life was like for the ordinary American who elected to live in the Islands. Part of the hiatus is filled nowadays by the efforts of scholarly associations, from one of which, a little volume published by the Historical Conservation XXIV Society, I have already quoted the reminiscences of Captain Betts. There is another article in the same book, "Recollections of Mr. Elmer Madsen," which is even more enlightening. Madsen was born, in 1880, to Danish parents

Admiral George Dewey *(UPI)*   Emilio Aguinaldo *(UPI)*

First U.S. flag hoisted in the vicinity of Manila, August 13, 1898 *(Courtesy of the American Historical Collection in Manila)*

William Howard Taft, Governor-General 1901–1904 *(The Bettmann Archive, Inc.)*

William Cameron Forbes, Governor-General 1909–1913 *(NYT Pictures)*

Baseball game at Baguio Teacher's Camp, circa 1910 *(Courtesy of the American Historical Collection in Manila)*

Veranda of the Baguio Country Club *(Courtesy of the American Historical Collection in Manila)*

Francis Burton Harrison, Governor-General 1913–1921 *(UPI)*

(Left to right) Secretary of the Navy Edwin Denby, Governor-General Leonard Wood, and Major General Omar Bundy in Manila, 1921 *(UPI)*

Henry Stimson, Governor-General 1927–1929 *(UPI)*

Dwight Davis, Governor-General 1929–1932 *(UPI)*

Manuel Quezon, first president of the Commonwealth of the Philippines, elected in September 1935 *(UPI)*

The Asiatic fleet in Manila Bay *(UPI)*

The internment camp at the University of Santo Tomas in Manila during WW II *(UPI)*

General Douglas MacArthur wading ashore at Luzon, Philippines. January 25, 1945 (*UPI*)

Independence Day Ceremony, July 4, 1946 (*NYT Pictures*)

who had emigrated to the United States and homesteaded in Nebraska. The family lived for some years in a "sod house," i.e., a house built of turf with grass on top, the roof balancing on a few branches from their fruit trees: there was no other building material available, but at least it was warm. The livestock was protected in the same way, with straw pressed down on sod. "Those shelters were very satisfactory," said Mr. Madsen. "Straw is very warm, much warmer than grass." Oddly, in tropical Manila he often thought of the warmth of that straw.

After he finished school he went to a business and normal school and studied typewriting, bookkeeping, and commercial law. Then he taught high school for a year, after which he worked for a small country bank.

"When my people settled in that part of the country," he said, "there were Indians about. They were among the first settlers. There were no roads. There were no bridges. The place was far away from the town. Winters are very, very cold . . . The implements they had for working their land were very primitive. They did not have horses but had oxen instead. These farmers used plows and harrows. . . . School began at 9:00 in the morning. The children had to get up early particularly the older children because these older children did the chores before they went to school. They had to feed the cattle, the pigs, the cows, chickens and had to milk the cows. After that was done they changed their clothes and went to school. In the evening after they had finished their work, they got their books and studied their lessons. They had to get up early the next morning . . . To heat themselves they had small heating stoves and it was very, very cold so they kept close to the stove. Some other kids were very small, and they went to kindergarten. The teacher had to teach all of them, kindergarten up to high school. When the kids returned from school they got busy at once, started attending to household chores consisting of feeding animals and milking the cows. After these were all done, they had their dinner. And after taking dinner they studied their lessons. During those days they studied with a strong will.

When these children grew up some of them remained in that part of the country and kept on farming. Others ran away to distant places, working at almost any trade . . . However, those old fellows deserved a great deal of credit more than has been given to them for opening the frontier. They had really hard times. There were no doctors. When they got sick, they simply stayed in bed without any medicines and no nurse. Medicines could only be gotten in town and the only town was very far from their place."

Exactly the kind of background, one would say, for a man who went to a far-off place like the Philippines. The Spanish-American War broke out while he was still in business school, and he volunteered, but was not accepted by the army. However, others made it, and the Nebraska Volunteers got to the Islands. There was a lot of publicity about them, and Madsen saw some of the photographs they sent home. He was tempted by the coconut trees and other strange bits of scenery, and made up his mind to get there somehow.

"I then applied for a government position and took a government examination," he said, presumably referring to the period when he worked in the bank. "The Civil Service people wrote me saying that they had no vacancy in the United States and offered me instead a position with the Philippine Government which I accepted since it was what I wanted." The long adventure had begun.

He went to San Francisco by train and embarked there on the S.S. *Coptic*, of the Pacific Mail Steamship Company. "The accommodation was very poor but the food was good." It was June 10, 1904. Fellow passengers comprised schoolteachers, mining engineers, architects, "and others." Some, like Madsen, were going to Manila for the first time; others were returning to the Islands. Everything, of course, was new and delightful for him. Honolulu was "a wonderful place." In Japan, he watched women do the work of refueling in Nagasaki, passing the coal baskets from hand to hand in a chain, so that the vessel was refueled in twelve hours: it looked as if serpents were boarding the ship. He found Shanghai more interesting even than Japan; there were more Europeans there than Americans. He remembered a train in Hong Kong that went up and down the mountain, carrying passengers to and fro. Hong Kong was his getting-off place: the *Coptic* didn't go any farther, so he had a little time to look around. "The English and the Chinese had great respect for each other, and treated each other decently," he observed.

Then he and the other Manila-bound passengers boarded their ship, the *Tean*, which also carried a large number of cattle: at that time meat was imported into the Philippines. The trip from Hong Kong to Manila took three or four days. They arrived at night and he and "some of the other boys" went to what was then the Bay View Hotel, which was located directly in front of the present hostelry of that same name.

"There was no Dewey Boulevard then, nothing like that," he said. "The hotel stood up right close to the Bay. . . . Coming as I did from Nebraska, I knew nothing about mosquitoes. None of us had a mosquito net so we fought the mosquitoes all night. In the morning I was unable to recognize myself because of the mosquito bites."

There were no automobiles in Manila, just various kinds of conveyances called *carruajes, carretillas,* and horse-drawn buses. Getting anywhere was very slow, especially as it was July when it rained most of the time. He used to walk to work, which was in the Treasury Department: he was there for three years. For the first few months he lived in a boardinghouse.

"However, I came to prefer to live in one place and to eat out in restaurants so a friend of mine, Mr. Holson and I both took a room in the Walled City in Calle Palacio opposite the plaza of the old San Augustin Church. I lived there for quite some time. There were a few restaurants in the Walled City and mostly they were run by Chinese. I took my meals in these Chinese restaurants. Meals were not bad and were very cheap. As a matter of fact everything in those days was very cheap. I remember we had a laundryman. He came across the bay to get our clothes and charged each of us P5.00 a month. I remember buying twelve suits, all of them with coat and pants for a total of P96.00 or P8.00 a suit. The Walled City was very nice then."

Madsen's friend Mr. Holson wandered about a bit. He went to Canton and didn't like it and came back. He went to Santo Domingo, was transferred to Washington, D.C., and while there took law courses at Georgetown University. "He came back again when Harrison was governor," said Mr. Madsen. "At that time he was appointed director of Civil Service. Holson left when Harrison was still here because Harrison made it a policy of dismissing most of the Americans who were then in the Service. After leaving the Philippines, he was appointed American adviser to Persia. Subsequently, he became adviser to Emperor Haile Selassie of Ethiopia. I want to say that he was one of my best friends during those early days in the Philippines. We used to go out together for long walks near the sea which was then the favorite place for people to walk. Holson and I oftentimes went out to see the big waves coming. We enjoyed those long walks."

Old men don't forget; they remember, and often they repeat. Madsen was no exception. He said again that transportation in 1904 was very slow, and he listed again the sorts of carriage available— *carruajes*, *carretillas*, and *carromatas*. "The Filipino horse is a small animal but it can travel quite well," he continued. ". . . We had a few streets like Escolta which were paved with wooden blocks. In rainy days they became slippery and so the horse would often fall down. Outside Manila there were very few roads. In most places however there were trails and on those trails we used carabaos. We had the Manila–Dagupan Railroad which went out to Sta. Mesa and then to Malabon. People who had come with me and who were stationed in the provinces had difficulty in getting to their station. I remember one school teacher who was assigned to Cagayan Valley, in Tuguegarao I think. He took the train from Manila to Cabanatuan and from there on he got a horse for himself and a carabao for his belongings. He went up during the rainy season and of course had quite a hard time getting there, although once there he enjoyed his station notwithstanding the fact that all he had for food was rice, fish, chicken and eggs."

We have another valuable witness to life in Manila in the early days of the century: Dr. Victor Heiser, who has already appeared briefly in these pages. He was born in Johnstown, Pennsylvania, in 1873 and orphaned at the age of sixteen by the disastrous Johnstown flood, which he survived because he was young and nimble. Through the following (surprisingly few) years he made his way into government service as a doctor, first in the Immigration Department and then, in 1903, in the Philippines, serving first as chief quarantine officer and then as director of health. Already experienced (though he was only thirty when he arrived in Manila), he had done a lot of public health work in other countries. For example, he had stopped up the escape holes through which diseased immigrants were slipping from Canada into the United States, and he had traced outbursts of bubonic plague in New York to bundles of rags that were routinely sent from Egypt for processing. Obviously he was, or had reason to be, a hardened health officer by the time he arrived, but the Philippines and its problems of hygiene awed him. As has been said, he scorned the old Far East hands, the British, French, and Dutch, who said it was a waste of time and money to "sanitize" the Oriental. One couldn't let people suffer if one had the means to relieve them, Heiser reflected. Besides, it was simply uneconomic to leave disease unchecked, as it never stays at home, but wanders outside the original filthy breeding-place to infect others. Cholera, malaria, and smallpox ruined all the chances Filipinos might have to make a living, and thus ruined the possibility of any thriving industry. Look at what happened to the Spaniards when they tried to run the place, he said; over and over they failed to produce sugar on a large scale, though cane grew well.

One might ask why so much emphasis was placed, from the beginning, on health in the Islands. Heiser explains it to a degree we can't understand until we know the background. At the end of the war we suddenly found an unsought duty on our hands. Though the British, French, and Dutch had had years of experience in the unhealthy tropics, we Americans had not. The only exception we could point to was a recent one: our successful fight against yellow fever in Cuba, a disease we had long tried without success to keep out of our own country.

"To prevent this danger was one of the principal reasons for our going to war with Spain," wrote Heiser, and even today that is a surprising remark, but only because most of us don't look at history from the health officer's point of view. Our military governor, Leonard Wood, with the Yellow Fever Commission headed by Walter Reed, and Major William C. Gorgas of the U.S. Army Medical Corps, conducted this battle against yellow fever in Cuba. Then the United States was drawn into the construction of the Panama Canal, where the French for years had unsuccessfully struggled against the inroads among their workers of yellow fever and malaria. Gorgas was put in charge of supervising sanitation in this venture, in which U.S. engineers intended to cut across the Isthmus, while his friend and colleague, Victor Heiser, carried the benefits of their experience to the Philippines.

In 1903 the population of the Islands had been at a standstill for some time: it was even on the downgrade. War had weakened the people and left them easy victims to disease. Their health, he decided, must be improved. What with plague, cholera, smallpox, tuberculosis, and beriberi, it was no wonder the Philippines had the biggest infant mortality rate in the world: every second baby born there died soon after birth. There were ten thousand lepers wandering about uncared for because the Church tended only a few hundred. The Filipinos had no system for treating the insane. Overcrowding was gross. One ancient, polluted water system had been installed in Manila by the Spanish; otherwise they had no reservoir, no pipeline, not even an artesian well in all the Islands. It was a health officer's nightmare. And the Filipinos, superstitious to a frightening degree, seemed resigned to their lot. Heiser at the beginning set himself the goal of trying to save fifty thousand lives a year, but later he was to say that he could have made it a hundred thousand.

One of the first tasks, he decided, was to rid the city of the great twenty-five-acre moat around Intramuros. Like the Walled City itself, it was very picturesque and pleasing to the romantic eye, but to the nose it was another matter. Four sewers emptied into it: it was noisome, filthy, and a breeding place for snakes and mosquitos. Only the carabaos really loved it, because they could wallow in the mixture it held of swamp and human excrement. The whole city of Manila, if it came to that, was unsanitary to a degree. Worcester's description was even more vivid than Heiser's: if one was out in the city at night, he said, it was wise to keep to the middle of the street, and even wiser to carry a raised umbrella.

"Immediately after the American occupation, some five hundred barrels of caked excrement were taken from a single tower in one of the old Manila monasteries. The moat around the city wall, and the *estaros*, or tidal creeks, reeked with filth, and the smells which assailed one's nostrils, especially at night, were disgusting."

Cemeteries were often located in the very middle of the towns, or near the local water supply. There was not a single modern operating room, let alone a modern hospital, in all of the Islands.

Apart from the moat, the Walled City's houses were themselves unhealthy places, old as they were: dysentery, tuberculosis, and cholera flourished within those picturesque walls. Under Heiser's direction the Americans filled the moat and covered it over with turf, changing the area into parkland. They punched holes in the thirty-foot-thick walls and opened Intramuros to air, light and traffic. In his enthusiasm Heiser even considered pulling down the whole Walled City, but this suggestion brought forth such an outraged clamor of protest from antiquarians and historians that he had to relinquish the idea, and in the end he and his corps contented themselves with pulling down the river wall. Most of Manila's inhabitants did not live in Intramuros anyway, but in houses of a kind they could afford, the wealthier in sandstone buildings and the workers, such as farmers and fishermen, in nipa huts—"airy baskets on stilts" Heiser called them. Many still live in such huts on the outskirts of the city. The nipa palm provides roofs and sides with its leaves, and the frames and floors are of bamboo, the wood of which is not attacked by termites. The whole edifice is tied together with vegetable fiber. In short, said the health officer, apart from the fact that in those days each hut had its own sanitation, simply dropping all unwanted substances into the space on the ground underneath, no more suitable dwelling for the climate could have been devised. The bamboo poles, split and laid face down, were cool and elastic enough for hot nights; the Filipinos merely spread their sleeping mats on them.

The peasant farmer of the Philippines, who made up the bulk of the population, was called the "tao." Unofficially he was ruled (at uncomfortably close quarters) by the rich man of the village, the "cacique" or chief. The cacique owned everything in the way of land, and farmed it out, taking part of every crop—and a good part, too, so that the tao was virtually a peon. When they came, the Americans were indignant about the situation but could hardly do anything effective in changing it: this would take time. And in the health service, as Heiser said, they had to recognize the cacique's power and work with him, as otherwise nothing would be done. The cacique had to be convinced that he would get nothing from them, the health people, directly, but when he saw, as he soon did, that there were advantages in a system that kept his peons healthy, he cooperated. Dr. Heiser had nothing but praise for the superior officials through whose agency he was given the work he did with such zest. In his book he quoted with much approval President McKinley on the subject of taking on the responsibility of the Philippines: "There was nothing left for us to do but to take them all, and to educate the Filipinos, and uplift and civilize and Christianize them, and by God's grace to do the very best we could by them."

Of course—it seems necessary to say it more than once—they were already Christianized, but perhaps McKinley forgot that. At any rate his motives were pure, and so, in Heiser's opinion, were those of his representatives, Taft first as governor-general, then Luke Wright, then Henry C. Ide (though Ide held office only a short time). But the best of the lot, in Heiser's opinion as in Worcester's, was William Cameron Forbes, who, already on the commission, was appointed governor-general in 1909, the year Taft became president of the United States.

As Forbes saw it, the matter of first importance in developing the Islands' resources was transport. He wanted to create an efficient road system, and this, in spite of having inadequate funds for such a project, he managed to do. It was not an easy task, because even after the roads were built and paid for they were in constant need of repair. This is true of roads generally, but the Philippines climate exaggerated the difficulties to an extent it is not easy to imagine unless one has lived in the tropics. Forbes kept on each stretch of road a permanent "caminero," or roadman, who carefully inspected his own few miles every day and filled in every hole he found. Cameron Forbes was so insistent on this business of building and repairing roads that the Filipinos, punning on his name, called him Caminero Forbes (or Forbess, which is how they still pronounce it). Joking apart, his judgment proved sound: trade immediately improved. As Dr. Heiser declared, wealth began to flow along those highways as soon as they existed. In one year, for example, sugar production rose from fifty thousand tons to a million and a half. The copra industry developed with equal speed, as did that of Philippine tobacco. The progress of the latter industry was so marked that it aroused the jealousy of those American merchants who dealt in Havana cigars. They spread such horror stories about Filipino cigars that for years it was impossible, or at least very difficult, to buy this really good tobacco in the United States. It took the Cuban crisis of the twentieth century to help the tobacco growers of the Islands to come into their own in North America.

Opinion about Forbes was not unanimous—President Manuel Quezon was later to say that Forbes was rather stupid—but two chroniclers, Heiser and Worcester, agree in their hearty admiration of him. For one thing, as Worcester said, he didn't need the job, which always helps, because he had an independent income. For another, he really liked the Philippines and their people, and was familiar with them through having served since 1904 as secretary of commerce and police on the commission. (This affection is amply evident in his history of the Islands.) He had had a good deal of experience in business before coming out to the Philippines: it was a strong sense of duty that had impelled him to accept the first appointment. And he had other enthusiasms as well as a fondness for roads. A fact that was bound to endear him to Dean Worcester was that he was truly interested in the non-Christian tribes. He traveled widely to see such people—the Moros and Bukidnons in the south, and the Negritos, Benguit Igorotes, Ilongots, Ifugaos, and Hugaos in the north. Repeatedly, said Worcester approvingly, he visited subprovinces in the Mountain Province. He had great faith in the outdoor sports that he himself enjoyed as a health-giving, peaceful way of life for the natives; he stimulated interest among the Filipinos in baseball, golf, and polo. He was honest, generous, and imaginative, said Worcester, and under him the Islands flourished as never before.

One of his actions, which seemed at the time controversial (and continued to stimulate argument among his successors) was the construction of a road to Baguio, in the highlands of northern Luzon about 150 miles from Manila. Baguio itself was Worcester's creation, though Forbes fought sturdily to build and protect it. It was obvious to him (and to most other thoughtful Americans in the colony) that what foreigners there badly needed was an occasional break from the hot weather. Why shouldn't they find a place that would afford some relief, a sort of summer capital? The English in India sent their women and children to "the Hills" of Simla during the hottest season. Even at home, residents in New York and other places subject to the pitiless heat of the continental summer managed to find cooler resorts where they could repair now and then, and one could scarcely claim that Manila was any easier to live in during the hottest days of the year than New York. When they were in pursuit of Aguinaldo, some American troops had noticed that the mountain regions where he took refuge afforded cool weather. For that matter, the Spaniards in their time had discovered the same thing in a certain region north of the city, five thousand feet in altitude, and one or two of them mentioned it to Worcester. He in turn spoke to Forbes, who investigated that part of the province and found Baguio, a lovely region where it actually got cold at night. It would make a fine health resort, the men agreed: the only drawback was that it was so very hard to reach. Very well, said Caminero Forbes, we will build a road, and he started things rolling.

Building that road cost a lot. The months and the seasons moved on, each bringing its own kind of catastrophe. There were washouts over and over. Bridges were barely finished before they were destroyed. Falling boulders made deathtraps. In the end two million dollars were poured into the project, and Forbes was attacked by his enemies on all sides for wasting Philippine money on such a harebrained scheme. Loudest among his critics were the Filipinos. But the road was finished at last, and Baguio was built up into summer houses and clubs and hotels, and people found health and pleasure there, until even those Filipinos who had been loudest in their complaints had a change of heart. According to Dr. Heiser, when Francis Burton Harrison supplanted Forbes as governor-general, the Democrats who had put their new man into office said to the Filipino critics of Baguio, "This is your road. Since you dislike it so much, you may abandon it if you wish." To which the Filipinos replied, "This is a beautiful road. We love it dearly."

On one of his visits to the Islands, William Howard Taft found Baguio and its environs very salubrious. He wrote back to Elihu Root that he had ridden part of the way to the mountains on horseback, and felt much better for his visit. Root cabled in reply, "How is the horse?"

Chapter Eight

We might wonder who these people were, these Americans who decided to stay on in the Islands, and how they managed it, but these are easy questions to answer. They were simpler times than ours, when a volunteer soldier could follow his impulse and take his discharge there and then. He could not exactly move in on another man's land, but the Philippines were not so crowded that he couldn't find a foothold, especially out in the country. Or, as was more likely, he might go into business for himself with his payoff. As Gleeck says, many of these Americans were adventure-minded, coming as they had from the Western or Middle Western states, where people were mobile by nature and willing to take chances. "Seeing vast areas of unsettled and undeveloped land . . . [they] were beguiled both by the adventure and profits which seemed to await those bold enough to wrest the riches of unexploited minerals, lumber and plantation crops from mountain, plain and jungle. . . ." It would never do with us today, but this was yesterday. Those who stayed divided themselves into three waves, as it were: the first were demobilized soldiers, the second were those who lost their jobs with the government after the Republican administration in Washington was unhorsed in 1912, and the third took up an offer embodied in the Osmeña Act of 1921, which awarded bonuses to such Americans in government service who voluntarily retired and left their posts free for Filipinos.

Apart from the retailers in the towns, the new settlers went in for growing crops such as abaca, coconuts, and rubber in the area around Davao Gulf, prospecting for minerals in Rizal-Quezon, the Mountain Province and Camarines Norte, lumbering and growing sugarcane in Negros, and growing rice in Nueva Ecija. A few Americans also went in for cattle ranching, but they were not many.

For most it was a hard life; in Gleeck's words, the first planters worked and often lived like animals. He cites "Jake" Jacobson, who arrived at Cebu in 1900 with General Kobbé, came to Davao in 1906 to manage a new coconut plantation for another American, Frank Crowhurst, and lived there for seven years, saving his money. With this he was able to buy a ranch of 460 hectares on the east side of the Gulf. "For some time, working to the point of exhaustion, he lived in a tent, then moved to a nipa shack. Davao in 1906 was little better than a swamp cleared out of the jungle. Sickness (with no doctors) and hardships were the rule; ice was a luxury for which Jacobson waited thirty years. Many of the original pioneers died. Some settlers mated with wild women; a handful imported wives, but few of them could stand the life. O. V. Wood's wife went crazy." Yet O. V. Wood had what was called the finest hemp plantation in the Islands.

The rubber planters in Mindoro had high hopes for their future, as Harvey Firestone was interested in developing a great plantation in Mindanao and Sulu, taking over these vast tracts bodily. But the Philippine government at last turned Firestone down, and he carried his capital to Liberia. In 1936, says Gleeck, "the back-breaking toil was far behind Davao and the pioneers. Other foreigners—the Japanese, with their incredible industry and organizational skills, were beginning to put their stamp on Davao." At that time there

144

were fifteen American plantations around the Gulf, some of them surpassing the best of the Japanese holdings.

In Zamboanga and its hinterland the American plantations were on a smaller scale, for various reasons including the obvious one that the Moros did not welcome settlers. Gleeck quotes some fascinating passages from the saga of a coconut plantation belonging to Stephen Juricka, hardware merchant and broker in Jolo, and his wife Blanche, who managed their coconut plantation at Sibuco sixty miles away from Zamboanga. (The climate there is better suited to the production of copra than rubber.) Mrs. Juricka grew angry when some newspaper writer from the States spoke of her enviable life in the "languorous East," and wrote a retort to show just how languorous existence was for a woman who made a regular monthly trip to the plantation. Twenty-four hours before writing the letter, she said, she had started out as usual in her ten-foot vinta—a light little sailboat—with three Moros, two to paddle and one to manage the sail. They set out at dusk to avoid the sun's glare, and stood out to sea a mile. Then, avoiding reefs and currents if they could, they headed for the plantation, which entailed sailing all night and arriving at dawn tired and cramped and cold and hungry. On that trip a storm broke over them when they were nearly there: they had to reef their sail by rolling it up, and with a half sail they scudded on before a constantly shifting wind. The shore was blotted out. But at five the next morning the weather cleared, and they saw they were only ten miles beyond the plantation. That was lucky, said Mrs. Juricka: they could equally well have fetched up at Jolo or Hong Kong. They had to paddle back against a strong current, and landed at their own beach at eight.

The plantation people were net fishing when they arrived, but ten minutes later one of the women rushed out of the water to the beach in order to give birth to a child, Blanche and the foreman's wife acting as midwives. For some time then she did her usual duty of attending to various ailments ("I am not a trained nurse, I have only the knowledge which comes to every woman who raises a large

145

family"), treating sores and skin diseases, dispensing quinine and such, and giving advice on everything "from warts and women to coconuts and the Koran." She then walked and rode over the plantation until three in the afternoon, when it was time to sail back to Zamboanga, stopping on the way to ask if she could do anything for various planter neighbors. One always pulls up for a minute, she explained, to find out if the others had mail to send in and to visit for a bit. A few minutes' visit in that isolation is incredibly valuable, and when reading matter gives out "you actually find yourself absently reading over and over the labels on fruit tins and soap wrappers." This time, stopping at a lumber mill, she found the owner agitated because one of his laborers had a terribly sick baby, and he didn't know what to do for it. Blanche Juricka brought out her first-aid kit and examined the baby in the laborer's shack, listening to its chest: clearly, she said, it had acute bronchial pneumonia, and had been ill for three days. At eight, when she saw that it was dying, she asked the mother, Marta, if the infant had been baptized. Blanche got a glass of clear water and marked the baby with the sign of the cross, and baptized him in the name of the Father, Son, and Holy Ghost. She said, "Now, Marta, the baby is all right." But the lady was Protestant, wailed Marta. Blanche promised to bring her a letter from the padre to the effect that the baptism was all right.

Then, back to Zamboanga.

Camp Keithley, on the shores of Lake Lanao, was a lovely spot in spite of the Moros with whom the soldiers often battled, and in 1914, after the First World War, sixty-eight American soldiers were discharged in the Philippines by their own choice, and went homesteading in that vicinity, in Mumungan near the Maria Cristina Falls. There they cleared the land and went in for mixed farming. They all married natives, either Christian Filipinos in Luzon or, when they arrived in Lanao, Moro girls. Their children all spoke the local Maranaw dialect, and a reporter from the *Free Press* of Manila reported rapturously in 1940, "Among the settlers in Mumungan today besides the white Americans, are American Negroes, Japanese and Chinese. People from Cebu, Bohol, Leyte and Luzon, especially

146

the Ilocos region, live in Mumungan too in peace and content."

But many developments had occurred before this halcyon interlude was possible.

In spite of his excellent record and his popularity, Cameron Forbes had one inexpungeable black mark against him in Washington when the new administration took over in 1912 and Woodrow Wilson became president. He was a Republican and had been appointed by a Republican president who had occupied his place for only one four-year term. It is true that in the early days when the commission first went out to Manila, it had been solemnly decided among McKinley, Taft, and the others that politics should play no part in the American administration of the Islands. There were to be no pork-barrel handouts and no abrupt changes of personnel such as one usually sees after a political upset at home. But no dead man can govern the actions of his successors, and it could not be expected that the Democratic party would follow meekly in the Elephant's footprints. Besides, Forbes believed in slow, careful ways to bring in Philippine independence: he thought it should be well and solidly built, the country governed by men who had been trained for their new positions to a degree that no speedy indoctrination could accomplish. The Democrats took the opposite point of view.

Wilson himself, after some irresolution, thought the Philippines should soon be granted a form of independence. *The American Historical Collection Bulletin* for January–March 1978 carries an article on this matter by Charles M. Farkas, "Relieving the White Man's Burden," in which the author declares that Wilson had no Philippine policy in 1912, and so was lucky that the Philippines had not been an election issue and that his ambivalence on this subject had no effect on the voters. During the earlier debate on American imperialism, in 1898, Wilson asked himself in a memorandum, "What Ought We to Do?" and had not quite answered the question by 1912. On the one hand, we could do a lot of good to lesser nations if we possessed them and governed them properly. ". . . he advocated a policy of what I call 'softcore imperialism'—that is, a policy of positive intervention in world affairs that was the foreign affairs manifestation of the domestic social uplift movement that we label progressivism," said Farkas. ". . . Wilson recognized in the Philippines an opportunity to 'square our theories with our practices . . . We have been enjoying liberty. Now we are going to give others liberty.'

"Filipinos were to benefit from democratic institutions, *'spread by the people who have them.'* But the Philippine people must learn 'self control,' 'self-mastery,' and 'a thoughtful care for righteous dealing.'" Anything less would result in chaos: "'if we sent to the Philippines our institutions in manuscript they would suffer the same fate which befell a dress suit once captured by the savages. The coat was worn by one savage, the vest by another, and the trousers by a third. Each savage had part of the suit and all were unconventional.'"

By 1902, said Farkas, Wilson had rationalized American colonialism in the Islands, accepting the superiority of American democracy and believing that the Filipinos were like undisciplined children. "Democratic government and institutions would be the vehicle to bring peace, justice and stability to the Philippines." Then, from 1902 to 1913, he didn't think much about the Islands at all, any more than most other Americans. He was busy with other matters. On New Year's Day, 1913, when he was president-elect, he had a letter from Walter Hines Page, soon to be ambassador to Great Britain, suggesting that he commission some man in whose judgment he had confidence to go and make a study of the Philippines and see whether or not U.S. policy should change. Cameron Forbes wrote making a similar suggestion, as did later the secretary of commerce, William Redfield. Before he got these second letters Wilson had already sent the man of his choice, a former political science professor named Henry Jones Ford, of Princeton, to make the survey. Ford visited, talked with people, and wrote a confidential report to Wilson strongly urging that drastic changes be made as soon as possible, to avoid the trouble he said was brewing. He saw the Filipinos as ripe and ready for self-government, and the American officials in the Islands as discouraging to their wishes.

A good many of his impressions he received from Manuel L. Quezon y Molina, who had been stationed in Washington since 1909 as one of the two resident commissioners in the House of Representatives. Quezon, one of the most interesting Filipinos in American-Philippines history, was, like his nearest rival Sergio Osmeña, born in 1878. A Spanish mestizo (as were both his parents), he was good-looking, audacious, and intelligent. He fought with Aguinaldo in the insurrection, went into the practice of law, and inevitably became a politician. According to his own account, Wilson consulted him after the first version of the Jones bill, providing for Philippine independence, was defeated in 1912. (Wilson became President in 1913.) Osmeña, then speaker in the Assembly in Manila, had proposed that the Filipinos hold a constitutional convention and then proclaim independence, but Wilson turned it down, and he was wise in doing so: no such movement would be effective without Congress's backing. However, he did have several talks with the Filipino representatives, to one of which Quezon brought along Dr. Alejandro Albert, who happened to be in the capital at the time—as manager of a Filipino baseball team, of all things. Wilson asked the two men what they thought of Cameron Forbes as governor-general. Their reply was guarded. Personally they liked Forbes all right, they said (though later, according to Quezon's biographer, he admitted that he disliked him intensely), but they thought another man, more sympathetic to the cause of independence, would be preferable. At their next meeting Wilson asked them to suggest another name. Quezon named Jacob Gould Schurman. But he was a Republican and so would not do. Moorfield Storey? He was head of the Anti-Imperialist League and known to be friendly to the Filipinos. No, said Wilson; Storey at sixty-eight was too old to start a new career.

One day, said Quezon, Congressman Francis Burton Harrison stopped in to his office to suggest to him the name of a friend for the job. All of a sudden Quezon had a brilliant idea—why shouldn't Harrison himself have the position? At first it seemed a poor idea. Harrison was on the way to becoming chief of the Ways and Means Committee, one of the most powerful—perhaps the most powerful—

of places in Washington politics. But the more he and Quezon thought it over, the better the proposition sounded. Secretary of State William Jennings Bryan liked it, too, and said so. This, of course, is Quezon's version of the matter, but in Harrison's diary there is an interesting paragraph: "Feb. 3, 1936: . . . Talked with Under-Secretary Albert, who remembers not only the Philippine Revolution against Spain, but later on an interview he had with President Wilson; he came back here sharing a cabin with Quezon when I arrived in the *Manchuria* in Oct. 1913. He said that Quezon was much excited when he secured my appointment as Governor General through Secretary of State William Jennings Bryan in 1913—and then he said: 'now we are sure to get independence.'"

The entry was written a long time later, and we need not take everything Quezon said for gospel. At any rate such games of musical chairs are no novelty in government circles, and Cameron Forbes may well have expected to be replaced as soon as Wilson took over the presidency: that is the way things are usually done. But it is possible that he did not, by reason of that agreement made at the beginning of the commission's existence—no politics, no pork barrel. There is no denying that Harrison was a very political choice—a New York congressman, even a member (though not a typical one) of Tammany Hall. He may have seemed the obvious man for the post because of a speech he made four years earlier in favor of independence for the Filipinos. Nothing could have sweetened the pill for Forbes, probably, but the manner in which it was administered made things a lot worse. It was in no way gentlemanly. A cable arrived out of the blue, signed "McIntyre"—that was General Frank McIntyre, new chief of the Bureau of Foreign Affairs—simply saying to Forbes that Harrison was the new governor-general; his appointment had been confirmed on August 21 (the cable was dated August 23) and that the president would like him to sail on September 10. For this reason it "would be convenient" to have Forbes's resignation accepted on September 1, as this would give the new governor-general the chance to take his appointment formally on the second.

"The President desires to meet your convenience," continued

General McIntyre. "Should Harrison take linen, silver, glass, china, and automobiles? What else would you suggest? Wife and children will accompany him. Please engage for him servants you leave."

A couple of days afterward, belatedly remembering his manners and protocol, Woodrow Wilson did write a personal letter to the outgoing governor-general, thanking him for all he had done, etc.

All this was not surprising, considering what had gone before. While still president-elect, Wilson had said in a public address toward the end of 1912, "The Philippines are at present our frontier but I hope we presently are to deprive ourselves of that frontier."

"The effect of these few words was disastrous to the Philippine Islands," wrote Cameron Forbes. "They settled down like a wet, cold blanket over the merchants, manufacturers, and other men of business. Up to the date of that speech the imports had exceeded the official estimates so that the customs revenues of the Islands were more than one-half million dollars more than had been figured in the forecast of the preceding year. Acting on this unexpected prosperity, the Legislature had been quite liberal in its appropriations, confident that the increase would continue. Beginning with the first of January, 1913, the customs fell off at the alarming rate of about two hundred thousand dollars per month, until by July 1 the loss of revenue reached a total of more than a million dollars."

So things took their course, and on March 4, 1913, Wilson became president. In his first annual message to Congress he spoke of the archipelago and announced that his government would more and more put the control of the native citizens over the "essential instruments of their life, their local instrumentalities of government . . ." Literary style, it seems, was not the president's long suit, but the meaning was clear. There followed the appointment of Francis Burton Harrison—"the first to be appointed without any previous experience in the Islands to equip him for the complicated duties he was to undertake," wrote Forbes. Careful as he was to be scrupulously fair, he could not help making this criticism, nor to comment on Wilson: "He proceeded to inject party politics squarely into the government of the Islands."

151

Worcester repeated a story he was satisfied was true: that Harrison, when being interviewed by reporters in Honolulu as he made his way to Manila, said, "For years I have been of the minority in Congress and have seen the Democrats kicked about, trampled upon, and otherwise manhandled by Republicans, so that I must confess it gives me a saturnine pleasure to see the Democrats in a position to do the same thing to the Republicans."

As soon as Harrison arrived, on October 6, he asked for the resignation of Frank A. Branagan, the American commissioner, and four Filipino commissioners, described by Cameron Forbes as able, loyal, and high-minded gentlemen who had faithfully served the American government. . . . The Filipinos, he said, were thunderstruck. Harrison's policy, wrote Farkas, consisted of three sections. He wanted to accelerate the Filipinization of the Civil Service, give Filipinos greater autonomy in their own affairs, and promote the economic independence of the Islands. He made a stirring speech telling the Filipinos that it was the beginning of a new era for them— "The door of opportunity stands open," etc.—and reported to Lindley Garrison, secretary of war in Washington, "The bureaus here are top heavy with Americans and the Filipinos really have little share in the management of their own government."

Soon he had changed all that, and Farkas gives statistics. When he arrived there were 2633 Americans occupying the 9000 positions available in the insular government. Twenty-one of twenty-four bureau chiefs were American, as were twenty-nine of thirty-five assistant chiefs. Americans, said Farkas, dominated both the upper and lower levels of the Philippines bureaucracy. By the end of his first year in office Harrison had reduced their number to 2148, and increased the number of Filipinos to 7283. By the end of his administration (eight years later, in 1921) only 582 Americans held insular positions: the Filipinos had also gained a majority of the higher offices in the government.

Forbes and Worcester, and no doubt many others, wrung their hands over the plight of such Filipinos as lost their places, but even more were they upset over the hapless Americans who were so unceremoniously dumped. They had given their all to the work, said Forbes. They had become accustomed to living in the Islands: they were used to the climate; their health had been impaired in the service. How then could they go back to the States and settle down? Among others who lost their jobs in the sweep Harrison instituted on his first day in office were the collector of customs, director of lands, chief of police of the City of Manila, and many assistants. The panic caused by these actions can hardly be imagined. "This feeling became so intense," wrote Forbes, "that Governor-General Harrison authorized Executive Secretary Carpenter to call a meeting of the bureau chiefs and inform them that no further resignations would be requested. The reassuring effect of this, however, was in large measure nullified by a peremptory call for two additional resignations on the following day."

And because the Filipinos demanded "insistently" that American salaries be reduced, this was accomplished just as remorselessly: Harrison supported a bill of appropriation, unanimously passed by the reorganized legislature, providing an across-the-board cut in higher salaries. The result was probably gratifying to the governor-general, as many more resignations were immediately proffered.

"His [Harrison's] motives were twofold," explained Farkas, "first, to extricate the United States from the Philippines, and second, to create a body in the Philippines capable of advancing social, political, and economic reform."

Forbes says that even those Americans who had not immediately sent in their resignations were so disturbed that Harrison made a further statement, meant to be reassuring, which said in part, "I know of no reason for apprehension on the part of government employees as to the permanence of their offices excepting as they may be affected by the consolidation of bureaus under plans which are already known to the public . . . I wish, therefore, to make it plain that this administration does not contemplate a wholesale reduction in either American or Filipino employees. . . . I hope this

153

announcement will settle finally the unrest and uncertainty which I am told has followed certain changes deemed necessary soon after my arrival here, and put down the unfounded and dangerous rumors which I am now told are in circulation. I wish government employees to continue to enjoy that sense of security, which I promise shall surround them so long as they deserve such consideration. . . ."

Nevertheless, sackings continued. "Of the more than 2600 American employees to whom he addressed his [Harrison's] assurances in the fall of 1913," wrote Forbes, "only eleven percent were on the roster eight years later, and of these nearly one-half were teachers."

In these circumstances it was natural that the American civil servants were glad to support a "so-called" retirement act proposed by the governor-general, which provided a retirement allowance for those who had a record of six years' service graded upward to a maximum of a full year's pay to those who had been in the service for ten years—always provided that the officials tendered their resignations in writing before the ensuing July 1. After that, resignations fluttered in thick as the leaves of Vallombrosa, which of course was the effect desired by the governor-general.

It should come as no surprise that Harrison was held in far higher esteem by the Filipinos than the Americans, and was probably the most popular governor-general during the American-Philippine history of the Islands. He even persuaded them to increase taxation without trouble. And one American, at least, found some favorable words to say about his incumbency: this was Dr. Victor Heiser, who wanted to get Filipinos to take responsibility for their own affairs whenever possible. To be sure, Heiser looked on matters as a medical officer would rather than from a politician's point of view. In 1914, as he said, the change from military to civil government was at last brought about, with the happy result that Frank W. Carpenter came into prominence. Carpenter, who had spent ten years in the Medical Corps, came out to the Philippines and became secretary to General Lawton, who was killed in the insurrection. He was then secretary to other military governors, and was at length appointed secretary of the Executive Bureau, which had the task of supervising Filipino officials. He had a great talent for getting on with these men, partly perhaps because he was dark, like them, but mainly because he had learned to speak Spanish and several native dialects. Arthur S. Pier in *American Apostles to the Philippines* described how he would cope with recalcitrant charges:

"He pointed out the necessity for honest and tactful administration and unconsciously revealed in his talks the model of what a public servant should be. Some abuses of office were too grave to be condoned or corrected by reprimand; those he did not hesitate to punish by suspension, removal or prosecution in the courts. In ten years, he dealt with more than 2300 cases. Very soon, under his teaching, the officials in the municipalities and provinces learned to clean house. The last thing they wanted was to be summoned to Manila by Carpenter to explain matters that would not bear explaining."

A valuable man anywhere, but when he was put in charge of the Moros (by Harrison), there was much headshaking. The Moros, as everybody said, were different. General Pershing, who until Carpenter took over, was governor of their provinces, had his hands full and could not claim much progress. But Frank Carpenter took hold and made a success of it, showing the same sagacity (said Heiser) as he had displayed in Manila when counseling the governors-general.

"Tremendous progress was made toward pacifying this race of warriors under his administration," said Heiser; "the bolo and the rifle were replaced by the hoe and the plow. Much time was also spent trying to organize schools to which the Moro women could go, but the men always retorted, 'We don't want our women educated.'"

Heiser is interesting on the subject of women in the Philippines. Except for those in Moro country, he found them to be surprisingly influential, and he respected their abilities. He had cause to think hard about this when, after having built a "fine hospital" in Manila he had to staff it with imported American nurses. This, he had thought, was a merely temporary expedient, but as time went on, in spite of all his blandishments he failed to interest Filipinas in taking the

Americans' places and letting them go home. Why should this be? They couldn't depend forever on American nurses, any more than they could on American officials. Besides, he had hoped that through the Filipinas the men in time would take more of an interest in health problems: Heiser had already noticed what influence they had on their men. Rarely did a Filipino take any action without first consulting his wife. It was she who held the keys to valuables in the house. It was she who ran the business in most cases, and showed most intelligence. (This, of course, excepted the Moros, who didn't give their women a chance.) As a matter of fact Filipino men often did the cooking, washed the dishes, made the beds, and—as well— worked in the fields, while the women did a lot of the hard thinking for the family. Their status was a fascinating study, but the difficult fact remained that hospital nursing was not among an upper-class Filipina's talents: she had simply never considered it.

"This prejudice had to be overcome," Heiser decided.

He managed, after a lot of talk, to persuade a group of five young girls of good family to come and help out at the hospital. They came, they wandered about the wards for an hour or so, they chattered with each other, and after a day or so they didn't come anymore. This, he knew, was because nursing meant working with their hands: he was up against this prejudice again. Having thought it over, he tried a new tack, and got the amateur dramatic society to put on a play making heroines of nurses. It had the desired effect: the next day all five girls were back in the wards. Everything went well until their parents objected. Being a nurse, they said, was not *nice,* and Heiser played his last card: he pretended to explode into a temper.

"All right," he said, "take them away. Take them away. I don't want to see them around here anymore."

It was like the Baguio road all over again: the parents swiftly changed their minds and begged him to keep their daughters.

In the years that followed a number of other girls did their training, enjoyed it, and passed on their sentiments to the next lot. In time Filipinas were going regularly to the United States for their training. Then they either came back to staff hospitals in the Islands, or stayed in America. Either way, they were excellent nurses. They still are.

It might be remembered that Heiser at the beginning, when he was quarantine officer, had his trouble with the management, or lack thereof, of foot-and-mouth disease and rinderpest. The latter was particularly vicious in its effects on the tao, and the officials found it necessary to keep a close watch and enforce quarantine regulations wherever this seemed advisable. But now, with so many American heads rolling, the quarantine people, too, were shorthanded, and the Filipinos who took over their duties had a different way of regarding the situation. Quarantine was a nuisance, they said; quarantine was a waste of money and very hard on the people. Wasn't it time for the governor-general to relax these tiresome regulations? Harrison looked at the record and agreed, saying that after two years of strict surveillance he could see no noticeable improvement in the situation, so they might as well scrap the whole thing. Very quickly the authorities saw the opposite of improvement. In the final year before Harrison took office there had been 2787 cattle that died of rinderpest, but in 1921, when he was relieved of his post, the number of dead animals was 35,750. We can imagine how eagerly and balefully his enemies took note of this catastrophe and chalked it up against him.

Never mind. The Filipinos loved Harrison, and continued to revere his memory long after he left. In an edition of his diary (made up of extracts rather than a continued account), Professor Michael P. Onorato published a revealing foreword:

"Francis Burton Harrison resigned as governor general the last day of President Woodrow Wilson's second term. He left Manila after virtually eight years as the sole architect of a unique relationship between the representation of the metropolitan power and the Filipino political leaders. His departure from Manila and his high office was personally heartwrenching for Harrison. As governor of nearly eleven million people, he had possessed both the office and duties that enabled him to make his life, as he saw it, meaningful. As the ranking Democrat in line to succeed to the chairmanship of the House Ways and Means Committee in 1914, he sacrificed, in the view of many of his colleagues in the Congress, much to go out to the Philippine Islands. Even General Leonard Wood, then Chief of Staff, advised him not to waste a promising career in public service upon an alien people when his government had neither policy nor plans for their future relationship with the United States. We know now, however, that Harrison was restless for the challenge of more arduous and demanding work in the service of his country. The post of governor general was considered by many at that time to be the highest public office that any American could hold."

We know, too, that he loved his life at the Malacañan Palace, and thoroughly enjoyed his popularity. A tall, good-looking man, one of the Fairfaxes of Virginia, he even entered with relish into the occasional jokes told against him, as for instance the one about his innocent announcement, when he arrived, that he would wear formal morning attire for his inaugural address—cutaway coat and top hat. The various dignitaries could not muster enough proper morning dress between them, especially the mandatory top hats. They settled their quandary after a fashion by wearing ordinary tropical whites. Professor Onorato is not exaggerating, therefore, when he writes that Harrison's eight years in the Islands were personally fulfilling as well as tragic. Perhaps "tragedy" is too strong a word, however.

"He was vilified by Manila Americans before he left for his post," wrote Onorato, and one is tempted to retort that after all, that's politics. "Republicans at home and in the Philippines made his work unnecessarily difficult. His second marriage floundered under the stress of life in Manila. . . ."

The second marriage, not to mention the third, and the fourth, and the fifth—the governor-general must have added a good deal of spice to life in what remained of American society in Manila during the years that followed, both before and after his term expired. (He served four Filipino presidents in his post–governor-general time as adviser—Quezon, Osmeña, Roxas, and Quirino—and after the Second World War he was to advise the Philippine Foreign Office whenever he was asked to, until 1951.) As to the marriages, let Professor Onorato speak:

". . . his third marriage to the just-turned eighteen-year-old daughter of an American professor teaching in the Philippines did not enhance the prospect of returning home in March 1921." Especially when that marriage soured and he married his bride's sister.

Elting E. Morison, author of the life of Henry Stimson, described Harrison as a sophisticated, imaginative, and utterly charming man—also lethargic, or as one man put it, excruciatingly lazy. Partly from principle, partly from apathy, he permitted the Filipinos during his term to acquire more and more power over the government and economy of the Islands. Because he believed completely in the justice of the Philippine claim for independence, he allowed the Filipinos great freedom in the direction (and misdirection) of their affairs. As a result, said the Republicans, the system of American administration so carefully built up by Harrison's predecessors rapidly disintegrated, the health services dwindled to a point where the well-being of the community was endangered, and the financial and industrial structure of the Islands was placed in a precarious balance. Again it seems necessary to mention politics here—and here, too, is the moment to speak of the Jones Law which was passed by Congress during the Harrison term of office, in 1916.

Congressman William A. Jones from Virginia, who gave his name to the bill, was chairman of the House Committee on Insular Affairs. In 1913, in the House of Representatives, he savagely attacked Governor-General Forbes and the whole Philippine administration, basing his allegations (says Forbes) on misinformation he got from people who had recently been discharged from that administration. He said, inaccurately, that the American commissioners and their assistants had voted themselves large raises in salaries, which was totally untrue. Much of the public money of the Islands, he declared, was needlessly and shamelessly wasted. Cameron Forbes replied

159

with a published paper refuting these allegations, and both Roosevelt and Taft (with Senator Warren Gamaliel Harding, who was later to become president) backed him up sternly and strongly. Roosevelt later wrote to Forbes, "As you know I administered the Islands absolutely without regard to politics. Both Luke Wright and Smith were Democrats and you, when I appointed you, were, as I understood it, either a Democrat or a Mugwump."

Be that as it may, Jones favored independence for the Philippines, and in preparation for it submitted his 1916 bill to reorganize the Islands government on a basis of extended autonomy. The Philippines administration could have lived with that: after all, the original idea of taking charge of the Islands was to educate them to the point of handling their own affairs. But Senator Clarke of Arkansas now came forward with an amendment that would have placed a time limit on this period, granting complete independence at the end of not less than two and not more than four years from the time the bill became law. The Senate vote could not have been closer—41 to 41—and Vice-President Thomas Marshall then voted in favor of the adoption of the amendment, which decided matters. But with that vote the Senate brought down around its collective ears such noisy protests that the amendment never went through. New York and Boston newspapers spoke out against the whole bill, not to mention the amendment, and Secretary of War Garrison declared in a letter to President Wilson that he considered the principle embodied in the Clarke amendment an abandonment of national duty and a breach of trust toward the Filipinos. Wilson refused to come out and agree with him openly, so Garrison resigned. The storm died down when the House of Representatives, through the influence of Catholic congressmen, voted the amendment out, but the Jones Bill itself survived and became law on August 29, 1916.

Without going into detail its effects can be summed up as follows: the members of the Philippine Senate, as well as those of the House of Representatives, were now to be elected. There was no longer to be quite so much difference between legislative control over the Christian Filipinos and the non-Christian tribes: Moros and tribal people would now be represented in the Senate and the House of Representatives, but their senators and congressmen were not elected, but appointed by the governor-general. In the matter of finances things would go on much as they had before: that is, if the legislators failed to vote those appropriations necessary to carry on the government, the figures of the last appropriations made would be considered in force once more. The governor-general had the right to veto legislation or items in the appropriation bills: if any measures were passed over his veto they had to go up to the president of the United States for veto or approval as the case might be. The Senate—that is, the Philippine Senate—could confirm or refuse to confirm all the governor-general's appointments except those of representatives of the Moros or tribal peoples. The Philippine government had the power to legislate every matter in the public domain except such laws as applied to land, timber, and mining. These acts, when passed by the Philippine legislature, would not be laws until they had been approved by the president of the United States. There would still be a governor-general with general supervision and control of all departments and bureaus of the government in the Islands; he would be commander in chief of all locally created armed forces and militia. There was also to be a vice-governor at the head of the Department of Public Instruction, which should include the Bureaus of Education and Health.

"Throughout the Taft régime," wrote Forbes, "the line between the legislative, executive, and judicial functions had been carefully drawn," except that the governor-general and commissioners with portfolios had both legislative and executive duties, as did provincial officials and municipal presidents, though the legislative functions of these were limited. "In no case had these officers failed to defend their executive or legislative prerogatives against encroachment. The Speaker of the Assembly had always had executive control of the legislative body over which he presided and its secretariat. His executive powers stopped there. Repeated efforts had been made by the Assembly to give its committees executive functions, above all to place the expenditure of the money appropriated for irrigation under

161

control of a committee of its members. In 1916 the Philippine legislators began a series of progressive encroachments upon the executive power, and, in spite of an injunction by the Secretary of War to permit no such encroachments, Governor-General Harrison failed to exercise the veto power in a single instance to prevent measures carrying invasion of the executive power from becoming law."

The encroachments continued, sometimes with enactments of new laws that required executive officers—including the governor-general—to obtain the consent of the presidents of the Senate and the House of Representatives before performing certain functions. These executive officers were required to enable the National Bank to guarantee bonds of some corporations, to reduce the weight and fineness of Philippine coins, and to issue temporary certificates of indebtedness. They were required to suspend construction on certain public works, to use unexpended appropriations in other projects, and to issue bonds for public improvements. To none of these requirements did Governor-General Harrison make the slightest objection. He may not have wished to bother reading the relevant documents, or he may have wished to give the Filipinos everything they wanted, without fuss. In either case matters reached a point where the United States government realized that it must take a hand and reverse the trend. When Wilson left office in 1921 the Republican Warren Gamaliel Harding was elected, and among other matters he decided to find out what was going on in the Islands. He appointed the Wood-Forbes Mission, so called, to go and investigate. From Forbes's book we see the results—he and Wood found little to approve in the state of the Philippines as it was under Democratic control.

Chapter Nine

It was obvious that even now, with the Democrats out and the Republicans in, the clock could not be turned back. So much progress had been made toward granting the Islands independence, so many promises implied, that the Republicans could do little but blow where the wind took them, though they did try to temper it a little. Incidentally, we had had the world war, and even Harrison's (and Wilson's) critics had to admit that the good feeling engendered in the Philippines was fortunate at that time: we owed the governor-general a debt. "Many Filipinos enlisted; some fought in France, and many served in various capacities in the navy," wrote Forbes. "In 1917 the Philippine Militia was created and a National Guard division was organized. The complement of officers included many from the United States Army and the Constabulary. About 28,000 enlisted men were enrolled . . . Moreover, the Philippine government voted to build and pay for a destroyer and a submarine and these boats were built and placed in commission. They were not completed, however, until the war was over . . . But the generous loyalty which prompted the building is as much to the credit of the Filipinos as though the United States had seen fit to draw upon the Philippine treasury for the cost."

During the war Leonard Wood, through the inevitable intrigue and wire-pulling of army life, had a bitter disappointment. With his record he had every right to expect that he would be sent to Europe in command of the U.S. forces, but General Pershing beat him out of it, and the two men were never on good terms again. At least, however, Wood was not condemned to idleness. Because he was a hero, some political experts persuaded him to run for the presidency against Harding in 1920, and it was probably only the traditional dislike of American voters for generals in high public office that kept him from getting in. Once esconced, Harding asked him to undertake the governor-generalship of the Philippines. At first Wood declined, preferring to accept an offer that would have made him provost of the University of Pennsylvania. But he was, after all, an old Philippines hand, there were many things there crying out for attention, and in the end he said yes. It was a popular choice.

"If Wood can't do it, nobody can," people said. No doubt, too, Wood was influenced by the summary he and Forbes had just made of their mission, in which it was said that the Islands needed time to absorb and master what was already in their hands. The authorities had to build up an informed public opinion, a stronger sense of civic responsibility, a better appreciation of the obligations of citizenship . . . Most Christian Filipinos had a very natural desire for independence, but though a very small number of them wanted this independence to be contingent on a complete break with the United States, the large percentage desired independence under the protection of the States. The Moros and tribal peoples, however, like the Americans who lived there, nearly all wanted American control to continue.

Forbes and Wood found far too many people in the administrative departments of government who were all wound round with red tape. They needed supervision and more personal contact. There was a general opinion among the people—Filipinos, Americans, and foreigners—that the public services had become inefficient. The dispatch of business had slowed down. There was a "distinct relapse" toward the bad habits of former days in administration. In large part, the report said, this deterioration was due to bad example, incompetent direction, political infection of the services, and lack of competent supervision and inspection, brought about by surrendering, or failing to employ, the executive authority of the governorgeneral. There was a tendency on the part of the legislature to demoralize the Civil Service: there were numerous exemptions from the requirements of the Civil Service and many provisions for temporary employment. But at any rate the constabulary was in fine shape, and the Supreme Court could have been worse, though justice was doled out far too slowly. The land court should be reestablished: land registration, too, was in a mess.

Education was in good shape—better than good. The missioners recommended stepping up the processes by which the English-speaking teachers could be trained, and urged that the school of tropical medicine, which had disappeared, be reestablished. Health appropriations were insufficient and there was a shortage of medical personnel. But people were learning to save their money in the banks, business was increasing, and the worldwide depression had not yet arrived to arrest this trend.

Summing up, the commissioners decided that the Filipinos were not yet ready for independence. The United States should not be in a hurry to withdraw, because many of the Filipino leaders said they ought to stay. This was to be the leitmotiv of American pronouncements for some years to come, but it does not mean that the United States officials were not sincere: save for a few American settlers whose immediate interests were involved, they were quite sincere. They couldn't see the Islands hacking it alone. They feared for them, like overanxious parents.

As Wood saw his task, it divided into three parts. He had to restore economic stability—that is, after he had managed to collect

165

around him a group of American men on whom he could rely. He had to inaugurate administrative reforms. He had to get back much of the executive power that had been taken away from the governor-general as long as Harrison, that charming playboy, was in a position to let it go. It took Leonard Wood a long time to do it, but he succeeded in all these aims. He had energy and incisiveness. He reduced the direct involvement of the government in the industries that had been established in Harrison's time, thus taking away much of the power of the Filipinos and restoring to himself (as governor-general) the authority prescribed in the Jones Act. In so doing, naturally, he antagonized most of the influential Filipinos in the legislature. When in 1923 they refused to confirm his appointments, he simply did away with the Cabinet and went ahead on his own. He accomplished a lot for the good of the Islands, but, as was to be expected, he earned much enmity. Quezon, after he became president of the Philippines, stated more than once, with typical braggadocio, that he had killed Leonard Wood. He hadn't, of course, directly or indirectly. Wood's death in 1927, at the age of sixty-seven, was a natural calamity brought on by an old wound received in the Cuba campaign, added to the trials of hard work in an unfriendly climate, but it was natural that Quezon should feel vengeful. If it had not been for Wood, the Philippines would have got their independence in 1924. Yet—did Quezon really want independence that early? Many of his friends and rivals doubted it. Independence would have cost the Islands dear, financially speaking.

Henry Stimson was actually favored by Quezon and Osmeña when the incumbent president, Calvin Coolidge, asked their advice. There was a considerable list of candidates for the job of succeeding Leonard Wood, including Schurman and McIntyre, but Quezon and Osmeña, both of whom had met Stimson in 1912 when he was secretary of war—he had visited the Islands then—liked what he had said about promoting the welfare of the Filipino people. They went to Washington to tell Coolidge what they thought, and Stimson went out to the Islands in 1927, arriving on March 1.

Stimson had said himself, fifteen years earlier, "Until our work in the archipelago is completed, until the Filipinos are prepared not only to preserve but to continue it, abandonment of the Philippines, under whatever guise, would be an abandonment of . . . our responsibility to the Filipino people and of the moral obligations which we have voluntarily assumed before the world." It was his belief that he had two ultimate objectives: first, to reestablish the government of the Islands as a cooperative enterprise, rehabilitating the procedures and institutional forms that regulated the relationships between the executive and legislative branches of the government, and second, to rejuvenate the economic and industrial structure of the Islands. He said as much, forcefully, in his inaugural address on the evening of March 1. He spoke of "what we have to accomplish together." By his opening words, as one Filipino lawyer said—"Fellow countrymen"—he gained their souls. But, as he himself wrote to a friend at home, history is not often changed by speeches. There was a lot of slow, careful work ahead.

Next morning at eleven thirty he held the first of the conferences on which his method depended: this time he met with Sergio Osmeña and Manuel Roxas y Acuña. Quezon was in the hospital in America, suffering an attack of the tuberculosis that was one day to kill him. Stimson began by saying that he did not intend to discuss the question of independence: such discussion lay beyond the scope of his official powers. In any case, as he wrote in his diary under the date of March 2, "the ultimate solution . . . would depend upon considerations far beyond the personal influence of either myself or of them." He told the officials that it was his primary duty to protect the small man in the Islands. Unlike the United States, the Philippines possessed no educated, organized body of opinion to ensure this purpose; therefore it devolved upon him, the governor-general. They would therefore have to develop, first, an effective executive office with procedures to enable the executive and legislative branches to work closely together. For days the three men talked it over. One of his first needs, Stimson thought, was a staff of

167

experts to guide him, to keep him informed of the needs and conditions of government departments and bureaus. He had tried to get such experts by means of a bill that had recently been before Congress in Washington, but the Filipinos, jealous of their own powers, had opposed it, as did many American congressmen who felt that such an act was a reflection on the Congress as not being sufficiently well informed already. The bill failed, so Stimson would have to let the Filipinos supply the experts. If he got them, he said, he would appoint Cabinet members from the majority party. (Wood had refused to do this.) He would also consider resurrecting the Council of State, abolished by Wood, which had been made up of the governor-general, his Cabinet, and leaders of the legislative houses.

For months Stimson, Osmeña, and Roxas discussed these matters "cautiously." They also discussed some economic proposals, which for a long time during Wood's stay had been very sensitive. Stimson found three things: that the Filipinos were afraid of large private corporations (he reassured them as to that), that they feared any reorganization of landholding procedures—a hangover from the bad days of the friars; at the time of the discussions no individual was permitted to hold more than thirty-two acres—and that the Filipinos really did resent America. It was not just something whipped up by rabble-rousers: it was a genuine resentment based on racial sensitivity.

Apart from the discussions, Stimson traveled widely in order to learn more about the Islands. When his own church refused to admit a Filipino member, he left it and joined the Episcopalians, first explaining why. He went out and shot with the army cadets. When the time came to open Malacañan for social occasions, he invited Americans and Filipinos together. His wife carefully learned to dance the ancient *rigodon* with the party leaders—and with Stimson, though it was observed that he was not nearly as good at it. Small wonder that the Filipinos very quickly responded with liking and admiration. But in certain matters it was still necessary to move very carefully and slowly.

The June elections had taken place, and everyone felt hopeful and cooperative, but one thing was not yet settled—the governor-general's group of experts. Since the bill had failed in Washington, Osmeña and Roxas agreed, the Filipino government must find the men and the wherewithal. Senator Belo introduced a bill to set aside half a million pesos to pay these assistants, and it passed, though with difficulty. For that reason the experts were called "the Belo Boys." Stimson's second project was the development of Filipino economy. He suggested to the legislature that they change the laws controlling corporate behavior, banking procedure, and landholding, so that private capital would be attracted to the Islands. Most of the laws, he explained, were antiquated, having been formulated thirty years before when America didn't know much about industrial development. Some of the Filipino legislators didn't like to face the fact that it would be necessary, in order to improve their economic conditions, to attract private American capital, so Stimson moved very slowly and tactfully. Anyway he did not want to move quickly: there were aspects of American capitalism unsuited to this country. Private companies manufacturing rubber, for example, should not have the right to create huge plantations in the Islands. All that was needed was to let them hold larger parcels of land than thirty-two acres on short-term leases, and to organize private farms more efficiently around series of processing plants, which were called "centrals."

Through the autumn and early winter of 1928 these matters were slowly but carefully thrashed out. Quezon had come back in July, and he, with Osmeña and Roxas, worked constantly with the governor-general, and carried his suggestions to the legislature. It was not always easy to get new laws and regulations past the legislators' suspicious eyes, but much of it, though thickly embellished with amendments, finally got passed. The national banking structure was improved, among others, but what really did grow was mutual trust and respect. Then came the test, the Timberlake Resolution. Representative Timberlake wanted to limit the amount of sugar that had until then been imported into the United States

169

duty free. This law, if enacted, would have been a terrible blow to Philippine economy. Quezon said furiously that if it went through, "If the United States retained the Philippines under the American flag and taxed our products entering the United States while keeping open the Philippine market for the free entrance of American goods, I would start a revolution against the United States!"

"I would not blame you," said Stimson with a smile. "That will never be tolerated by the American people and I will fight it to the end." He firmly opposed it, no matter who said what to whom, and the matter was forgotten. Quezon said one night, "What we need more than anything else is certitude. What we need more than independence is the knowledge that the situation as it now exists or could be made to exist will continue to exist. We are constantly being subject to changing administrations in Washington, changing attitudes on the part of the American people, changing procedures on the part of American businessmen here. Give us certainty and we will take dominion status. Give us certainty and we will take a dependent status. But for heaven's sake let's get organized so we can run the thing with some assurance that it will continue to run for a while and forget the independence issue . . . Like your President T. R., if you quote me on this, I will say you lie."

Unfortunately democracies aren't run like that. Stimson could not give Quezon certainty. Anything else, but not certainty.

Still, he didn't do too badly. When he was recalled and left on February 23, 1929, his ride from Malacañan to the pier was a triumph, with cheering crowds and blowing whistles and ten thousand "friendly brown faces" along the way. And when he got home, after what *The New York Times* said had been a brilliant administration, President Herbert Hoover named him secretary of state. At first, said Morison, Hoover didn't know much about the Philippines, but he learned fast. Virtually Stimson's first act as secretary of state was to tell the House Committee of Ways and Means that certain proposed tariff restrictions on imports from the Islands represented a betrayal that would damage American credit

170

throughout the Orient, and would raise once more all the ancient agitation about independence. He did help to ward off the tariff restrictions, but though he tried for the next four years to work out a permanent relationship between the United States and the Philippines, in this he failed.

The next governor-general did not make much difference one way or the other. Dwight F. Davis was available. He had been secretary of war under Coolidge, and was known chiefly for his prowess in and love of sports, as witness the Davis Cup for tennis. He was no rebel: he behaved as Stimson would have liked him to. The Filipinos had no complaint against him except for the fact, which was hardly his fault, that sugar interests in the Islands were producing too much of the stuff for their financial health. "Diversify," he said warningly.

But another appointment was very nearly disastrous, when President Hoover in 1930 named Nicholas Roosevelt, a family connection of Theodore, to the post of vice-governor of the Islands. The Filipinos hated Nicholas Roosevelt. They already knew him as the author of a book, *The Philippines; a Treasure and a Problem*, based on travels he had made in the Islands in 1925–26. It was not a flattering book. Among other statements that made the Filipinos grind their teeth, the author had said that it would take at least a century before the Philippines were ready for independence. And he dedicated it to General Leonard Wood. One is forced to conclude either that President Hoover was badly advised or not advised at all, and couldn't read.

Protests seemed to be of no avail. The Filipinos at home burned Nicholas Roosevelt in effigy, along with copies of his book. They marched in processions of protest. They made furious speeches. They sent cables, they sent letters, but Hoover went on not reading any of these things, or at least not reacting to them, until at last Quezon, who was again in the hospital, this time in California, for his tuberculosis, wrote personally to the secretary of war, Patrick Hurley, setting it out for him in plain terms and asking him to

171

intercede with Hoover. Quezon spoke of his very serious concern that the appointment of Roosevelt would exacerbate racial antagonisms, and that letter did the trick: Hoover withdrew the appointment. (Roosevelt was made minister to Hungary instead. He probably liked Hungary better anyway.)

The stock-market crash of October 29, 1929, had had a direct effect on the Philippines not only because every nation in the world suffered in the Great Depression—the Islands' gross revenues, for example, showed a decrease of five million dollars for 1931—but because Americans more than ever resented the competition of the Islands' industries: sugar, of course, but also hemp, cordage, cottonseed oil, and dairy products. More and more, Americans found the idea of Filipino independence attractive. It would get them out of our hair, it would make life much less expensive (at least so they hoped), and it was what the Filipinos wanted, so why not? A sudden termination of free trade, warned Governor Davis, would have a disastrous effect, and the outlook was not all black. Gold mines were being developed and would be active for years to come, with profitable results. Landing fields were being constructed on different islands and in many provinces under the Department of Commerce and Communications.

Davis's term of office ended in February 1932, when he resigned and was replaced by Theodore Roosevelt, Jr., son of Teddy. Forbes said it was a suitable choice, as he had been governor of Puerto Rico and spoke Spanish well (though why this was considered important save for a few of the old-fashioned aristocracy and Spanish mestizos such as Quezon is not clear). TR, Jr., was a good administrator, but he probably attracted most attention when he set to work to eradicate discrimination in Manila schools. There were two so-called public institutions between which Americans could choose, Central High School and the American School. Central was intended—at least by some people—for American children, those of army and business people mostly, and its curriculum was slanted to meet the requirements of such children as they grew up and went to the

172

States. Nearly all of the teachers were American, some, naturally, from the Thomasites. At first the enrollment included many students who were half Filipino.

"Some 625 students, nearly all of whom were American citizens, attended Central, but only 275 had American parentage on both sides of the family," wrote Gleeck of the years between 1914 when the school opened and 1925. "By 1925–26, enrollment was down to 470."

In 1921 there was objection among the town's Americans that Central should be reserved for "full-blood" American children, and a committee set to study the matter suggested that Central be turned into a primary school which excluded all but Americans, the children's later education to be undertaken by the Brent School in Baguio. But Dr. Luther Bewley, the director of education, refused to consider such a recourse.

At any rate there was another institution, called the American School, opened in 1920 and supported, if not lavishly or without anxiety, by Americans, whereas Central received public funds. "Central was also *de facto* segregated," wrote Gleeck, "it admitted only a few talented and high-status Filipinos until 1932 . . ." when Governor-General T. R. Roosevelt, Jr., put an end to this snobbish arrangement by decreeing that competence in English rather than race or citizenship would determine who should attend class there. This left only the American School segregated by race, and since it was maintained by high tuition fees, the general public, including Filipinos, did not feel wronged—or at least need not feel constantly irritated. Though, no matter how one rationalizes, such matters as exclusive clubs and schools in foreign countries *are* an irritation.

Roosevelt proved a good administrator in that he managed the faltering Islands economy and improved relationships between tenants and landlords. The Depression was biting. Americans did not feel it as sharply as they would have in the United States, but it was there. Roosevelt also established a Fish and Game Administration under the Department of Agriculture, the object of which was to

173

manage the breeding of fish, open and closed seasons, and the regulation of collecting of shells (very important, always, in the Philippines, where they are used for window glass and other purposes), sponges, and turtles.

"The fact that there was quite a large infiltration of Japanese fisherman into the Islands made these measures very appropriate," commented Forbes. If it comes to that, the infiltration of Japanese in all walks of life was becoming more and more obvious; it was a situation that could not be ignored and was often mentioned. But the subject that most preoccupied Filipinos and Philippine Americans was the 1933 political turnaround in Washington after Franklin Delano Roosevelt was inaugurated President and took firm measures to halt the Depression. Governor Roosevelt in Manila belonged to the wrong party (the two branches of the family were, of course, politically opposed), and he resigned in March. Frank Murphy was his replacement.

For two years Congress had been discussing and then forgetting the subject of the Islands and what to do about them. Osmeña and Roxas, the resident commissioners in Washington, favored a bill dealing with the Philippines that went under the name of Hawes-Cutting, because amid all the confusion it was relatively simple in its aim to grant independence to the country, a consummation most senators now devoutly wished. Hawes was Harry B. Hawes, senator from Missouri; Cutting was Bronson M. Cutting, senator from New Mexico. The bill acquired a new name in the course of preelection 1932 and became the Hare-Hawes-Cutting bill because it was reintroduced by Representative Butler Hare of North Carolina. Among many lesser clauses this bill provided for independence for the Islands after a transitional period of fifteen years, an increasing restriction on Philippine imports to the United States, a gradual application of United States tariff on these imports, and a limit on Filipino immigrants to one hundred a year. (Free trade for and unlimited immigration from the Philippines had long been a grievance to Americans at home, exacerbating, so they thought, their

174

depressed economy.) That, at least, is a rough description of the original bill. In the course of discussion, naturally, it was altered in many respects. The transition period, for example, was shortened to eight years and the immigration quota reduced to fifty. The Democrats in the government were anxious to see it passed—it, or a reasonable facsimile thereof. As Carlos Quirino said, when the matter was dropped in June and everybody started girding themselves for the presidential elections in November, the situation was this: if Roosevelt won, it was almost a certainty that the Democratic Congress would approve the Hare-Hawes-Cutting bill, and it was just as certain that Republican President Herbert Hoover if he got in would veto it. Roosevelt, of course, got in.

In Manila there was much discussion during the waiting period. Quezon found much in the bill to object to, especially the provisions for U.S. naval and military bases, the economic restrictions, and the powers that were to be granted to the U.S. high commissioner, who was to take the place of the governor-general in title but not, evidently, in influence. He was not appeased by the clause that awarded Malacañan Palace and the executive mansion at Baguio to the incoming Filipino president. Well, of course, he implied, but there were other far more important matters to settle—such as, for example, whether or not Osmeña and Roxas were doing any good in Washington, and if it was worth the expense of keeping them there until the H-H-C bill matter was settled. In July 1932 he told them to come back and talk things over. They retorted that they considered it their duty to stay right there. Observers hazarded the wise guess that the three leaders were jockeying for position in the coming era. Quezon was not sure he wanted to be stuck in Manila when, or if, Osmeña and Roxas triumphantly brought back independence. *He* wanted the credit.

Senator King of Utah had submitted a bill two years previously, during the worst of the Depression, providing immediate independence for the Philippines. Suddenly Quezon decided to interest himself in that bill rather than Hare-Hawes-Cutting, and he cabled

Osmeña and Roxas, asking what chances it might have of passing. "None at present," they replied.

On January 13, 1933, the lame-duck President Herbert Hoover rejected the Hare-Hawes-Cutting bill, as had been expected, and in equally expected fashion his veto was overridden, so enthusiastically that the Republicans themselves were surprised. All was joy among the Filipino representatives, all was champagne—except for one sour note from Manila, where Quezon declared that the mission had not obeyed instructions in accepting the bill, and thus wasn't actually empowered to accept it. They were not to go home, he said; they were to meet him in Paris for discussions. They did meet, and then, instead of returning to Manila, the whole party went to Washington. It was a large party, for Quezon had brought with him a mixed group of five, including Carlos P. Romulo, editor of the *Manila Tribune*.

They weren't glad to see Quezon in Washington. A number of the senators who had fought for him felt let down. If he didn't want the Hare-Hawes-Cutting bill, what the hell *did* he want? At least one senator accused him openly of not wanting independence at all, and Quezon denied the charge. What he didn't want, he said, was all those bases for the American army and navy. If they took out those clauses the Philippine legislature would probably accept the H-H-C Act—not that he could be sure.

Neither could President Roosevelt, and he wanted to be sure before any more offers were made. In May the missions (which had swollen to enormous size what with all the assistants, journalists, and whatnot) sailed for Manila. They arrived in July in time for a party caucus, and then the real fun began. Osmeña challenged Quezon to resign, which Quezon promptly did. He made a magnificent speech about it, which took three days. (Stamina, then as now, was well thought of in Filipino politics.) Osmeña's speech, too, was very splendid, though not quite so long, and he, too, resigned. In the end Quezon's resignation was not accepted, but Osmeña's was, along with those of two of his colleagues. Then for ten weeks nobody voted on the Hare-Hawes-Cutting bill. The masses were confused. They

176

loved Quezon, but the bill looked fairly good to them: what was all the argument about? And back in Washington the senators were tired of the matter—they had other things on their minds. Quezon, who knew how to bide his time, held on. At last the Philippine legislature, worried about some of the aspects of the sugar quota, voted on October 17 to reject the H-H-C on the grounds that its trade provisions would seriously imperil the Islands' economic, political, and social institutions; the immigration limitations included in it were offensive to Filipinos; the powers of the American high commissioner were too indefinite; and the military and naval reservations were inconsistent with true independence. At the same time Quezon announced that he was going back to Washington to negotiate a better law.

He had a friend at court in Senator Millard Tydings of Maryland, new Democratic chairman of the Senate Committee on Territories and Insular Affairs. Not realizing that the next election in the Islands would probably unseat Quezon, Tydings asked him to talk seriously about the new terms for independence so that the matter could be cleared up.

"I bluntly told him that the new administration in Washington must deal with me in connection with the Philippines," said Quezon.

Tydings and Congressman John McDuffie of Alabama began work on a new instrument of independence for the Islands. On December 27 Quezon had an interview with FDR himself, and President Roosevelt asked him to write a memorandum of all the points discussed. Two weeks later Quezon was summoned again to the White House, where he was surprised to find that Roosevelt had digested the contents of the memorandum and was ready to discuss it in detail. He agreed that the maintenance of American army reserves after independence would make a mockery of that independence, and added, "After all, the American military force in the Islands is too small to protect the Philippines against foreign invasion, and after we have been in the Islands all these many years, it will be impossible to induce Congress to appropriate the necessary funds for

177

the military defence of the Islands and the maintenance of any army of sufficient size to keep the enemy at bay."

He agreed on the other important points as well. On March 2, 1934, he transmitted to Congress a new bill asking for a change in the terms dealing with military and naval bases in the Islands. The rest of it, he said, need not be changed at that time, as any other points that came up could be dealt with in due course.

On March 10 Congressman McDuffie brought in a new instrument that was exactly like the H-H-C bill with two changes: the time the Philippines had to act on it was extended to October 17 of that year, the army bases were to be given up on the day independence went into force, and the naval bases were to be negotiated. It was quickly passed with the required two-thirds vote. In the Senate where it was introduced by Senator Tydings it was passed almost as expeditiously, though some amendments were suggested. On March 24 President Roosevelt signed it at last. The Philippines would soon be a commonwealth, on their way to independence. It probably didn't matter as much to most Americans as it had seemed to do some years earlier, but to the Filipinos it mattered a good deal. During the height of the agitation, we are told by Victor Heiser, a schoolmaster asked a small Filipino boy to write an essay on The Cow. The boy wrote,

"A cow is an animal with a leg on each corner. It has horns and gives milk, but as for me, give me independence."

Chapter Ten

The terms of the Tydings-McDuffie bill that affected resident Americans in the Philippines most closely were the dates involved. It had been agreed that the Islands should become a commonwealth as a sort of trial period. This commonwealth should last for ten years beginning November 15, 1935, by which time the Filipino legislature should have produced a constitution satisfactory to both governments. On November 15 the American governor-general would suffer a sea change, becoming high commissioner, with certain changes in his duties and perquisites. He was still to be paid by the U.S. government (as his opposite number, a Filipino official who resided in Washington, was to be paid by the Philippine government), but he was no longer to live in Malacañan Palace, this being reserved for the new president of the Philippines. Ten years later, on July 4, the Philippines would be a full-fledged republic and the high commissioner could go home. Of course there were many small rearrangements, but that was the general outline.

In 1934, when these agreements were made, the resident Americans—or at least most of them—were too preoccupied with business troubles to pay much attention to 1945 and the threat it imposed. A number of them, in fact, gave up in advance and went away. Gleeck tells us that in April 1933 there were only about five thousand Americans at the most left in Manila, some five hundred families having departed since 1929. The problems of the Depression and consequently reduced income for Americans had now become bigger in the Islands than in the States: there was not so much that a housewife could do to cut down on spending in Manila compared with the chances her sister in the Midwest might have to make economies. He quotes the *Journal of the American Chamber of Commerce in Manila* for April 1933:

"If an American family has another American family as neighbors it is accidental, something more or less true of all nationalities here. Americans live in New Manila, miles east of town, and in Pasay and Parañaque, miles south of town. But their churches are well toward the town's center . . . The schools, the Central and the American, are in Ermita . . . Half an American family's use of its motor car is between home and school and Sunday school . . . In an American city a school would be nearby, a church too. In Manila, on the contrary, even the movie theatre that is presentable and sanitary is downtown; that is to say, from 2 to 5 to 7 miles away from most American homes, and it is the same with clubs. . . ." It was estimated that gasoline for the average family car in Manila cost two hundred pesos annually—one hundred dollars, a shocking sum for those times.

"The standard of living an American maintains may not be elaborate," went on the *Journal*, "but it is expected by other Americans, including his employer, to be wholesome and dignified. There is no artisan class of Americans in town, no laboring class, only a professional class, families ambitious most of all for the well-being and education of their children. Decreased earnings make this paramount problem one of anxious concern in many American homes, more so now than at any earlier time in the American period."

Still, for those who could afford it the standards of living were going up. Screens and air conditioning were a great help to comfort, and there was also telephone service to the States, though it was very costly—thirty dollars for three minutes to California, thirty-nine dollars to New York. This service completely altered the psychological life of the community and took away the chief horrors of isolation. It cost a lot, but it was very reassuring to be able to get in touch with the people at home, or the head office. It really revolutionized existence. The development of the telephone may even have outweighed the cheer generated by the gold-mining boom that took place when Roosevelt raised the price of the metal. After all, there was gold in the Islands—everybody knew it—and now mining activity was stepped up to unheard-of heights. Some people became millionaires; certainly a good many became richer. Speculation in gold stocks occupied the thoughts of most Island Americans in 1934 when Quezon was battling it out with Osmeña and Roxas: who cared about native politics anyway?

More thoughtful than the Americans, however, was Quezon, who had Japan on his mind. When the Tydings-McDuffie Act had been signed, one of his first actions was to get in touch with Major General Douglas MacArthur, until recently the chief of staff and still at the War Office. MacArthur, as we know, had spent much of his youth in the Philippines: he and Quezon were old friends, on a first-name footing. Quezon was on the point of leaving Washington, he told the general, but there was one important question he would like to ask: did MacArthur think that the Philippines, when the time of independence had arrived, could be defended?

Yes, said MacArthur promptly, but there would have to be enough money to prepare the defense. As both men knew, six million pesos a year was now being devoted to the upkeep of the Philippine constabulary. In MacArthur's estimation they would need ten million pesos more every year for the next ten years to build up a worthwhile defense. He cautioned Quezon that he should not think of maintaining a big regular army because that would be too expensive. They would have to create a citizen army on the basis of universal compulsory service.

Quezon then asked another question: "Would you be willing to come to the Philippines and be the man to put into execution the ideas you have just expressed?"

Yes, said MacArthur, of course, if he was not needed at home and his superiors permitted it. But Quezon had first to be elected president, there was the new constitution to formulate—all kinds of things had to happen. Nevertheless, the two men parted well satisfied.

The Filipino legislature worked for nearly a year on the constitution and approved it on February 8, 1935. There were to be three divisions under a president and vice-president. Presidential terms were to last for six years, after which the president was to be ineligible for reelection for the next term, as was the vice-president. (Obviously this law was to remove the danger of a dictatorship, but Quezon in office was soon worrying about the shortness of a six-year term, and he found a way to change the constitution in that respect.) On March 28 President Roosevelt approved the paper, and it was submitted to the Filipino people by plebiscite. They ratified it almost unanimously.

Now Quezon and his most formidable rival, Osmeña, agreed to merge their parties in a coalition and run for election as president and vice-president. This move, they explained, was desirable because of the dangerous times they lived in, the threat of Japanese conquest. They were not unopposed, and the name of Quezon's chief challenger might well startle the public, because it was Emilio Aguinaldo. Another candidate was Gregorio Aglipay, a religious leader who had split off from the Roman Catholic Church and founded his own church. He had many followers—for that matter he still has, though he himself is dead. Aguinaldo was quite old by that time, but he put up a vigorous fight, and when Quezon won overwhelmingly (Quezon, 695,332; Aguinaldo, 179,349; Aglipay, 148,010), he objected loud and clear that there had been fraud at the polls. He himself had won only one province, and that, which was to be expected, was Cavite. Two others went to Aglipay, and the remaining forty-seven were Quezon's. Aguinaldo complained to Governor Murphy, demanding a thorough investigation, but when he was invited to present his evidence he refused to attend the proceedings.

"Undoubtedly, frauds had been committed," wrote Quirino, "as they had been perpetrated in about every Philippine election held since the Filipinos were granted the ballot. Such frauds were usually committed by desperate candidates on the barrio, municipal, and even the provincial level, and were limited to small localities or even to certain regions where political rivalry was bitter. But since they were usually committed by both sides, nobody was free from blame. . . ."

Aguinaldo did not take such an indulgent attitude, nor did his followers in Cavite. There was talk of assassinating the winners, or at any rate demonstrating on November 15 to mar the celebrations of the commonwealth inauguration. Governor Murphy said, peremptorily, he would not hesitate to use force to preserve law and order. To prove that he meant it he put twenty-four-hour guards on Quezon and Osmeña (election results for vice-president, Osmeña, 812,352; Raymundo Melliza, 70,899; Norberto Nabong, 51,443), and General Aguinaldo subsided.

Francis Burton Harrison was invited to the festivities, and came eagerly. For fourteen years, said his editor (of the diary) Michael Onorato, he hadn't done anything in public life, not since he resigned from his post in Manila. Perhaps he felt that his work there had been too controversial, and in any case the Democrats were out and the Republicans were in. Most of the time he spent in Scotland, where his cousin Lord Fairfax helped him to lead the life of a country squire, though he did emerge and come to the States long enough to write his own book, *The Cornerstone of Philippine Independence.* (Published 1922. He later told Quezon he wrote the whole thing in five weeks—in longhand.) But now the Democrats were in again, and his old friend Quezon had invited him, and he was glad to come back and see the place. He brought with him his latest and fifth wife, an Englishwoman named Doria. Harrison had left in 1921 and now it was 1935. It was an emotional time for him.

It was pleasantly exciting to be back and have Quezon making much of him. It was gratifying to see how right he had been and how wrong the bad guys, to be assured over and over again that if it had not been for him everything would have taken much longer, and to know in his heart that this was true and not just the flattery of diplomats. He had arrived in time to be in the know about a flurry of temper on the part of Quezon just before the inaugural ceremonies began. Some weeks in advance, preparing for them, MacArthur had stated that there would be a twenty-one-gun salute for the president: twenty-one, he explained, was the courtesy always extended to heads of state. But the high commissioner-to-be, Frank Murphy, objected that Quezon was not yet a genuine head of state, and would not be until the commonwealth became a republic. As chief executive, he said, Quezon was entitled to a mere nineteen-gun salute. MacArthur and Murphy could not agree, so they referred to Washington. That was no good either: the secretary of state agreed with Murphy, whereas the secretary of war, as might be expected, was on MacArthur's side. Finally they took it right up to the top, to President Roosevelt. He was probably annoyed at being bothered with such a trifle. Anyway he cabled, "Nineteen-gun salute or nothing."

Very well, said Quezon furiously, it would be nothing. He wouldn't come to the party: they could have it without him: he could take his oath of office wherever he liked, even in his bedroom. It took the pleas of practically everybody to change his mind, but at last, on the evening of the fourteenth, he yielded. He would not, he said, disappoint hundreds of thousands of his people: half a million of them were swarming into Manila for the festivities. Quirino lists the dignitaries—seventeen U.S. senators led by Vice-President John N. Garner; twenty-six representatives led by Speaker Joseph W. Byrne; scores of diplomatic representatives from foreign countries; and two dozen American newspapermen, led by Roy Howard, William Allen White of the *Emporia* (Kans.) *Gazette*, Marlin E. Pew of *Editor and Publisher*, and Dean Carl W. Ackerman of the Columbia School of Journalism. At ten past eight o'clock Governor-General Frank Murphy and President-elect Manuel L. Quezon appeared, to the applause of the crowd. The official representative of the U.S. government, Secretary of War George Dern, came in last. The band played "Hail to the Chief" and "The Star-Spangled Banner," as the Stars and Stripes went up the flagpole. The archbishop of Cebu, the Most Reverend Gabriel M. Reyes, delivered the invocation. Murphy made a speech introducing the secretary of war, and *he* made a speech, and so on.

Murphy read aloud President Roosevelt's proclamation, and Quezon took the oath of office and made his inaugural speech. At two minutes past nine, Secretary Dern proclaimed, "I do hereby announce that the heretofore existing Government of the Philippines is now terminated, and that the Government of the Commonwealth of the Philippines is entering upon its rights, privileges, powers and duties." Et cetera. Some observers thought the new president was looking strained. He was: he was still fuming over that twenty-one-gun salute. At this point in his book Quirino took time off to discuss the prevailing attitude of the Americans toward the Filipinos, which he said was patronizing, and continued to be until after Bataan. "American clubs in Manila before the war, for example, were decidedly off limits to Filipinos: not only were they excluded as members but were not welcome even as guests." Filipinos were not allowed to be members of the Baguio Country Club until the 1930s when Quezon suggested that their lease need not be renewed unless the discrimination ceased—after which, of course, it did cease. In

Manila the Army and Navy Club and the Elks Club also barred non-Wasps, and the Manila Polo Club, which had admitted the wealthy and powerful Elizaldes (they were of pure Spanish blood), only removed their discriminatory rules when the Elizaldes threatened to resign if they did not. Later, when some of their candidates were turned down because of being Filipino, the Elizaldes resigned anyway and organized their own club, The Tamaraws. Furthermore, as soon as the Independence Act was accepted, they took Filipino citizenship.

Harrison enjoyed the inaugural ceremonies, the more so as he felt needed again after years of being out of things. Quezon had asked him to stay on as an adviser. Harrison was never to decide just what kind of adviser, but never mind. The trouble with the situation, he concluded after some months of vague fiddling around in his office, was that he still didn't feel needed except as a sort of confidant of Quezon's when the president wanted to talk or ask questions or play bridge or merely reminisce about the old days. Privately Harrison and his wife, who had taken a house in Manila, thought they should give it a year and then move on. In the meantime life was pleasant and often interesting, especially when Quezon would suddenly scoop him up for a trip somewhere outside the city. At the end of his planned year, more or less, he joined the directorship of several corporations in the country, and in January 1937 the Harrisons went away, not to return until autumn of the following year. They now had a baby daughter, born in Baguio.

Lewis Gleeck thought it worth mentioning that after the applause and echoes of the nineteen-gun salute had died away, while the Americans and Filipinos were busy rearranging Malacañan Palace for its new tenant, it came time to move some of the pictures from the walls of the governor-general's office. The American team took away, first of all, Governor-General Wood's photograph. But Quezon happened to drop in, and noticed the omission at once. He roared, "What's happened to General Wood's photograph?"

186

The Americans said that they had taken it down because they took it for granted that would be the president's wish. He swore at them, and said, "You bring it back. He was a good man!"

They brought it back.

On November 29 there was great excitement when the first Pan-American Clipper flew into Manila's airport. Think of it, from California to the Philippines in two days! It had been three weeks at the shortest until then. Said Gleeck, "1936 was the first year of the Commonwealth, the year the mining boom reached its height, and a year of the usual quadrennial activity by Republicans and Democrats in the American community looking toward the American Presidential elections."

Things could have been a lot worse for the Americans, it was agreed: the calamity howlers were proved wrong. It is true that the new high commissioner was out of the official residence, but Quezon came forward with the offer of the government's residence at Baguio as a temporary expedient (he certainly didn't need it: Mrs. Quezon had a fancy for gathering real estate, and they had plenty of houses). There was a period reminiscent of 1913 when lots of Americans were removed from office, but this time it wasn't so painful, either because the officials had expected it, or the community was getting used to it. The four remaining American members of the Supreme Court departed, but other people were asked if they wanted to stay on, and they all did.

Gleeck said, "For the American community, the granting of Commonwealth status to the Philippines by the United States meant that the off-again, on-again perspective with which its members had over the years since 1901 viewed their future now seemed fixed, definite and irreversible. They were now faced with simple choices: to accept total Filipino sovereignty after ten years or to leave. If they chose to remain indefinitely, they must first of all think of themselves as guests in an alien land and accept the Filipinos as arbiters of their destiny. This was by no means an intolerable prospect, particularly under Quezon."

Certainly business and play went on much as usual for some years. The fact is indicated by a somewhat complicated memoir acquired not long ago by the American Historical Collection, a set of souvenirs of the institution that used to be known in Manila as Liberty Hall. In the Collection *Bulletin* for April–June 1980, Tom Carter has described it conscientiously—photographs, papers, handbills, and all, including the box these things were stored in, a beautifully designed and executed little wooden chest. (They do wonderful woodwork in the Philippines, and they have rare wood to do it with.) Though the record is scrappy to say the least, it covers a period of forty-seven years, and is summed up by Carter as "2 photographic albums, 1 bound accounting/correspondence record for the year 1952 party, correspondence files for the 1933 and 1936 parties, and a few oddments."

There must have been more, he comments, which did not survive the years and the occupation. One can imagine a busy man or the man's busy wife, cleaning out the office or the house desks before leaving Manila, wondering what to do with the box before finally deciding to hand it over to the American Historical collectors because nobody else, obviously, would be interested in all that old stuff. But the people in the Collection building knew a lot more about it than that.

The moving spirit of Liberty Bell (not so much a building as a concept) was T. J. Wolff, hereafter known as Tommy Wolff. He arrived in Manila, aged nineteen, in 1898 with the Quartermaster Corps, and like many of his fellows he stayed when the war was over. With two compatriots, in 1908 he opened the Sanitary Steam Laundry, and in that country where clothes must be washed every day it did very well. Soon he was manager, then he bought out his partners. By the time Francis Burton Harrison arrived as governor-general, Tommy Wolff was one of the regulars at Clarke's famous restaurant, who like the other important citizens sat at the Round Table. As Gleeck says, he personified the spirit of spending characteristic of the gold boom. The "party-giving laundryman" was no millionaire, but he made plenty of money. He didn't depend only on his laundry by this time, but bought mining stocks and real estate, and owned an export-import firm.

He was director general of the Philippine Carnival in 1917, and during the First World War he joined the Philippine National Guard and saw service: for the rest of his life he carried a silver plate in his spine. In 1918 Governor-General Harrison appointed a Defense Council of some of Manila's leading citizens, and among them was Tommy Wolff. By 1921 the *Journal of the American Chamber of Commerce* referred to him as one of the live wires of Manila's younger business set. He loved to give parties for distinguished visitors and have his picture taken with them. He loved to give parties. He had a big house in Pasay and used to throw enormous bashes for his employees there once a year—which brings us again to Liberty Hall, described by Gleeck as "a smoker-stag party featuring strip-tease entertainment."

It was claimed, Carter tells us, that Liberty Hall was Tommy Wolff's personal story in that he and another American named Walter Olsen were from its inception (in 1905) to at least 1936 the only two survivors. Some old-timers argued that the first celebration was actually 1903, but we know what old-timers are. At any rate the original entry in the collection was on December 31, 1905, and was a list of signatures with various comments, such as:

J. E. Morton—"a pig"
C. W. Hughes—"2 pigs"
Sidney Thomas—"a has been"
Stuart (illeg.)—"Honi Soit qui mal y pense"
O. A. Pritchett—"too Full to say anything"
Mark Hanna Evans—"Busted two buttons by 12:30"
T. F. Robson—"Send my remains home"
T. E. Burd, Jr.—"Call no man unhappy until he is married"
N. R. Donaldson, USN.—"May the unhappiest days of your future be as the happiest days of your past"

189

The next entries are dated 1907, 1910, 1911, and so on till 1916, where a letter "unfortunately almost illegible" is signed by a few names: Rosenthal (Jake), Wolff (T. J.), and Diehl (Theobald), and "Approved—J. W. Markey and W. E. Olsen—the surviving members of Liberty Hall." There is also a poem signed "Wolff, the Washman," which goes as follows:

Here
With my beer
I sit,
While golden moments flit;
Alas!
They pass
Unheeded by,
And as they fly,
I,
Being dry,
Sit, idly sipping here,
My beer.

The record continues scrappy. Here and there Carter found and studied imperfect pictures of strippers at their work: was a censor responsible for these bad specimens of photography? Bills for the 1931 party gave a staggering list of the food consumed: well, it was a big party—

"168 pounds of bread; 200 dozen Large Parkerhouse rolls; 100 Apple Pies; 25 lbs. Salted peanuts; 1 case Salad Dressing; ½ kilo. Whale Clovers; 150 lbs. Amer. White Beans; 3 cases Cooked Hams; 50 lbs. Hamburger Steak; 50 lbs. Tenderloin Steak; 200 lbs. Potatoes"—but why go on? The most important item is the last: "Total cost—only P724.98."

From then on the parties got larger. Until then the biggest crowds amounted to six hundred, but on July 15, 1933, there were as many as fifteen hundred guests, and most of this growth was obviously due to Tommy Wolff's efforts. From that time on, too, the party was always at his house. (There was a Mrs. T. J. Wolff: she must have gone out that night.) Among the signatures for this occasion was Frank Murphy's, who was then governor-general.

But the biggest bash of all was held on March 7, 1936, the year of the inauguration of the commonwealth. There survive a few printed programs, invitations, and handbills for it, one of the latter reading, "Dewey or Don't We? If we do you will find out how on March 7. If we don't you will learn why on March 7. The Hammer-Headed descendant of a distinguished line of BACHELOR VETERANS Will Appear and Disappear March 7."

One is not quite sure what all that means, but no doubt Mr. Wolff's contemporaries knew. At any rate somebody had saved newspaper clippings of the party, or some other one. An undated headline ran,

Husbands Missing After Whoopee at Liberty Hall
Wives organize Manhunt for Disappearing Espouses:
Luz Last to Reach Home

The text included some descriptions of what went on: "Assembly-man Manuel Roxas was introduced and he spoke of Filipino gratitude to the American people and assured the local Americans that under the new government, 'what is good for the Filipinos is also good for the Americans.' There was a falsetto note in his voice [T. J. Wolff] when he explained the purpose of the annual gathering of the Liberty Hall-ers, saying that out of the eleven original hosts, only two have survived the rigors of time, and (there was a tremor in his voice as he said it), I am older than the other one . . . Senator Fairchild, being a good Republican, took care of Commissioner Murphy, and Ewald Selph, who still had his speech against the Democrats in his pocket, stood at a safe distance away . . .

"Pedro Campos and Consul Espinos were inseparable, both of them staying behind the stage, explaining that in some instances it is

191

better to see from the rear . . . The sun shone Sunday morning on Tommy's lawn showing the wreckage, debris and human flotsam in the form of several guests snoring in unison.

"Arsenic Luz arrived at his home at 8:56 in the morning."

Whatever the date it is clear that (a) the party took place before Pearl Harbor, and (b) by this time the membership was well and truly binational.

There were no more parties after the war intervened, of course. But the chest holds souvenirs of the next and last one, in 1952. Tom Carter observes that General Douglas MacArthur, who arrived in 1935, could have made the 1936 gathering, but if he did he left no record of it. Francis Burton Harrison was invited to that bash, but probably he didn't come. In fact, the only governor-general (or high commissioner) who did leave his mark was the one, Frank Murphy. (Tommy Wolff died of cancer in 1956.) Murphy seems to have made his mark in other directions as well. A Filipino gentleman in Manila recently told this writer that the governor-general used to cruise through the shops, and when he saw a salesgirl he liked the looks of he would buy something in the shop, then ask the proprietor to send her along to his residence to deliver it.

"And when she got there," recounted my informant, with relish, "he would receive her in his drawers. Sometimes he was successful, sometimes not."

Inevitably the American community was changing, especially after the inauguration of the commonwealth. New settlers came in and their attitude was not the same as that of their predecessors. They were still predominantly businessmen, but one encountered fewer adventurers and picturesque drunks, flotsam of the Great War. Gleeck has counted among the postwar group only twenty-four men who had jobs when they arrived; the rest were looking for work.

"Seven had been recruited from the United States by local firms," he wrote. "Only four were employed by the government (two teachers, two U.S. army medical corpsmen.) Two were ordained ministers. Just over half were college-educated. Nearly all were in their late twenties. Only a handful were church members or regular churchgoers. In temperament, nearly all were rough and ready types, unpolished, fond of horseplay, ambitious, generous, friendly and direct. Nearly all would remain in the Philippines through most of their career . . . They knew what they wanted, and they did not doubt the traditional values. They were not adventurers, but solid bourgeois, seeking to better themselves at what was for them an American frontier . . ."

They seem to have got on better with the Filipinos than did their predecessors, because they didn't preach so much. Even Americans live and learn.

Fourteen months of life as a commonwealth went by comparatively smoothly, with a definite improvement in the country's economy. A man who had left in 1931 came back in 1937 to be staggered by the changes that had been wrought in Manila. So many new buildings! Skyscrapers! Roads for more and more cars, and traffic jams as a result! Manila, said the returned resident (A. V. H. Hartendorp, who had first come to the Islands as a teacher), had become a real city, and there was now a definite Filipino middle class.

High Commissioner Frank Murphy was relieved of his office on April 1, and was replaced by Paul V. McNutt, another tall, imposing American who by his appearance projected the image Americans wished to project. There was still no official residence for high commissioners, though plans were afoot: the McNutts rented El Nido, a large house on Dewey Boulevard that had a very interesting history. E. A. Perkins, a successful attorney, and his wife had built El Nido before they quarreled and began divorce proceedings. They owned as joint property valuable gold-mining stocks which Perkins claimed as his exclusive possessions, basing his claim on Spanish marriage laws that were still valid in the Philippines. His wife, Ilona Slade Perkins, refused to give them up. Perkins brought suit against her, and she was put into Bilibid prison. Mrs. Perkins was a strong-minded, eccentric woman. She went on a hunger strike, and her case attracted a lot of sympathy from both American and Filipina women. Perkins alleged that she was insane, and the case was still unsettled when Mrs. Perkins, in 1941, went of her own accord to the National Mental Hospital, insisting that she be placed under observation. She appealed to the women of the Philippines to rise up and change the laws of property for wives, and she was on the road to success for her campaign when the war came along and interrupted all these matters. After the end of the war the case went on, and at last she won the day—represented by a rising young lawyer named Marcos. But we are still in prewar Manila, and McNutt, with his family, has just settled in at El Nido.

What might have been a diplomatic contretemps deliberately engineered by the Japanese representative was narrowly averted when, at a public banquet, the Japanese proposed a toast to President Quezon. That was right and proper except that he proposed it *first*, before drinking to the United States representative Paul McNutt. Quezon quickly corrected the Japanese and did the proposing all over again.

"As the representative of the President of the United States," he explained to the party, "the High Commissioner naturally takes precedence over the President of the Philippines, even though they are of equal rank."

Actually the two men got along very well, both before and after this demonstration of solidarity. They probably felt that it was vitally important even if they hadn't liked each other. Japan was making threatening noises, especially in China where she did more than make noises: she moved in on Shanghai, or at least her forces flowed around the city, filling the countryside and cutting off the metropolis from the rest of the mainland. On August 17, 1938, word came out from McNutt's office that a large contingent of American refugees from China was expected to arrive in the Philippines— thousands, the office said—and the high commissioner appointed a committee to deal with them, get them settled down, and if necessary find jobs for them. In the event it was not thousands but a mere 900 who arrived, and of those 250 were homebound Filipinos. Moreover, most of the American refugees did not seem interested in remaining in the Philippines, but moved on to Australia or other countries. Probably some of them went back to the States. At any rate they didn't stay in the Islands.

Here and there a Manila American took fright and departed, but the general feeling among the settlers seemed to be that it didn't do to borrow trouble, and if you stopped looking, the danger would probably go away. Besides, General MacArthur had everything under control, didn't he? He was training the Filipino army, and, in the last analysis, Washington wouldn't let them down.

Chapter Eleven

It was not that simple. MacArthur had had a run-in, not his first, with some of the people in Washington. They warned him that he could have only two years off to act as field marshal in the Philippines, after which he was expected to come back to the States and resume his American duties. MacArthur promptly resigned from the army's active list. This worried Quezon, who had hoped that the general's close connection with U.S. Army headquarters would be a profitable shortcut for his own nation's military supplies just when it looked very much as if they would need extra help. The Japanese were making great advances in China, almost as if nobody opposed them, and one did not have to be a pessimist to see how dangerous the situation was becoming for his own country. He and MacArthur at the beginning had talked of a ten-year defense plan, but it was becoming clear that ten years was more than they could expect, and in any case the material for defense was simply not there. Quezon contemplated giving up all thoughts of defense. He even went to Tokyo to discuss the possibility of neutralization of the country. In

197

American Caesar, William Manchester recounts the deterioration of relations between the general and the Filipino president. Morale declined among the Filipino troops, who were already dissatisfied because their pay was much less than that of the American soldiers, and those Filipinos of military age began evading conscription. MacArthur's standing army dwindled to 468 officers and 3697 men— a pitiful handful. "Between 1936 and 1940 the number registering for the draft dropped to 42 percent."

Francis B. Sayre was now high commissioner, having succeeded Paul McNutt. Though he was one of those officials who believed in his heart that the Philippines were indefensible, he was startled when Quezon spoke to him of dismissing MacArthur and, furthermore, said in a public speech that in spite of all the talk, the Philippines could *not* repel an invasion, and couldn't be defended even if every Filipino man were armed with modern weapons. Even more startling was the fact that when MacArthur tried to see Quezon, he was told that the president was too busy.

"Jorge," the General told the secretary who brought the message, "some day your boss is going to want to see me more than I want to see him."

The reason for neglect from home, of course, was that FDR and his Cabinet were worried about other aspects of the world war that was obviously brewing, too worried to pay special attention to one corner of the problem like the Islands. But MacArthur, naturally, looked hardest at his corner and tried his best. In 1938 he sent Dwight Eisenhower, his chief of staff, to the States to see what he could do with the situation. Eisenhower reported that they were unsympathetic in Washington. "As long as the Philippines insisted on being independent," he said, "the War Department's attitude was that they could jolly well look after their own interests." A natural reaction, no doubt, but shortsighted considering the situation. In America, Eisenhower scratched up such munitions as were available and bought a few planes, then returned to the Islands. Later, when the general asked to borrow some arms from the United States, the authorities turned him down with the commonsensical argument that arms wouldn't do him any good without ammunition, and they had no ammunition to spare: they didn't even have enough for themselves. Even when MacArthur begged, in 1940, for an annual payment of fifty dollars for each Filipino who was drafted, the answer was in the negative, and later the Philippines were not included in the Lend-Lease program.

There is an old Japanese proverb, "Bees sting a crying face." In 1939, when the Germans invaded Poland, Eisenhower decided that he must go home and help prepare for the war he was sure was on the way. MacArthur had to give in and let him go, however reluctantly. He was replaced by Lieutenant Colonel Richard K. Sutherland, who was never to be as popular as his predecessor.

The Japanese occupied Vietnam in 1940, and in September they joined Germany and Italy in what was called the Tripartite Pact, according to which each was sworn to come to the assistance of the other two in case of need. The Japanese diplomat, Yosuke Matsuoka, made a speech on this occasion, inspiring the *Punch* humorist who signed himself EVOE to write a poem that included the following lines:

Mr. Matsuoka! Riddle deep for solving,
Tell us what you mean now in hard cold fact
When you talk of your homeland's policy revolving
(Wonderful picture) round the three-power pact.
All night long has my bosom been debating.
Mr. Matsuoka, you fascinating elf,
How can a thing keep constantly rotating
Round three other things, one of them itself?

Then they got the news in Manila that of the annual appropriation they had been promised by America when the commonwealth was declared, only one-eighth was actually being paid. Quezon declared a limited state of emergency in the Philippines, and MacArthur felt impelled to resign. But Quezon, doing a right-about, begged him to stay, and the general consented, saying, "This is a call of duty I cannot overlook."

Of course he had a plan of defense: he had had it for at least two years. The trouble with it was that he did not take air power into account. Luzon, he declared, had only two coastal regions in which an army of any size could land, and if they were properly manned and prepared no penetration would be possible. Anyway, he said in 1940, Germany had told Japan not to stir up trouble in the Pacific, as this might interfere with her European campaign. He might have believed it himself when he said it, but as the months went by he seems to have begun to wonder. The commonwealth might build up a respectable defense, he said, if it was prepared and determined to repel attacks, but in any case it was the ultimate responsibility of the United States to assure the safety of the country. His little army was merely a reserve to the small contingent of American forces stationed there. Now at last Washington was willing to listen. Indeed, they had listened and discussed the situation—now and then, at least—for two years, but they hadn't told MacArthur about it because he was no longer with the U.S. Army. The division was admittedly absurd in the circumstances.

"On the one hand," says Manchester, "there was Field Marshal MacArthur with his native troops. On the other hand there was the Philippine Department: American soldiers and Philippine Scouts, the scouts being carried on the rolls as members of the U.S. Army. Under these circumstances, much depended on the relationship between the commonwealth's Field Marshal and the U.S. general commanding the Philippines Department, and MacArthur's record for sharing authority was not encouraging."

But things got better for the field marshal in spring 1940, when the new head of the Philippine Department proved to be Major General George Grunert. Grunert was an old friend of MacArthur's and was on his side in the debate with Washington. It was time, he said, to take Japan seriously. Conditions would improve as soon as the

Filipinos saw this happening, he was sure. He thought there should be more American officers training the Filipinos, more American soldiers in the Islands, and a really strong air and submarine force based in the Philippines. The two officers got Quezon to write to Washington himself in October, asking for more U.S. war personnel. In November, Grunert wrote again to Washington denying a newspaper story that the commonwealth had twelve divisions preparing for combat. Not so, said Grunert: MacArthur's target date, through no fault of his own, was still six years away. It was as well for the two friends' peace of mind that they did not realize what was going on at home, or the desperate plans their superiors were making. At first the War Plans Division was in favor of "the Orange Plan," which entailed withdrawing all U.S. forces in the Pacific east of the 180-degree meridian, leaving out the Islands with Guam and Wake. As Manchester said, "It would have entailed forfeiting Manila Bay, the finest anchorage under the American flag in the western Pacific. . . . The Orange plan had assumed a conflict between just two powers, the United States and Japan. But the present war was global." Accordingly the British and Americans agreed on a war plan later known as "Rainbow Five," which in essence was that in case of war the United States would conquer Italy and Germany before tackling Japan. Even then, our strategy with Japan would be defensive, not offensive: the United States, said the Americans, did not intend to add to its military strength out East.

"The Philippines, in short," said Manchester, "were being abandoned before the opening shot. No one put it quite that way, and there were no plans for evacuating the Americans on the islands, but that was the gist of it."

Ignorant of all this, the generals in Manila talked, and talked, and talked. Grunert agreed with MacArthur that the archipelago could be defended. One thing had to be remedied, they realized: MacArthur was still outside army circles and had been for three years. In February 1941 he wrote to the chief of staff, General George C. Marshall, about it. He outlined his program for defense, saying that he would soon have 125,000 trained troops, which should be supported by aircraft and a naval corps whose primary striking element would consist of thirty to fifty high-speed motor torpedo boats. With this force he was sure he could defend the beach against a landing operation of 100,000, which he believed would be the maximum "initial effort" of the most powerful enemy. He intended to block all straits leading to the Philippines' inland sea, but for this he needed more equipment—mines, guns, searchlights.

He had not had an answer to this suggestion, nor was he likely to get one, when by a fortunate chance he wrote to Roosevelt's secretary, Stephen Early, an old friend, suggesting that Early talk to Roosevelt about making MacArthur commander of all the military, American and Filipino, in the Islands. Though there was again no reply, we have it on Stimson's word (written in his diary) that Marshall had mentioned to him that "in case of trouble out there" they were thinking of recalling General MacArthur into the service and putting him in command. However, the word seemed to have stopped in the diary, and on May 29 MacArthur wrote to Early that he was coming home, and had already reserved a stateroom on the steamer: he was going to shut down the Manila operation and move to San Antonio. This letter did get action. FDR really wanted MacArthur out there in charge of operations, and at last he was willing to say so. The president's military aide cabled MacArthur to stay put until he got further word from the White House. On July 26 the president announced that the American and Filipino troops were to be merged into one army, and MacArthur, now a major general (in the American army, of course) was to command it.

Though the general would not have said so, the president was not exactly doing him a favor. On the same day FDR made a few other decisions. He ordered that all Chinese and Japanese assets in the United States be frozen: he closed the Panama Canal to Japanese shipping, and forbade Americans to sell oil, rubber, or iron to Japan. Britain and Holland, at his request, joined in the embargo. This made war with Japan inevitable, since as they themselves said to their Allies there was an ever-strengthening chain of encirclement around them which they would have to break. Obviously they had to find their raw materials elsewhere, in Malaya and the Dutch East Indies. The Philippines, they said, were a pistol aimed at Japan's heart. They would have to have military bases in Thailand where they could get rubber, tin, and rice. In the meantime they occupied Saigon, and MacArthur read the news of the occupation in the same paper that brought him word of his new command. It was July 27 in Manila, still July 26 in Washington.

About five minutes later the official cables arrived with the story of his appointment and the welcome addition that he was permitted to spend ten million dollars on defense.

Sutherland, typically, did not join the jubilation in MacArthur's office. He was always cautious, always looking on the dark side. "It all adds up to an almost insurmountable task," he reminded his superior officer. But Quezon at least was happy. He came straight over from the palace, embraced MacArthur, and said, "All that we have, all that we are, is yours." He ignored the facts that dismayed Sutherland—a Japanese army of six million seasoned soldiers who had already been fighting in China for four years, compared with the Philippine forces of twenty-two thousand U.S. soldiers and Philippine Scouts, plus the commonwealth army of, at best, eighty thousand untrained Filipinos, "many of whom," said Manchester, "had never seen a rifle and most of whose military knowledge was limited to saluting." MacArthur himself did not ignore the facts of the situation, but he never hesitated: he started planning with renewed vigor, and probably he was as happy as Quezon.

What would Japan do? Everybody in the know—except for George Marshall—was convinced she would attack (Marshall said she wouldn't dare), but they disagreed as to when. Stimson, as it happened, was the nearest to the right solution when he said it would be in January 1942. MacArthur thought it would be in April because the monsoon would be over by then. This would give him much more time to build up his men and matériel, and things did begin to happen: fourteen companies of American soldiers arrived by transport in September. In November the marines who had been in Shanghai joined them. Fifty thousand more men were to arrive in February 1942, and ammunition for them was expected to get there *seven months later*. The fact was, MacArthur's forces were increased, by the day Pearl Harbor was attacked, by only 6083 American regulars: half of his Filipino troops were on other islands than Luzon. There was a scarcity of shipping between islands: American Admiral Thomas Hart had only three cruisers, thirteen destroyers, eighteen submarines, and six PT boats. Equipment . . . It was being turned out faster and faster, then slower again as it was improved, but it all took at least six weeks to sail from California ports to Manila. What with no spare parts for new planes and very bad old ammunition, MacArthur's equipment was almost pitifully inadequate when the time came to use it.

The Philippines only first-class defensive fortification, "the Rock," was on Corregidor, a new hundred-foot-long tunnel called the Malinta, which had laterals (or wings, like stories), ventilators, a trolley line, aid stations, and reinforced concrete walls. Corregidor itself looks on the map like the rock it is called, just off the tip of the Bataan peninsula, but it is not merely a rock: there is some land around the fortification. In spite of its formidable aspect, it was vulnerable to cannon shots from Luzon and, of course, to air bombardment—the one branch of modern warmaking that Mac-Arthur still did not take quite seriously.

In the entire archipelago, Manchester tells us, there were just two radar sets to warn Manila of approaching aircraft: MacArthur relied, rather, on Filipino lookouts with crude telegraph sets, situated on the beaches nearest to Formosa.

Nobody except the general seemed to take the situation seriously. Life went on, as life does in such moments—and after all, why not? What else could the Americans have done but give parties and go to parties? But in Washington they might perhaps have taken a more sober view of things. In September they instructed the major general in Manila to confer with his British and Dutch opposite numbers over integrating defenses in the Islands, Australia, Singapore, Port Moresby, Rabaul, Borneo, Java, and Sumatra. He couldn't: he was far too busy to go jaunting off over immense distances like that. It wasn't until the following month that they showed him Rainbow Five.

"When MacArthur saw it, he didn't like it," Manchester says. "Though it had been revised to provide a limited defense of key Philippine positions, the entrances to Subic and Manila bays, he thought its 'citadel' concept too 'negativistic': he believed he could keep the Japanese out of the Philippines altogether and use the archipelago as a base to menace enemy shipping." He predicted that the Japanese would try to land at Lingayen Gulf and cross the central Luzon plain to Manila, in which belief he was correct: what he didn't realize was that he could not stop their landing. He still thought they would not come until April, by which time he was confident that he would be ready, and he convinced even the skeptical Tom Hart that his plan was feasible. Then he asked Washington's permission to let him carry out his desire to fight the Japanese fleet, and even they approved. The beaches must be held, he instructed his officers: they must prevent a landing. Surprisingly—surprising, at any rate, in retrospect—nobody thought about planes and attacks from the air. But then, as Manchester observes, since history began, fighting forces have been slow to accept new inventions, and of them all the admirals are the most conservative.

It was MacArthur's misfortune that the great powers, though slowly and cumbersomely changing their ideas on air power, had not yet come to the proper conclusion and accepted it. In February 1941 it was suggested by some daring young modern that heavy bombers be sent to Luzon, but the War Department vetoed the idea. In August, however, the British had nothing but praise for their own heavy bombers, the Flying Fortresses, in battle against Germany, and Roosevelt accepted the idea, so nine heavy bombers flew to Manila from Hawaii. The chief of the Air Corps, General Henry

(Hap) Arnold, ordered that all the B-17s that could be amassed should be flown to the Philippines "as soon as they could be made available," and in expectation of their arrival, MacArthur put his people to work expanding three airfields: Nichols Field just outside Manila, Clark Field sixty-five miles north, and Del Monte Field on Mindanao, five hundred miles south. He figured that by December 7 he would have 207 planes, which were 76 more than they had in Hawaii. It was believed, at least by Stimson and probably the others in the government, that this array would be enough to deter the Japanese from attacking. Air Commander Lewis H. Brereton came out during the last week in November to join the general, and if he had been given the necessary time he would have found many things wrong with the planes already there—no spare motors, few maintenance tools, Nichols Field too short for heavy bombers, and so on. But he was not given the time: MacArthur for some reason sent him straight off on the sort of trip that Washington had earlier commended to MacArthur himself, to talk to his opposite numbers in Rabaul, Port Moresby, Melbourne. It took Brereton two weeks. Not until November 21 did he advise MacArthur to move the B-17s away from Clark Field to Del Monte, out of Japanese flying range. MacArthur told Sutherland to see to it, and Sutherland for some reason didn't do a thorough job, so that only half the bombers were moved by December 7.

They were warned from Washington on November 27, and no wonder, that an attack was doubtless imminent. Great Japanese convoys were plain to see, steaming along toward some destination not very far from Manila; one in particular, out of Shanghai, seemed to be aiming straight toward them, and a final warning was sent to MacArthur. On December 1, the watchers spotted unidentified aircraft near Clark Field, and on the next day another plane was seen over the field, while one of the radar sets reported strange planes off the coast of Luzon. Getting the range, said one of Brereton's men. "Next time they won't play," he added. But by the fourth nothing had happened. The Americans sent up planes on nightly patrol, and the pilots spotted Japanese planes within twenty miles of the beaches of the Lingayen Gulf: "Presumably trial flights," said Brereton.

On Friday (December 5) the British Admiral Sir Tom Phillips, known to the media as "Tom Thumb" because of his small stature, sailed in from Singapore to talk things over with Hart and MacArthur about strengthening all their forces: more Japanese fliers were in the vicinity, though they departed when they were spotted. On Saturday, MacArthur doubled the guards at the airfields and ordered that his planes be dispersed on the fields, but there they were in full view, neatly lined up, wing tip to wing tip on the ground. There was no more talk of April, but MacArthur still spoke about a future date, say January 1.

Everybody knows about Hawaii on the morning of Sunday, December 7, or if you prefer, December 6 in Hawaii. But MacArthur did not get the news about Pearl Harbor until 3:00 A.M. Afterward they all seem to have scuttled around like ants in an anthill. Manchester says MacArthur's inactivity was due, sheerly, to "input overload," to use anachronistic computer jargon. "The Hawaiian disaster and the need for momentous decisions in Manila may have been too much for MacArthur. Hart agonizing over his vessels, Brereton over the threat to his planes, and above all Quezon begging him to keep the Philippines neutral—these were but a few of the urgent demands being made upon him in the turmoil of those predawn hours. And Sutherland, who as chief of staff should have been his strong right arm, was no help at all." Brereton wanted to attack Formosa, but when he tried to see MacArthur, Sutherland said that the general was too busy. He said when Brereton told him what he wanted, "All right. What are you going to attack? What's up there?"

This was an extraordinary question, considering everything. According to Brereton, Sutherland then said that he would have to wait for MacArthur's permission, as Washington had forbidden any offensive action. Ants in an anthill . . .

MacArthur was informed at 5:30 that Japan and the States were at war, and Rainbow Five was to be executed immediately. Some of the general's champions insist that it was Quezon who prevented any offensive action for as long as he could, out of a stubborn notion that the Islands could maintain their neutrality. The sun rose at 6:12, finding the forces and their leaders still in disarray, with no aircraft shelters on Clark Field, U.S. warships at anchor out in the open, and none of the troops with any orders to follow. Japanese planes were bombing Malag in Davao Gulf, but not doing much damage— probably, as Manchester said, because Formosa was fogged in and these planes came from carriers. The records are confused, but in outline it can be made out that for six hours after Pearl Harbor, even though some sensible actions were suggested, nothing was done— nothing, that is, by the Americans. There was an alarm when Japanese planes flew close by, but they flew off again. In northern Luzon several places were bombed by the Japanese. Perhaps MacArthur did at last approve a photo reconnaissance of Formosa, but later he denied having done so. There were still seventeen Flying Fortresses on Clark Field, and for a while sixteen of them were in the air to be out of the way, though the seventeenth couldn't get off the ground because of engine trouble. At eleven they were told to come in to Clark, where three were equipped with cameras and the others loaded with bombs—for bombing missions had at last been authorized. However, MacArthur now called in all his P-40s for refueling, which meant there was no fighter cover over Clark Field— just as Japanese planes, freed at last by a lifting of the fog over Formosa, flew toward the Islands. Filipino watchers on the coast reported this activity by radio, but their reports never got through owing to static, though this excuse, like so much about that day, is hard to verify.

What is not hard to verify is that the enemy swooped in on an undefended Clark Field and did whatever they liked, brushing off like flies the few antiaircraft shells the Americans managed to fire. They got three Fortresses first, and after that picked off everything worth hitting—planes, hangars, fuel tanks, everything. That was on Tuesday.

On Wednesday the Japanese concentrated on the naval base at Cavite. The Japanese bombed where they wanted to. The United States had lost practically all her planes in the Philippines. The enemy also torpedoed and sank Britain's *Prince of Wales* and *Repulse* off Malaya, taking to the bottom of the sea Admiral Tom Thumb and the crews. Two weeks later Admiral Hart took what was left of his fleet to the Dutch East Indies. His decision to do so startled MacArthur, because he firmly believed that the *Pensacola* convoy, full of troops and supplies, which had been diverted for a time toward Hawaii, was actually on its way to Manila at last. Hart didn't think it could make it, because the Japanese had blockaded the Islands. Nonsense, said MacArthur (now over the first shock), it was only a paper blockade, and his strategy called for the lanes to be kept open by our ships—or such of them as remained—but he could not change Hart's mind.

The general's daring behavior, standing out in the open to count Japanese planes and always refusing to take cover, captured the American public's imagination, and instead of blaming him for his hours of dithering at the beginning, which at any rate were not honestly reported, they revered him and made him a hero. The public began to demand relief *now* for the gallant General Mac-Arthur and the poor little Filipinos, who trusted us.

Chapter Twelve

MacArthur's headquarters at this time were located in the ancient Fort Santiago, on one of the walls of Intramuros, but his living quarters remained in the penthouse at the Manila Hotel, where he had lived since his return to the Islands. Here his wife and little son still lived. During those first two weeks after the Pearl Harbor attack the general behaved as if he had dug in, well and truly. He issued orders that the civilians of Manila should get out of the city (but where could they go?), or at least prepare bomb shelters. Schools were closed and important buildings sandbagged. MacArthur got in touch with the prime minister of Australia, John Curtin, to make quite sure that country would support him if it came to that, and Curtin promptly agreed that Australia was depending on the United States, never mind her British background. Obviously, they were afraid in the capital at Canberra that the British would not be able to halt the Japanese progress toward their country. Churchill didn't like MacArthur's going over his head in this manner, but he could do nothing about it. The general also thought that Russia should now take a hand and draw off Japanese fire, but Stalin put off the subject, as he said, until spring.

Undismayed when the Japanese made small landings at three widespread beaches—Legaspi, Aparri, and Vigan—MacArthur refused to react, saying that these were attempts to divert his strength. He would wait, he said, until they really did attack in force at Lingayen, as he had always been sure they would: he would hold his defenses until then. Eventually, he admitted to Sutherland, Quezon, and Major General Jonathan M. Wainwright that they would doubtless have to move sooner or later, army and all, to Bataan. In which case, said his critics during the postmortem, he should have begun preparing for this move by stocking up on supplies on the peninsula of Bataan, but instead he spent his time driving around the front lines encouraging the Filipino troops. Manchester lays this mistake in tactics to the general's vanity. He was determined to show himself correct by keeping the men on guard at Lingayen, ready to repel the invaders as he planned and push them back into the sea. But all this, of course, is hindsight, the easiest game in the world to play.

On December 19 the U.S. submarine *Stingray* reported that it had sighted an armada of Japanese troopships and heavy cruisers only fifty miles off the northern Luzon coast. There were four Flying Fortresses still available: they bombed the ships without effect and then flew down to Australia where Brereton already was. Finally, on December 22, the Japanese began disembarking and landing at three points on the Luzon coast, and encountered resistance at only one, Rosario. It did not last long. Reunited, the Japanese troops began marching toward Manila. Still MacArthur held out, trying in vain to get matériel from Washington. Most of the Filipino troops now scattered to the hills, later to fight as guerrillas, a technique they had not forgotten. Or at least they hid in the jungle. Ten thousand more Japanese made landings while the general hesitated because he so hated to accept the plan laid down by the Allied commanders, but at last it was obvious that he had to give in or risk being caught between the two monster columns of the enemy. He gave commands. The next day it was announced that in order to spare Manila from any possible air or ground attacks, the military authorities were considering declaring it an open city, "as was done in the case of Paris, Brussels and Rome during this war." In Fort Santiago, MacArthur busied himself ordering that all supply depots and storage tanks be destroyed, razed to the ground.

When at last the troops were moved to Bataan, he had executed a masterly maneuver to get them there without being bombed. Many of them crossed the Calumpit Bridge, twenty miles northeast of Manila, beating off a ground attack on New Year's Day, and got to safety, after which Wainwright blew up the bridge. In a similar move, another bridge at Layac was also destroyed, on January 6. As Manchester says, "Counting troops already withdrawn from other parts of Luzon, [MacArthur] now had eighty thousand fighting men in Bataan—fifteen thousand Americans and sixty-five thousand Filipinos—in addition to twenty-six thousand refugees. Now the problem was, not the enemy, but food." He had to put them on half rations.

MacArthur himself was already on Corregidor, along with Quezon and his family, Carlos Romulo, MacArthur's family and staff (including Francis Sayre), and various other people, including Ah Cheu, little Arthur MacArthur's amah, or nurse. It was Christmas Eve when they got there. They had come by the steamer *Don Esteban*, accompanied by the Islands' store of gold and silver bullion, for looting had already begun in the city—not by the Japanese, not yet, but by the Filipinos. The move was made in the dark of night. The Quezons were put straight into the Rock's hospital section, for the president, no longer a young man, was gravely ill with the tuberculosis that would in a few years' time kill him. MacArthur refused to live in the cave, which, it must be admitted, was not inviting. The garrison's commanding officer, Major General George Moore, had quarters in a cottage on top of the fort, and MacArthur announced that he was going to live there, though Moore warned him that his rooms were exposed to air attack. It was two days before the Japanese, who had just arrived in the city, discovered that he had gone. They knew where he was, of course, and soon they were bombarding the Rock. The first raid went on for nearly four hours, and during it all MacArthur, typically, stood outside by a hedge, watching. The cottage where he had intended to live was blown to pieces. When Quezon scolded him, he only laughed and said that the "Japs" hadn't yet made a bomb with his name on it. Seriously, though, he added, at the right time a commander had to take chances because of the effect on the men under him.

In the meantime the Japanese, regardless of the "open city" declaration, were bombing Manila. Lieutenant General Masaharu Homma, commander of the invading forces, seized the city when he judged it was sufficiently softened up, and the internment of Americans began. The pattern applied to all Japanese conquered places was followed in the Philippines, in general outline, but there were differences between them, depending in part on who was in charge and on what the special conditions of surrender were. If the Japanese had had a hard time during the fighting before surrender, they tended to be more brutal to the civilians when at last they arrived. Manila had caused them very little trouble; they should have been gentle there, but for a time they were not. There was a lot of unnecessary bombing after the surrender, and the Filipinos were treated worse than the Americans.

At first the Americans, or most of them, were rounded up and put into hotels and lodging houses. Later, having summed up the situation, the conquerors pushed them into the University of Santo Tomas on España Boulevard. Other internment camps in the rest of the Islands were at Bilibid, Los Baños, and Cabanatuan, but Santo Tomas was the largest. Let the guidebook in *Sightseeing In and Around Manila* take over for a little: Santo Tomas, as it proudly says, was founded twenty-three years before Harvard, in 1611, by the Archbishop Miguel de Benavides of the Dominican Order. [Fortunately for the internees, its original site was changed in 1911 and it

214

was enlarged.] It was originally located in Intramuros, but in that year the main building was located on a new site—"a giant city block bounded by Calle Dapitan at the back and España Street on the front, between P. Noval and Governor Forbes streets, a 21-hectare site in the Sampaloc area of Manila. . . . It was dedicated in 1927 when units of the university started moving to the new site. However, even during World War II the medical school was still in Intramuros . . . At that time (1927) there were 100 faculty members and 6,000 students.

"From January, 1942, to February, 1945, the campus was used as an internment camp for Americans, British, Canadians, and other allied nationals. In all, more than 10,000 internees spent some time there, although there were never more than 4,000 and usually less than that at any one time. . . . Starting on January 3, the internees were herded into the university compound—a huge city block surrounded by high masonry walls on three sides, with an ornate wrought-iron fence at the front, facing España Boulevard. Many who were interned were just passing through Manila when the war in the Pacific broke out. These included women from outposts on the islands who had come to Manila to do their Christmas shopping; entertainers, businessmen, sailors who had jumped their ships, soldiers who were trying to pass themselves off as civilians, and even prostitutes—the internees were really a cross-section of humanity."

The guidebook describes how the prisoners organized the necessary departments: a dispensary in the first-floor hall, for example— they used oil paintings from the college museum for partitions. "The mezzanine was used as a youth center where recreational activities were provided three times a week. Children under two years of age were moved out of the compound and cared for by nuns at a nearby college."

At first it went very hard. They were frightened, confounded, and hungry. The worst was that there was no hard news, only rumors. They had heard of MacArthur's removal to Corregidor, and they placed great hopes on the troops in Bataan. Surely, surely it would

215

not be more than a few weeks before the Americans triumphed and they could all go home? But those few weeks passed and there was no triumph. What kept them going psychologically as well as physically was the astonishing kindness of the Filipinos outside.

"The front fence proved to be a life-line for the internees," says the guidebook, "for their Filipino friends or former servants brought to the fence an average of 900 packages a day." Sometimes these Filipinos had to run the gauntlet of insults, threats, and blows from the guards, but they kept coming just the same. "Toilet, bathing, and laundry facilities were almost non-existent," the book continues, "but surprisingly enough, the internees were allowed to send their laundry out, and laundry packages became a means of transmitting messages and money."

In the course of time, too, the prisoners—or some of them— managed to achieve some measure of privacy by building sheds or shanties on their small allotment of campus ground. At one time there were over six hundred of these shanties, divided into so-called towns. Unfortunately, however, privacy was not complete even there, as the Japanese insisted that each shed should have only three walls, so that they could be sure of what was going on.

"Internment brought about many changes," wrote Gleeck in *The Manila Americans*. "Many of the members of the community had occupied positions of privilege, with wealth and servants. Behind bars, they were reduced to second class citizens. Sheer lack of space, with important secondary effects such as the limitation of privacy and the imposition of collective discipline, which the Japanese tried to enforce both as a security measure and because it corresponded to their own concepts of good citizenship, brought out other great changes to individual lives. . . . For the community as a whole, the most important adjustment required was to respond to the requirement that it provide the camp government. Instead of being subject to outside, responsible government which the members of the community could influence but of which it was not a party, the community was required to govern and police itself under strict Japanese control and supervision."

As always in times of war, there was a noticeable shift in the strata of authority. People who had been leaders in their field before the Japanese came in were not usually so authoritative in camp. The highest positions in the pecking order were usually occupied by men (and women) nobody had ever noticed in the old days. It was a new world with new standards: only the population was prewar, and they had to bow to circumstances. But after a certain amount of time the strata shifted back, and the bosses resumed their old positions, though naturally nothing in life was yet "normal." Ability in the former executive world made itself known in the new one, though men versed in technical matters probably took one step up the ladder and stayed there. Having money helped, too: those who had been able to bring quantities of currency into the camp had the edge on those who had been caught short. A. V. H. Hartendorp kept a journal in camp which he managed to conceal from the Japanese, and he commented:

"The possession of money or credit . . . soon divided the camp into the rich, or comparatively rich, and the poor. The former could afford to build shanties, the cost of which soon rose from a hundred pesos or so to several thousand; they could buy extra food; they were better dressed; they looked more fit. Shanties at first had been built of anything that was at hand, but after a few months the lowly bamboo and nipa construction of the native hut was found to be most suitable and became standard. Their owners, some 600, became the 'shanty aristocracy.'"

It was from another camp, the civilian one at Stanley, Hong Kong, that the following limerick came. After all, prison camps all over the Pacific had much in common:

There was a young lady of fashion,
Overcome by a frenzy of passion.
To her lover she said
As she slipped into bed,
"This is one thing the bastards can't ration!"

"But they did," my informant added bitterly. Certainly the Japanese did not encourage lovemaking among the internees: they probably thought it complicated matters.

Food was the first priority—how to cook what they had so that it would be edible, how to keep it sanitary, how to ration it fairly. A kitchen was improvised and people were given each his task in the process of getting the stuff from stove to prisoner. Then there was the problem of cleanliness, apart from those plutocrats who had the means to send out their laundry: they improvised a camp laboratory which produced soap, and one of its by-products, calcium hypochlorite, was used to treat drinking water and as a cleaner for floors and toilets. They were able to make alcohol, epsom salts, hydrochloric acid, and creolin, and in another department they studied the process of turning corn (of which there was a reasonable supply) into bread and even hominy.

Once the hope of instant release was forgotten, the prisoners turned to the problem of educating the many children in the camp. This was not nearly as difficult as making bread or hominy. The camp was full of educators, including Luther Bewley, the irascible gentleman who had arranged the pedagogues' distribution when they first came out, ex-principals, primary teachers, intermediate, high school—anything one needed. Classes were quickly collected, and there were books from whatever libraries were available. They even had trained librarians. They had everything but space and enough textbooks, which were shared among the pupils. By the time the children came out, their education had not suffered as much as one might expect. For the adults there were classes and lectures if anybody wanted to attend them, and so-called "forum" or discussion meetings. They played cards. They played games (until they got too weak from hunger to go in for sports). Professional entertainers put on shows for them. Some of them managed to smuggle liquor in, though it was forbidden to drink: still, some managed. All in all, said Gleeck, they did pretty well, though there were occasional troubles when the camp authority (not the Japanese) was resented and resisted.

*   *   *

MacArthur spent seventy-seven days at Corregidor, and this, along with the fact that his troops still held out on Bataan, hungry and tired as they were, made him even more of a hero in American eyes. He *was* a hero, too—he behaved like a hero, even though a foolish one, refusing to duck from bombs or take shelter even at times when it was obvious that he should be more sensible than foolhardy. Churchill praised him in the House of Commons, and when a Japanese submarine actually rose from the waters to shell Santa Barbara, MacArthur said, "I think I'll send a wire to the California commander and tell him if he can hold out for thirty more days I'll be able to send him help."

In fact, says Manchester, MacArthur and his garrison were caught in a gigantic trap. The Japanese kept moving on past Bataan and into the South Pacific. They took places that everyone else had been confident would never be taken, Singapore being the most vital. By the spring of 1942 they were in Siam, Burma, Sumatra, Borneo, the Celebes, Timor, the Bismarcks, the Gilberts, Wake, Guam, and most of the Solomons. Half of New Guinea was gone. Nothing lay between their presence in Java and the city of Darwin in Australia, or at least so it seemed. And in Europe their ally of the Axis, Germany, looked well on the way to Suez and Stalingrad. Only Bataan remained unconquered, but how long could it last?

There was much resentment among the troops on Bataan, hungry, crowded, and dirty, because they never saw the general. Only once, at the beginning, did he cross the short distance from Corregidor to visit Wainwright and look over the terrain. Thereafter he remained on the Rock. The reaction among the men, who dubbed him "Dugout Doug" and put his absence down to cowardice, was natural: their equipment was woeful, much of it no good, and their prospects really nil. If ever a body of men needed reassurance and pepping up, they did. Why didn't he visit them more often? Because, guesses Manchester, and it certainly sounds reasonable, he couldn't face them knowing that Washington was letting them down. Every day he hoped for more matériel and reinforcements, and they never arrived. It seems quite natural, now, that a man who took this situation to heart, as MacArthur certainly did, could not undergo the ordeal of facing his doomed troops. It is noteworthy that the Filipinos, unlike the Americans, never wavered in their faith. Their adoration of him as a hero remains even now in the Islands. And FDR was not sparing of encouraging words, at least. He cabled reassuringly to Quezon as well as MacArthur. In reality he seems to have given up the Islands, complete with its leaders, as a lost cause. Politically, however, he did not dare to sacrifice MacArthur (and Quezon, secondarily) because of public opinion at home. So an attempt was made to bring help through the only route that seemed at all possible, through Australia and by means of boats. But boats were difficult to find at the best of times, and this was not the best. Captains and owners were naturally afraid to risk encountering the blockade. One did arrive at Mindanao, and its cargo was broken into smaller loads which were carried by small boats. Ten thousand tons of supplies dwindled to one thousand that did actually arrive at Corregidor—enough for four days. And a few submarines brought ammunition now and then.

Quezon grew very restive, especially when he heard a Roosevelt broadcast to the effect that the European enemy must be defeated before the Philippines could be helped. He said to MacArthur that if this were true, he ought certainly to return to Manila and give himself up as a prisoner of war. MacArthur replied with calming weasel words. Then came more disquieting stuff, especially from the Japanese and—a voice from the past—Emilio Aguinaldo. They all said that Quezon and his cause were abandoned by the States.

"We must try to save ourselves, and to hell with America," said Quezon to Carlos Romulo. Hadn't the Japanese promised the Islands independence as soon as the war was concluded? His Cabinet joined him in demanding immediate independence, "with neutralization and the evacuation of all American and Japanese troops to follow." The message went to Roosevelt on February 8. Moreover, it had the support of Francis Sayre, who affirmed that if Quezon's premise was correct, that no help was coming, he believed his proposal for immediate independence, etc., was the sound course to follow. Washington ignored this message but paid attention to MacArthur's cable supporting the idea for various reasons, and saying calmly that Washington must figure soon, in any case, on the complete destruction of his command. The temper of the Filipinos, he said, was one of "almost violent resentment" against the United States.

Stimson, Roosevelt, and Eisenhower agreed that they could not accede to Quezon's demand. Help was on the way, they insisted. Quezon wrote out his letter of resignation, but was persuaded in the end not to send it. As for MacArthur, he was told, in essence, to hang in there until he no longer could. He replied that he had no intention of surrendering or capitulating, and that there was not the slightest wavering among the troops. Privately, he couldn't help agreeing with one of his officers who at last said flatly that Roosevelt had never intended to send help, but meant MacArthur to serve as a delaying factor in the Japanese drive to the south. When his usefulness was over, presumably, he was expected to surrender, but MacArthur had no intention of surrendering alive. If he had to die, he had to die: it was perfectly simple. As for his wife Jean and little Arthur, when Marshall offered to send a submarine to carry them away to safety, she flatly refused to consider it. They would all die together, she declared, if they had to.

According to Manchester, however, George Marshall was having second thoughts about the sacrifice of MacArthur. He was valuable because of his knowledge of the Far East, and he knew how to fight the Japanese. For FDR's part, the public adulation of the general, which was rapidly mounting, made any such action as letting him die politically unwise. But how were they to persuade him to leave his men? In Patrick Hurley's opinion only a direct order from the president would do it, and even then the matter must be handled carefully so as not to smirch his honor or his soldierly record. There is something funny, at this late date, in the picture of all these men treading so carefully in order not to disturb their temperamental star way out there in the Islands.

The deciding development, however, was that going on in Australia, where Prime Minister Curtin, alarmed by the swift approach of the enemy, demanded the immediate return of three divisions he had lent to the Allies, now at work fighting the Germans in North Africa. Churchill said they couldn't have them: the Australians were in a vital position where they were. In the argument that followed, Curtin said that he would moderate his demand for the men if they could have in Australia an American general to be supreme commander of their theater of war, with American troops to join him as soon as possible. Of course he meant MacArthur, and Roosevelt realized it. On February 22 he decided to save MacArthur, after all.

In the meantime, MacArthur had sent the Sayres and the Quezons into safety in the submarine *Swordfish*. During the time they were together something had occurred between Quezon and MacArthur that has only lately been exposed: the Filipino president allegedly presented MacArthur with a gift of half a million U.S. dollars—and MacArthur allegedly accepted it. To this date of writing there has been no further word on the transaction, but no doubt it will come to light in due course. At any rate, not long after the farewells had been said, on February 23 MacArthur received a surprising cable from Marshall telling him that Roosevelt was probably going to send him to Mindanao to organize the defense of the southern Islands. In a couple of hours the executive cable arrived, directing him to go at once to Mindanao, where he was to determine the feasibility of a prolonged defense. But he was to stay there only a week, after which he would go on to Melbourne and assume command there of all U.S. troops.

It was obviously a shock to MacArthur. Put at its baldest, he was being ordered to leave his men in the lurch; at least that is how he viewed it at first. He conferred with his wife, and then at a hastily called staff meeting he showed them the president's cable. It was an impossible choice, he said: if he disobeyed he would be court-martialed, but if he obeyed he would desert his men. Rather than face either eventuality he intended to resign, go over to Bataan, and enlist as a soldier. The staff officers didn't see it that way. No doubt, they said, a relief expedition was being organized at that very moment in Australia, and MacArthur was needed to lead it back to Bataan just in time to save the beleaguered men. He didn't quite believe it, but though he drafted a letter of resignation he forbore to send it until next morning, and by that time it all looked more reasonable. He cabled to Roosevelt saying that he would go, but that he wanted to pick his time himself, in order to forestall any sudden collapse. FDR said all right. Then MacArthur went through nine days' torturing indecision, until he heard again from Washington that the situation in Australia required his early arrival. On March 9 he got another cable, and that settled it. He sent word that he would be leaving on March 15, and would be arriving in Australia on March 18. He expected to be back by July 1, 1942, and his orders for food rationing were based on that premise. Wainwright was left in charge.

A slight change in plans. It was on Wednesday, March 11, that the MacArthur party boarded four PT boats to get through the blockade. With the general went his staff, his family, the Chinese amah Ah Cheu, two naval officers, and a staff sergeant who was a technician— twenty in all. They made it, though it was a rough trip to Mindanao where they were to be picked up by planes, and there were some tense times when the Japanese, sensing that something was up, tried to find them. Mindanao was not occupied by the Japanese, and there were twenty-five thousand troops there. They stayed there at Cagayan for four days, during which time the enemy bombed and strafed the island often, but MacArthur was happy, for he believed that Washington had changed its tactics completely and was preparing for "a great offensive" against Japan. In this he was mistaken, but he believed it. After Mindanao they had a violently uncomfortable, stormy flight to Darwin. It was in Adelaide that MacArthur made his famous statement,

"I came through, and I shall return."

It is debatable how long it took the American civilian prisoners to discover that MacArthur had escaped from Corregidor, but when Bataan fell, as it inevitably did on April 8, they soon heard the news. For a time it seemed that all hope must now be given up, but people are amazingly resilient, and soon the hopeful, lying rumors began again. It was starvation, of course, that brought about the surrender of Bataan. The Japanese occupied Corregidor on May 6 and moved the men still there over to the peninsula. On May 7 the prisoners began the notorious Death March north, during which from seven to ten thousand men, Filipinos and Americans together, died. But in the civilian camps, mercifully, they did not hear of these things until after liberation. They were (rightly) confident that MacArthur in Australia was working all out to collect the forces with which he could keep his promise. But it was to be a hard pull even for the civilians, and perhaps it was as well that they did not realize how much longer they would have to wait.

Not all of them got off scot-free, even so. An American named Earl Hornbostel, an electronics expert, was kept out of the camp, like a few others the Japanese found useful for their skills, and he worked fairly much as he had done before the war until he fell under suspicion. He is still furious and bitter over what happened to him then. The Japanese put him, with hundreds of other prisoners, into a stone chamber at Fort Santiago. According to a plaque now there for the benefit of visitors, eight hundred men were crammed into the room, packed in so tightly that when they slept—on the stone floor, of course—they did, literally, all have to turn over at once.

"A lot of the men had TB," he said later, "but I didn't catch it. So I know now that whatever I die of, it won't be TB."

However, he very nearly did die of another cause. During his incarceration, at less arduous times, he struck up an acquaintanceship with the daughter of the Filipino in charge of the prison, and in the course of time these two young people, regardless of the difficulties of the situation, managed to fall in love. At the end, when the Japanese were preparing to get out of Manila, there was a plan to kill all the prisoners before they left, so that nobody could tell tales on their captors. Word went out to the man in charge, Earl's jailer, to murder everyone in the camp, but his daughter pleaded with him to spare them.

"He wasn't such a bad fellow," said Hornbostel's sister, Mrs. Gertrude Stewart. "Anyway he listened to her and didn't kill anybody. Then, of course, we were all rescued, and my brother and his girl were married."

Chapter Thirteen

This phase of the Pacific war was a race between the Japanese to get to Australia before MacArthur was able to collect enough men and matériel to hold them back, and MacArthur with his insufficient forces going ahead just the same. It entailed guessing on the part of each side as to just what and where the other meant to strike. The Japanese managed to go dangerously far, beginning with their victory at Guadalcanal and continuing in New Guinea, where by superhuman effort they made inroads on a jungle hitherto believed to be all but impassable. But MacArthur outguessed, outplanned, and, in the end, outfought the enemy. It was a tough battle which we will not follow in detail. Suffice it to say that MacArthur improved day by day in predicting what the enemy would do, and then preventing it. In 1943 the tide was definitely turned: MacArthur had at last learned to use air power, and the Japanese were halted. They were only halted, not beaten back, but it was the beginning. If the Americans had had to retrace their steps of retreat, going back to reconquer the territory island by island, the task might have taken years, but that is not how it was done. Some of the islands were simply bypassed, so that the Japanese troops occupying them were isolated and flummoxed.

In July 1944 MacArthur received orders from FDR to meet him in Waikiki, flying over from Australia for a conference. He resented leaving his post, but orders from the commander in chief are orders, and he went. The two men discussed the best way to finish off the war, MacArthur being urgent in his recommendation that they retake Luzon. The president was against it: such an action, he said, would mean heavier losses than the United States could afford. Not so, said MacArthur: good commanders no longer "turned in" heavy losses. They argued the point for three hours, and in the end Roosevelt gave in; he was tired out.

"Carry on your existing plans," he said to his stubborn general, who would not even stay overnight, but was chafing to get back to his post.

No longer was MacArthur cut off from the Islands, if indeed he had ever been. Every month he received nearly four thousand radio messages: "his files held everything," said Manchester, "from the transcripts of executive sessions in Malacañan to the guest lists of the Manila Hotel. His submarines brought the guerrillas equipment, technicians, transmitters, and commando teams, and he personally interviewed each partisan who escaped into his lines."

Some of these people who escaped were Americans from the concentration camps, but most were Filipinos. The resistance kept growing.

Quezon's health had been getting steadily worse. At last he sought improvement at Saranac Lake, New York, but on the same day MacArthur returned from Hawaii the Filipino president died in the hospital, only a short time before the general had planned to bring him back in triumph to Manila. At any rate Quezon was able to see victory in the near future. At his death the vice-president, Sergio Osmeña, succeeded. In the meantime, however, the Japanese had followed their customary pattern in conquered countries and selected *their* choice for president of a puppet government. This was a man well known to the government in exile, José Laurel, who had gone to school with Quezon. His quisling activity was forgivable, the exiled Filipinos thought, and they made excuses for him even when, in obedience to Japanese orders, he and his regime declared war on the United States and the United Kingdom—for what the gesture was worth. But MacArthur was furious, and Quezon, near death as he was, had to argue for a long time to bring him round, pointing out that there was nothing else for the renegade to do. On the other hand, Quezon was not really fond of Osmeña, and much preferred another rising politician (and quisling), Manuel Roxas y Acuña. In the end Roxas, too, was to occupy the presidential chair. During the occupation, like Laurel he collaborated with the enemy, and no Filipino seems to have held it against him when it came to the day of judgement.

The Japanese were determined to keep the Islands, because if they were lost so would be their gateway to the oil and rubber of the Dutch East Indies, which were vital to their effort. They naturally assumed that MacArthur would try first to retake Mindanao, as MacArthur himself did until he changed his plans. They strengthened their defenses accordingly in the territory of the Moros. MacArthur's new plan was to concentrate on Leyte instead, but when the Japanese heard of all the activity around that island they were not dismayed, because they felt they were prepared everywhere. In the meantime, the margins of the war drifted farther and farther north with American planes. Manchester recounts the famous story of 3d Fleet commander Admiral William Halsey when the U.S. naval aircraft bombed Formosa. Japanese pilots flew at the invading aircraft and many were downed, but the survivors reported to their admiral, Shigeru Fukudome, that they had sunk eleven U.S. carriers, two battleships, three cruisers, and one destroyer. Fukudome passed on this splendid news to Tokyo, where Emperor Hirohito proclaimed a national holiday. Upon which Halsey sent a radio message to Admiral Chester Nimitz in Honolulu:

THE THIRD FLEET'S SUNKEN AND DAMAGED SHIPS HAVE BEEN
SALVAGED AND ARE RETIRING AT HIGH SPEED TOWARD THE
ENEMY.

MacArthur, aboard the cruiser *Nashville* on October 16, 1944, had
good reason to feel fine, with two hundred thousand veteran troops
under Generals Walter Krueger and Robert Eichelberger at his
command and a new battle plan which everyone has since agreed was
brilliant. They set out toward Leyte on the night of October 19.
When he had tired of pacing the deck he went below to his cabin and
read the Bible.

Next day the sun rose on the scene of U.S. warships lined up at
the beach near Tacloban. They immediately opened fire and small
boats raced toward shore, while Japanese planes thronged the skies,
trying to hit everything in sight. They did get some of the boats, but
the Americans were back at last on Philippine soil. MacArthur took
his time and didn't come ashore until after an early lunch. Then,
with Osmeña and Romulo at his side, he got into a barge and made
for land. Unfortunately fifty yards from the Red Beach, to where they
were aiming, the barge ran aground. They would have to wade the
rest of the way. MacArthur was too impatient to have the depth
tested: he stepped off the ramp straight into knee-deep water. But
the moment was too solemn to be ruined by this comedy: he simply
went on to the shore. Joyfully he wandered about, ignoring the shots
that landed all around him from snipers in the bushes. His own men,
recognizing him, paused in their fighting to gape. MacArthur
grabbed Romulo's hands and pumped them in an excess of jubilation:
"Carlos, we're home!" he announced. Then, as two flags were
hoisted—one American, one Philippine—to two tall coconut trees
nearby, he sat on a log to write to President Roosevelt: "—This will
be the first letter from the free Philippines. I thought you might like
it for your philatelic collection. I hope it gets through. The operation
is going smoothly . . ."

A microphone was provided for the general, and just as it began to
rain he gave an address he had already prepared aboard the *Nash-*

ville, the burden of which was summed up in the opening: "People of the Philippines: I have returned." His voice quavered with emotion.

When he had concluded, Romulo took over. They were not speaking into a void: a number of Filipinos from Tacloban had gathered on the ground to hear them, and one old man replied, "Glad to see you. It has been many years—a long, long time." They embraced.

Then the general returned to the *Nashville* to make plans and signal a guerrilla rising through the Islands. By nightfall Tacloban had been taken, and the general moved into a splendid house belonging to a wealthy American named Price, who at that moment was in the camp of Santo Tomas.

It took months of hard fighting and many hours of bitter squabbling between officers for MacArthur to get to Manila, but this need not concern us except for the fact that he did get there. The Japanese expected him to attack from the south, but he didn't: as they had done more than three years earlier he landed at Lingayen Gulf and marched his men down the roads toward Manila. His troops actually met with little resistance until they got to Clark Field. At the same time he landed men at Subic Bay on the west coast above Bataan. The Japanese could not keep up with his lightning changes. He put a regiment ashore at Mariveles, isolating Bataan, and the Japanese garrison had to surrender in seven days. Without a shot, American paratroopers took Nasugbu, on the other side of the Bay forty miles from Manila. The only place left around Manila to capture was Corregidor, and the defenders, unlike the Americans of 1942, were well supplied with provisions, not to mention ammunition. But MacArthur was not to be stopped. He sent a regiment of airborne troops to land on Topside (his old quarters on top of Malinta Tunnel), while at the same time an infantry battalion, arriving in Higgins boats, attacked the shore of Bottomside. Ten days later the Japanese commander, having lost 1500 men, retired with the rest to the tunnel and blew themselves up with all the explosives they could muster. Fifty Americans were killed in the explosion, but apart from them MacArthur lost only 160 men.

His headquarters were in Tarlac, which is sixty-five miles north of Manila, but he was now so eager to finish off the job that he drove everywhere, "doing everything but digging the foxholes and loading the machine-gun belts," as Manchester says. At one time late in January he actually slipped inside the grounds of Malacañan Palace and made a reconnaissance survey. By this time it was learned that General Tomoyuki Yamashita, who was in charge of Manila, had declared it an open city and withdrawn his troops. Some were still there, however, when on February 3 American cavalry patrols entered the city. On Tuesday, February 6, MacArthur was able to announce in a communiqué that American forces were rapidly clearing the enemy out. The defenders had been surrounded by MacArthur's converging columns. Everyone at home exulted, but they were a bit ahead of themselves: Manila had not yet fallen absolutely, and was not to do so for another month. The Japanese still had a few stings left to administer. They killed, raped, and burned: the streets were full of rubble and blood. In their rage they murdered nearly a hundred thousand Filipinos, strapped patients to their beds and set fire to the hospitals, mutilated the corpses of the men they killed, and killed babies in horrible ways. The blame lay with thirty thousand Japanese sailors and marines under Rear Admiral Sanji Iwabuchi, who ignored his orders to consider Manila an open city. The GIs had to fight them hand to hand. The Japanese retreated into Intramuros, which MacArthur refused to allow to be bombed because, he said, of the innocent civilians who had taken refuge within those ancient walls. The Americans shelled the place so thoroughly that it had practically the same effect. They managed to break down the northeast wall, but after they got inside they still had to battle Japanese, who fought like the demons they were.

MacArthur, sick at heart, left them to it and went to see the ex-prisoners at Bilibid and Santo Tomas. "At Santo Tomas," wrote Manchester, "he was surrounded by thousands of sobbing, emaciated men in rags. At Bilibid, many of the inmates made a pathetic effort to stand at attention. He wrote afterward: 'They remained silent, as though at inspection. I looked down the lines of men bearded and soiled . . . with ripped and soiled shirts and trousers, with toes sticking out of such shoes as remained, with suffering and torture written on their gaunt faces. Here was all that was left of my men of Bataan and Corregidor.'" Overcome, he returned to the battle lines. Later he attempted to visit his penthouse at the Manila Hotel, which was still in Japanese hands. Even as he watched, it flared up: they had deliberately fired it, and as he stood there helpless, he watched the destruction of his library and souvenirs, "the personal belongings of a lifetime." Then he and a group of American submachine-gun men fought their way into the hotel and up to the burning penthouse, leaving the Japanese colonel dead on the threshold.

It was really over, though much mopping-up, literally, remained to be done. Malacañan Palace was still unscarred, and in the morning of February 27 there was a ceremony there, when MacArthur formally restored Manila to the Filipino officials. The survivors turned their hands to cleaning up, so that on March 13 a sergeant was able to write in his notes, "The lights are going on all over the city."

The puppet government, which had remained safe in Baguio, was now in terror. On March 19 Yamashita flew Laurel and three of the others to Tokyo. Among those left behind was Roxas, who as the Americans drew near decided to go and give himself up. Much to the disgust of some diehards, MacArthur greeted him warmly. Later, in the first election, he won out over Osmeña, which is what the general wanted.

MacArthur's wife and little Arthur were already on the way in a refrigerator ship. They arrived in March, still within sound of the guns of battle, and Jean MacArthur was horrified by the desolation and destruction that she saw on all hands. She went to Santo Tomas, where the internees still lived—for there was nowhere else to go—

wearing their old rags, though now they were no longer hungry. She visited hospitals and, of course, the other camps. But little by little the sound of the guns died away, and one by one the erstwhile prisoners got out of durance. They were fortunate; of the last year's internment Gleeck reported that their behavior had slipped sadly:

"The abolition by the Japanese in February 1944 of the Executive Committee and its replacement by four functional committees ended such elective democracy as had existed in the camp . . . The remaining months were ones of lowered morale, reflected in increasing thievery and unwillingness to perform assigned work details, and in the growing hunger which in the last few months passed the stage of serious undernourishment and approached actual starvation. Even in such times, however, the sense of community was still strong enough to provide additional rations for children—at the inevitable cost of allowing some of the older, feebler camp members to die of undernourishment."

About three thousand people were left, though even so a few more died in those last hours of bombardment. The survivors greeted the American troops with "hysterical joy," though as Gleeck points out, not all the Filipinos outside shared in this emotion. They had been through too much: they could not welcome the liberators who, in many cases, had come too late for them. The government offered to repatriate the camp prisoners, and 3300 from Santo Tomas and Los Baños accepted the offer, though they would have preferred to stay in Manila if there had been sufficient food, medical care, and housing available. There was not. Even Filipinos had gone in for looting in those last days, as had some GIs: it is the nature of the army beast. But a few hundred American civilians remained, and soon they were hard at work organizing a rebirth of the city's financial and economic life.

"The Chamber of Commerce held its first post-liberation meeting in Santo Tomas only two weeks after the U.S. Army entered Manila," said Gleeck. President Osmeña urged Americans to stay and help build up the Philippines on the basis of a new relationship.

They listened willingly. Then the Army and Navy Club opened its doors, followed by the Manila Club, and one could, with luck, find a cot in the Manila Hotel. Some of the refugees even found their homes still standing. Inevitably, soldiers and sailors went looking for bars, and soon the Escolta reassumed the honky-tonk appearance of early days before everyone became rich and refined.

There were rough spots, of course. Some of the Filipinos were resentful of the discrimination which they claimed had begun to appear, feeling that they had earned the right to better treatment now that they were so nearly a fully independent republic. There were mutual recriminations and accusations of collaboration. But little by little these differences smoothed themselves out. The American School reopened. Old businesses, too, reopened, and new ones appeared. The Polo Club found adequate quarters. Newspapers began publishing again. Filipinos and Americans attended the same parties and after a while the old grievances were put away.

And on July 4, 1946, the independent government of the Philippines came into existence, bang on time.

Afterword

Once independence had been achieved for the Filipinos and the war was over, it stands to reason that life did not simply resume for the Americans as it had been before Pearl Harbor. Things were in a mess for everybody. Devastation in the towns, especially Manila, was so extreme that when the prisoners were liberated most of the so-called residents could not move back into their houses: many houses were simply not there anymore and many more were not habitable. The ex-internees had to go back, however unwillingly, to the United States. But soon the hardier souls came trickling back, and later arrivals found them actively rebuilding businesses, houses, and lives.

For a while it looked as if everything would return to the prewar normal, though wiser heads among the American community realized that this could never be. Vice-President Sergio Osmeña, who had succeeded Quezon, did his best to reassure the Americans, urging them to come back and help with the reconstruction of his country. He had most of the United States with him in this postwar sentiment. President Harry S. Truman in 1946 signed two important bills regarding the Islands: the Philippine Rehabilitation Act, which appropriated for the purpose $620 million, and the Philippine Trade Act of 1946, which extended the period of duty-free trade between the countries until 1954, and made clear that no change was to take place in the U.S. import quota of Philippine cordage and sugar for the following twenty-eight years. In addition, a military assistance pact between the countries was signed on March 14, 1947—after Osmeña's time—authorizing the establishment of U.S. bases on the Islands, and on August 30, 1951, the two nations signed a mutual defense pact.

In general things did not go smoothly among the Filipino politicians, then or later, but they had some weeks and even years to enjoy their new importance. Former officials naturally stepped straight into the higher places of government. Manuel Roxas, who beat Osmeña in the elections of 1946, died two years later and was supplanted by Elpidio Quirino, a circumstance which at first pleased the American community, with whom he was popular. They were soon forced to change their minds. Quirino was either too trusting or arrantly crooked, and fraud played a large part in his administration. During the elections of 1949 and 1951 it was so obvious that it could not be ignored, even by the most tactful of observers. Those gloomy souls among the Americans who had always declared that you couldn't expect Filipinos to run a straight government felt justified. Better friends felt it was all too bad, especially as when Quirino visited the States in 1949 he had been very well received by President Truman. So there was not much grief among Americans when in the election of November 1953 Quirino was defeated by Ramón Magsaysay, secretary of defense. Magsaysay was a controversial figure who came to the fore when he opposed the rebels who called themselves Hukbalahaps—Huks for short—and threatened the country's newfound peace. Under Quirino's presidency they had grown dangerously powerful, and were obviously slanted toward Communism. This did not endear them to most Filipinos, who were war weary—they lost a million lives during the war—and were not eager to embark on new hostilities. As president, Magsaysay settled the Huk leaders on Mindanao in 1955, after badly whipping their troops, and the rebellion subsided.

Magsaysay, consequently popular, seemed almost certain of re-election, but he died in a plane crash in March 1957. His vice-president, Carlos P. García, was elected as his successor the following November.

Diosdado Macapagal replaced García in 1961. In 1966 an able lawyer-politician named Ferdinand Marcos defeated him, and Marcos was reelected in 1969, which made a record: he was the first president to be elected twice.

All this time the Americans went their way in the new postwar fashion, paying attention to their own personal concerns rather than exerting themselves to gain influence or to follow shortcuts to power. Like their Filipino neighbors they were apprehensive of the Huks or any other revolutionary activity, and Marcos, who took a strong line with rebels, met with their favor. What the country needed, they told each other, was just such a firm hand, because lawlessness was on the rise again before Marcos's first election. Students, the traditional rebels of most Asian countries, had joined up with remnants of the old Hukbalahap forces and demonstrated, protesting the presence of U.S. troops on Philippine soil. (This was always good for a protest.) They kept everybody nervous, at least. An Englishman traveling in the East in 1970 reported to this writer that his Manila hotel displayed a sign in the lobby directing all people entering the building to leave their guns at the desk, and the sign was no mere indication of what conditions might possibly become, for that night his sleep was interrupted more than once by the sound of rifle fire.

On September 1, 1972, there was little criticism of President Marcos when he suddenly declared martial law. For some time, possibly a year, possibly more, the public accepted this measure as necessary. But as the years went on and Marcos showed no sign of relaxing his iron rule or giving up his presidential seat, the more

239

liberal among them wondered as loudly as they dared how long martial law was to continue. It had become evident that President Marcos was quick to apply pressure through his police. But at last, late in 1980, he declared martial law at an end. Nothing definite was said then, or up until now, about resuming free elections.

In 1981 the Americans in the Philippines, having had a generation to adapt themselves to the new order, are much like Americans in any other foreign country, with no voice in the government. Their numbers have decreased. Old timers among them may regret their loss of influence, but they can't do anything to alter the situation, and that is a healthy state of affairs for citizens of a nation that does not profess to be imperialist.

Notes

Chapter One

C. R. Boxer's comment on America's apparent lack of spices is taken from his article "The Manila Galleon: 1565–1815," *History Today*, August 1958. The statistics about the Chinese commercial holdings in the Philippines were found in William Lyle Schurz's *The Manila Galleon* (New York: Dutton, 1939).

Chapter Two

Father Nicholas Cushner's *Spain in the Philippines* (Rutland, Vt.: Charles E. Tuttle, 1972) provided much of the material about the Spanish influence in the Islands, particularly about the role of the friars and the rise of the anticlerical movement led by Rizal.

241

Chapter Three

The information about Theodore Roosevelt's followers in his drive for territorial expansion as well as the quotations from his speech at the Naval War College, his report to the president and his cable to Dewey are taken from Edmund Morris's *The Rise of Theodore Roosevelt* (New York: Coward, McCann & Geoghegan, 1979). The description of the town of Manila and its surroundings is from *The Philippines and Round About* (New York: Macmillan, 1899), by G. J. Younghusband. The sources for the accounts of Dewey's meeting with Aguinaldo are Albert G. Robinson's *The Philippines: The War and the People* (New York: McClure, Phillips, 1901), and Dean Conant Worcester's *The Philippines Past and Present* (New York: Macmillan, 1914).

Chapter Four

The description of the 2d Oregon U.S. Voluntary Infantry is from Thomas Carter's article "Webfeet Volunteers," which appeared in the *American Historical Collection Bulletin*, July–Sept 1979. And the report of the conditions that existed in Manila at the time of the American take-over is from G. J. Younghusband's *The Philippines and Round About*. Carnegie's comments on the annexation of the Philippines—as well as Younghusband's own—are also taken from Younghusband's book, and those of Frederic Logan Paxson from the *Dictionary of American Biography*. Frank A. Vanderlip's assessment of the commercial value of the Islands is quoted from *The Conquest of the Philippines by the United States: 1898–1925* (New York and London: G. P. Putnam's Sons, The Knickerbocker Press, 1926) by Moorfield Storey and Marcial P. Lichauco. The extent of American transpacific trade in 1898 is discussed by D. R. Williams in *The United States and the Philippines* (New York: Doubleday Page, 1926). Examples of American soldiers' contempt for the Filipinos are taken from *The Americans in the Philippines*, vol. 1 (Boston and New York: Houghton Mifflin, 1914) by James LeRoy. William Manchester's remark that the contempt was a provocation to war is from his book *American Caesar: Douglas MacArthur* (Boston: Little, Brown, 1978). The comment on American lack of skill at jungle warfare and the quotation from Mabini's interview with the *Chicago Tribune* are taken from Victor Hurley's *Jungle Patrol* (New York: Dutton, 1938).

Chapter Five

The comment on the anti-imperialism among American correspondents is taken from James LeRoy's *The Americans in the Philippines*, vol. 2, and the statistics on American casualties are from the same volume. Dean Conant Worcester's observations of the landscape, tribes, and customs of the Philippines are from his book *The Philippine Islands and Their People* (London: Macmillan, 1898), and the account of his meeting with McKinley is from his later book, *The Philippines Past and Present* (New York: Macmillan, 1914).

Chapter Six

The Frederic Marquardt quote is from *Before Bataan—and After* (Indianapolis: Bobbs-Merrill, 1943). Captain Arlington Ulysses Betts's description of his experience as a member of the Buckeye Regiment and as the founder of schools in the province of Tabaco is from his memoirs, published in the volume *Recollections of the American Regime* (Manila: Historical Conservation XXIV Society, 1973). The information about Betts's later life in the Islands is from *Americans on the Philippine Frontiers* (Manila: Carmelo & Bauermann, 1974) by Lewis E. Gleeck, Jr. R. G. McLeod's description of the bamboo structures used as classrooms appears in an article by Dr. Benigno V. Aldana in the *Philippine Magazine*, December 1929. The statistics on the increasing number of Filipinos among the teachers in the Islands were found in Gleeck's *Americans on the Philippine Frontiers* (Manila: Carmelo & Bauermann, 1974). Julian

Encarnacion's account of the history of education in the Philippines before the arrival of the Americans is from his article "From the Days of the Lakans to the Coming of the Transport Thomas" in the anthology *Tales of the American Teachers in the Philippines*, edited by Geronima Pecson and Maria Racelis (Manila: Carmelo & Bauermann, 1959). Dr. Gilbert S. Perez's comments on the behavior of Filipino students is in the same anthology in an article entitled "From Transport Thomas to Santo Tomas." Dr. Victor Heiser's observations on the diseases rampant in the Islands are from his memoirs, *An American Doctor's Odyssey* (New York: Norton, 1936). And Mary H. Fee's description of her experience as a teacher is from her book *A Woman's Impressions of the Philippines* (Chicago: McClurg, 1910).

Chapter Seven

The comments on early American policy in the Islands and of the powers granted the governor-general are taken from Cameron Forbes's *The Philippine Islands* (Harvard, 1945). The description of street scenes in Manila in 1901 is from *The Manila Americans* (Manila: Carmelo & Bauermann, 1977) by Lewis E. Gleeck, Jr. Elmer Madsen's account of homesteading in Nebraska and then taking a job in the Philippines is from *Recollections of the American Regime*. The descriptions of the unsanitary conditions in Manila and of the civic improvements made by Forbes are from Victor Heiser's *An American Doctor's Odyssey*.

Chapter Eight

The information about the Americans who decided not to return to the States and, instead, started plantations in the Islands is from Gleeck's *Americans on the Philippine Frontiers*. The material about Woodrow Wilson's early policy in the Philippines and about Harrison's execution of that policy is from Charles M. Farkas's "Relieving the White Man's Burden" in *The American Historical Collection Bulletin* for January–March 1978. Harrison's recollection of the circumstances of his appointment as governor-general is from his *Diary* (Ithaca, N.Y.: Cornell University Press, 1974), edited by Michael P. Onorato. The comments about the reaction to Harrison's treatment of Americans holding government jobs and about the erosion of his executive powers are from *The Philippine Islands* by Cameron Forbes. The praise for Frank Carpenter's supervision of Filipino officials is from *American Apostles to the Philippines* (Boston: Beacon Press, 1950) by Arthur S. Pier. The description of the progress made during Carpenter's administration is from Victor Heiser's *An American Doctor's Odyssey*. Michael P. Onorato's assessment of Harrison's career—both political and romantic—is from his foreword to Harrison's *Diary*.

Chapter Nine

The statement about the Filipinos' military service during World War I is from Forbes's *The Philippine Islands*, as is the reference to the infiltration of Japanese fishermen. Henry Stimson's affirmation of the American commitment to the Philippines and Quezon's plea for political certainty are taken from Elting E. Morison's biography of Stimson, *Turmoil and Tradition: The Life of Henry L. Stimson* (Boston: Houghton Mifflin, 1960). Quezon's objection to the Timberlake Resolution, his statement to Millard Tydings, and FDR's response to Quezon's memorandum are taken from *Quezon: Paladin of Philippine Freedom* (Manila: Filipiniana Book Guild, 1971) by Carlos Quirino. The figures of enrollment for Central High School and the American School are from Gleeck's *The Manila Americans*.

Chapter Ten

The comments on fraud at the polls and on the continued exclusion of Filipinos from American clubs in Manila are both taken from Quirino's *Quezon*. Much of the material about the political and social scene after the beginning of the commonwealth and the description of the new arrivals from America are from Gleecks' *The Manila Americans*. The description of Liberty Hall is based largely on Tom Carter's "Liberty Hall Philippines," which appeared in the *Bulletin of the American Historical Collection*, April–June 1980.

Chapter Eleven

The chief source for the account of MacArthur's activity as field marshal in the Philippines, through the time of the Japanese attack on Clark Field, is William Manchester's *American Caesar*.

Chapter Twelve

The figures for the size of the forces under MacArthur's command at Bataan are taken from Manchester's *American Caesar*. The description of life in the internment camp at Santo Tomas is from Gleeck's *The Manila Americans*.

Chapter Thirteen

The accounts of MacArthur's contact with the Philippines from Australia, of his eagerness on the battlefields after his return, and of his visit to the ex-prisoners at Bilibid and Santo Tomas are from Manchester's *American Caesar*. Manchester's book is also the source of Admiral Halsey's telegram. The description of the conditions at Santo Tomas during the last year of internment is from Gleeck's *The Manila Americans*.

Bibliography

Betts, Arlington, Victor Buencamino, and Elmer Madsen. *Recollections of the American Regime*. Manila: Historical Conservation XXIV Society, 1973.

Boxer, C. R. "The Manila Galleon: 1565-1815." *History Today*, August 1958.

Carter, Thomas. "Liberty Hall Philippines." *American Historical Collection Bulletin*, April–June 1980.

———. "Webfeet Volunteers." *American Historical Collection Bulletin*, July–September 1979.

Cushner, Nicholas. *Spain in the Philippines*. Rutland, Vt.: Charles E. Tuttle, 1972.

Dewey, George. *Autobiography*. New York: Scribner, 1913.

Farkas, Charles M. "Relieving the White Man's Burden." *American Historical Collection Bulletin*, January–March 1978.

Fee, Mary H. *A Woman's Impressions of the Philippines*. Chicago: McClurg, 1910.

247

Forbes, Cameron. *The Philippine Islands*. Cambridge, Mass.: Harvard University Press, 1945.

Gleeck, Lewis E., Jr. *Americans on the Philippine Frontiers*. Manila: Carmelo & Bauermann, 1974.

———. *The Manila Americans*. Manila: Carmelo & Bauermann, 1977.

Harrison, Francis Burton. *Diary*. Edited by Michael P. Onorato. Data Paper no. 25, *Origins of the Philippine Republic*. Ithaca, N.Y.: Cornell University Press, 1974.

———. *The Cornerstone of Philippine Independence*. New York: Century, 1922.

Heiser, Victor. *An American Doctor's Odyssey*. New York: Norton, 1936.

Hurley, Victor. *Jungle Patrol*. New York: Dutton, 1938.

Journal of the American Chamber of Commerce in Manila, 1923.

LeRoy, James. *The Americans in the Philippines*. 2 vols. Boston and New York: Houghton Mifflin, 1914.

Lichauco, Marcial P., and Moorfield Storey. *The Conquest of the Philippines by the United States, 1898–1925*. New York and London: G. P. Putnam's Sons, The Knickerbocker Press, 1926.

Manchester, William. *American Caesar: Douglas MacArthur*. Boston: Little, Brown, 1978.

Marquardt, Frederic. *Before Bataan—and After*. Indianapolis: Bobbs Merrill, 1943.

Morison, Elting E. *Turmoil and Tradition: The Life of Henry L. Stimson*. Boston: Houghton Mifflin, 1960.

Morris, Edmund. *The Rise of Theodore Roosevelt*. New York: Coward, McCann & Geoghegan, 1979.

Pecson, Geronima, and Maria Racelis. *Tales of the American Teachers in the Philippines*. Manila: Carmelo & Bauermann, 1959.

Philippine Magazine, December 1929.

Pier, Arthur S. *American Apostles to the Philippines*. Boston: Beacon Press, 1950.

Quirino, Carlos. *Quezon: Paladin of Philippine Freedom.* Manila: Filipiniana Book Guild, 1971.

Robinson, Albert G. *The Philippines: The War and the People.* New York: McClure, Phillips, 1901.

Schurz, William Lyle. *The Manila Galleon.* New York: Dutton, 1939.

Williams, D. R. *The United States and the Philippines.* New York: Doubleday Page, 1926.

Worcester, Dean Conant. *The Philippine Islands and Their People.* London: Macmillan, 1898.

———. *The Philippines Past and Present.* New York: Macmillan, 1914.

Younghusband, G. J. *The Philippines and Round About.* New York: Macmillan, 1899.

Index